The
DROP-OUTS

The DROP-OUTS

A TREATMENT STUDY OF
INTELLECTUALLY CAPABLE STUDENTS
WHO DROP OUT OF HIGH SCHOOL

Solomon O. Lichter

Elsie B. Rapien

Frances M. Seibert

Morris A. Sklansky, M.D.

SCHOLARSHIP AND GUIDANCE ASSOCIATION

THE FREE PRESS, NEW YORK
COLLIER-MACMILLAN LIMITED, LONDON

Copyright © 1962 by The Free Press of Glencoe

A DIVISION OF THE MACMILLAN COMPANY

Printed in the United States of America

Collier-Macmillan Canada, Ltd., Toronto, Ontario

Library of Congress Catalog Card Number: 62–11853

Fourth printing April 1967

PREFACE

FORTY PER CENT OF AMERICAN children drop out of school before high school graduation. Beyond these, tens of thousands of other youngsters are underachievers—do not function in school at the level of their intellectual competence. These drop-outs and underachievers represent a tragic waste of the resources of our young people at a time when our country needs their fullest productivity.

To study this unhappy situation, the Scholarship and Guidance Association, a counseling agency specializing in the treatment of the emotional and educational problems of adolescents, undertook a research project. It was designed as a study-in-depth, using casework treatment as the method of observation and data collection. The study centers around these issues:

Are there links between emotional and familial problems at home, underachievement and behavioral problems at school, and dropping out of school?

Are school problems reactive to the nonlearning aspects of school—the personalities of the teachers, school rules and regulations?

How does the student use school as a battleground to settle problems from other areas of his life?

Can counseling, by resolving the emotional problems, improve academic achievement and behavior, and prevent premature school-leaving?

What are the earliest danger signals of emotional disturbance that can be most easily detected in the classroom, which forecast poor school adjustment in high school?

The Drop-Outs provides answers to these questions. The answers come not only from our concentrated study of the 105 students in the Drop-Out Project itself, but from the experience in our general agency practice in which at least 90 per cent of the adolescents have school difficulties. We know that learning problems are complicated and tenacious and for those reasons are not fully understood by parents who have children with school problems, by educators who must teach the children, or by counselors who work to alleviate the problems. We know also that troubles at school bring unhappiness to the students as well as to their parents and teachers. Of equal importance, we know that a personality problem serious enough to interfere with school adjustment will subsequently interfere with work adjustment.

The treatment of the youngsters and their parents is also discussed in this volume. In its case examples and illustrations, parents, teachers, and social workers will recognize their own troubled and troubling children. It describes some treatment techniques we found to be effective in helping emotionally distressed youngsters become happier adolescents, better students, and high school graduates.

The Scholarship and Guidance Association had its beginnings in an agency founded in 1911. Although the specific function at that time was to help fourteen-year-old children, who could legally leave school, find work, an early report comments: "A peculiar employment bureau it is that does not want to give employment. Our first endeavor is to send the child who applies for work back to school." In 1961, the Scholarship and Guidance Association celebrated its fiftieth anniversary. Preparing the results of our study for publication seemed a particularly appropriate commemoration of the half-century mark, since the reluctant student was an agency and community concern in 1911 even as he is today.

ACKNOWLEDGMENTS

WE WISH TO EXPRESS OUR DEEP appreciation to the Wieboldt Foundation, who not only financed the project but also had a sincere and lively interest in the serious problem of early school-leaving.

We thank the many people in the Chicago public schools for referring students to the study and for working cooperatively with us for the benefit of the children.

Special acknowledgment is due Harry Brown and Mrs. Eleanor Dansky, members of the original research team who left the agency before the analysis of the material was started. We are most grateful to the agency's staff counselors for their interest, ideas, and criticisms; and to the clerical staff members for their patience and diligence.

Dr. Bernice Polemis provided some helpful consultation in the early stages of the study. Both of our research consultants, first John Gandy and then Dr. Benjamin D. Wright, gave very valuable guidance and assistance. Mrs. Jane Gottschalk was our able and devoted editor.

CONTENTS

CONTENTS

TABLES

THE NEED FOR AND

DEVELOPMENT OF THE

DROP-OUT PROJECT

Introduction

IN THE UNITED STATES, THE PROPER
education of our children and a re-evaluation of our educational
system are of major concern today. The concern extends from the
highest governmental levels to the parents and students themselves. The issues are varied and broad: they range from the
ability of our country to compete and survive in a tension-laden
world to the acknowledged duty of a democracy to educate its
citizens to their fullest potential.

Much discussion has taken place about ways of improving the
educational system, and many plans, such as suitable curricula,
accelerated courses, and more efficient methods of teaching, have
been instituted. Valuable as such measures are, any educational
system, however excellent, can only provide the means by which
a child may be educated—it cannot insure that a child will take
advantage of what is offered.

In contrast to this drive toward better school programs is the fact that 40 per cent of all children in the United States fail to complete high school; they are drop-outs. This is particularly alarming when one considers that in no other country is high school education so readily available and has so much emphasis been placed on high school graduation as a minimum educational goal. Leaving school before graduation is a sharp deviation from this common goal. Nor is it easy for youngsters to become drop-outs. The family, school, and community exert considerable pressure on children to complete their education and have mobilized an imposing array of facts to support their arguments. Ample evidence has been compiled to show that students who drop out harm themselves both culturally and economically.

Numerous educational studies have made it evident that school drop-out is a complex problem to which there is no simple solution. But from these studies a highly significant inference can be drawn: rarely do children who are successful in school leave prior to graduation. The high school drop-out is usually a child who has failed in his general school adjustment. This failure is not necessarily a matter of a specific learning disability but rather a broader "educational" disability.

The "educational" disability, moreover, cannot be attributed simply to limited mental endowment. Comparisons of graduate and drop-out groups show a full range of I.Q.'s for both groups, indicating that there are students of lesser intellectual capacity who complete high school, and that there are students with higher than average mental potential who leave before graduation. In most statistical studies somewhat more than half of the drop-outs have at least average intelligence. This half without question has the mental capacity to master a high school curriculum. Factors other than intelligence must certainly account for premature school-leaving among such adolescents.

Many previous reports have strongly implied that drop-out is an escape mechanism rather than a positive, if misguided, attempt at constructive action. Frequently, the student did express a wish to go to work, but very often this was a rationalization—an attempt to conceal from others, and perhaps from himself, his need to avoid school. High schools have been active in approaching the drop-out problem by remedial measures suitable to the school setting. Through such means as curriculum flexibility, vocational guidance, work experience programs, and some forms of in-school counseling, they have assisted many youngsters to remain in and to graduate from school. However, there are still children who, against their own best interests, either voluntarily leave school or have such difficulty that they are asked to leave. These children, whom the schools could not help, must be driven to this self-defeating behavior by powerful forces.

From our observations and experience in the treatment of adolescents, we speculated that with such children drop-out might be only a surface phenomenon, the final outcome of deeper social and emotional difficulties, and we decided to study the problem. The major hypothesis that we wished to test was whether intensive individualized treatment could effect a better emotional, social, and educational adjustment for drop-out or potential drop-out students. We hoped to prevent school-leaving where possible, but this was not our only intent. Ours was a wider approach geared to help the individual child and intended to modify those factors, environmental or personal, that were keeping him from realizing his potential for a personally rewarding and a socially productive life.

Through careful casework study of the child, we sought to gather material that might yield valuable clues for a deeper understanding of at least some of the basic factors causing students to drop out of school. We did not set up in advance areas to be investigated, since our primary aim was to help the child, and we had no way of anticipating all the important areas. It seemed, too, that material acquired in this way would be more revealing than superficial responses studied in specific areas in a routine way. We hoped to learn whether the youngsters could be helped; to discover the psychodynamics of their wish to drop out of school; and to acquire information that would be useful to educators, social agencies, and others coping with the problem of drop-out.

Description of the Study

Since our project was a pilot and demonstration study, it was designed to be small in scope with respect to the number of

clients. Two caseworkers, a man and a woman,[1] both with many
years of experience and demonstrated skills in the treatment of
adolescents, the agency's clinical psychologist, and its psychiatric
consultant, a psychoanalyst, made up the staff. A research consultant was added later when analysis of the casework material
began. The executive director of the agency served both as director of the project and as casework supervisor.

The basic orientation of the program was intensive, individualized service. For each client the entire scope of casework services
was available: regular interviews with the child and his parents;
careful, detailed study to assess the major factors involved in the
difficulty; and finally the setting up of a diagnostic evaluation as a
basis for treatment. In addition to individual counseling, we also
provided whatever supplementary help was needed, such as financial assistance to enable a child to remain in school, complete
psychological testing facilities, vocational counseling, employment
placement, and psychiatric consultation.

Cooperation with the schools was a vital feature of our program. We depended on them not only for referral of students
but for a sharing of their knowledge of the child and the way he
functioned in school. In turn, what we learned about the child—his
personality structure and the various forces in his emotional and
familial life—helped the school to deal with him beneficially.

We planned the treatment phase of the project as a three year
period, accepting referrals until approximately the last six months.
The project started in 1954; in 1957 we began to draw up a
schedule of areas and items for examination, study, and comparison and decided to continue the casework program for the
youngsters still in treatment until the schedule was completed.
The official closing date of the treatment phase was November,
1958.

As stated earlier, our aim was to discover whether casework
service could effect a better adjustment in a group of drop-out
or potential drop-out students. More specifically, we formulated
four hypotheses:

1. It is agency policy to assign boys to men counselors and girls to
women counselors.

1. School problems generally, and early school-leaving specifically, are often aspects of emotional and personality disturbance in the student.

2. Casework treatment can improve school performance by effecting a better emotional and social adjustment.

3. Casework treatment can prevent premature school-leaving.

4. School itself has a psychodynamic meaning of a conflictual nature that is contributory to early school-leaving.

Reaching the Sample

The Chicago public high schools were informed about our program and were asked to refer children. Information about our work was disseminated through meetings with the administrative personnel of the Bureau of Child Study and the Bureau of Pupil Personnel Services of the Board of Education. We also had personal contact in individual high schools with adjustment teachers, psychologists, and placement and attendance counselors, all of whom were directly in touch with the youngsters in trouble.

Although not refusing students who had been referred to us after already dropping out of school, we decided to concentrate our study on those students still in school who seemed to be in danger of dropping out. In this way we could investigate the factors that were immediately involved in the intent to leave school. Secondly, we could test the effectiveness of treatment in forestalling drop-out; and thirdly, potential drop-outs were more readily available for study.

The initial selection criteria given to the schools were:

1. Any student of average or better intelligence (I.Q. of 90 and up) who was openly expressing a wish to leave school at attainment of age sixteen.

2. Any child who was thinking of dropping out for economic reasons.

3. Any student exhibiting such prognostic drop-out signals as: (a) truanting and cutting; (b) serious academic underfunctioning, especially grade and subject failures; (c) marked lack of interest

in school; (d) behavior problems serious enough to interfere with school progress.

This special project was new, and we learned that in the initial stages of a service to another discipline the road to referral should be made as easy as possible. The very existence of a list of criteria evidently symbolized a psychological barrier creating more burdens for already overburdened school personnel. The result was a scarcity of referrals. Therefore, we modified our instructions: the schools were asked to send us any youngster who, in their opinion, was a possible drop-out and whom they hated to see leave school. Actually, this condensed our criteria in a single sentence; implicit in it was our limiting requirement that the student be intellectually capable of finishing high school, that is, of average intelligence or better. The problem of insufficient mental ability involves a totally different set of factors in school drop-out and was not within the scope of our program. Our common-sense criteria worked, and schools began to send us children who were, indeed, potential drop-outs. The referred students displayed all of the classic drop-out symptoms enumerated above.

Aside from the requirement of at least average intelligence, we set the lower age limit for adolescents in the drop-out project at fourteen and one-half years. No formal upper age limit was established; inasmuch as most of our study group were still in school, a natural selective age element was present, and no student over eighteen years of age was referred. The age of fourteen and one-half years was an arbitrary figure for the lower limit, but it seemed the most appropriate. We believed a child had to be that close, at least, to legal school-leaving age before he could be properly regarded as a potential drop-out. Moreover, we wished to study and treat the psychodynamics connected with drop-out, and we thought those factors would be most sharply in focus when the end of compulsory schooling was reasonably imminent. When children below fourteen and one-half were referred, they were placed in our agency as regular cases.

The schools followed the standard agency referral routine. After talking with us about a child, the referring person in the school communicated with the parents, usually the mother, explaining briefly the child's school difficulties and the counseling services of our agency and then asking the parents to call us for an appointment.

In all, 105 students from twenty-five different high schools were referred, sixty boys and forty-five girls. Table 1 in Appendix A gives the list of schools.

PSYCHODYNAMIC FRAMEWORK

FOR DIAGNOSING

PERSONALITY PROBLEMS

AFTER THE THREE YEAR PERIOD
allotted for treatment of the adolescents and their parents, we
began a systematic review and analysis of the case material. Our
hypothesis that social and emotional problems are the ultimate
factors in many school drop-outs led us to ask some broad questions: What were our drop-out youngsters like, how did they
come to be that way, and how did their school problems develop.
This meant a complete diagnostic study, if possible, of both child
and parents. We needed to understand many things about each
youngster: his intrapsychic life; significant interpersonal relationships with parents, siblings, and other important figures; and behavior at home, at school, and with peer groups. We needed to
understand the student's basic personality structure and its development, the kinds of ego defenses he was using to adapt to life,

and their effect on his adjustment. It was also vital to assess each parent's personality make-up to see how it interacted with the child's difficulties.

But a project like ours, which selected children on the basis of a common symptom, school-leaving, had to go far beyond the study of individual cases to realize its fullest value. The larger question was what similarities or differences existed in the group as a whole. Were there any significant syndromes, or did drop-out occur in widely variant individual situations showing no special patterning?

To begin the seemingly staggering task of analyzing such complex and detailed material, we developed some concepts to help isolate promising areas for examination. From previous experience with treatment of adolescents, we had noted distinct differences between the disturbed youngster without serious school problems and one whose disturbance resulted in substantial interference with school life and learning to the extent that he eventually left or was asked to leave school. These differences were not based simply on degree of pathology. Some of our most seriously disturbed youngsters outside the Drop-Out Project were pouring all of their energies into schooling successfully, to the detriment of other areas of functioning.

An adequate understanding of adolescence requires knowledge of the adolescent ego, which must perform several difficult tasks in the development of the personality. The instincts are intense in their urgency, and the ego must manage the impulses and needs that are their expressions. The family value system, its mores, and its morals come into serious question, and the ego must establish a new ego-ideal and superego. The adolescent ego directs itself toward emancipation from the family, and toward heterosexual object relations, social adaptation, personality integration, and identity formation.[1]

We felt for our special purposes it would be valid to study the nature of the adolescent ego as it relates specifically to school, for schooling is an important maturational occupation for the adoles-

1. Morris A. Sklansky and Solomon O. Lichter, "Some Observations on the Character of the Adolescent Ego," *The Social Service Review*, 31:3 (September, 1957), 271–276.

cent in our culture. An examination of our cases indicated it was feasible to describe the ego functions of our drop-out students in terms of personality diagnosis, outstanding ego mechanisms (defenses), and specific psychodynamic involvement in school.

System of Diagnosis

For the purposes of this project it was necessary to clarify the concept of diagnosis as it pertains to adolescence. The nomenclature in the disorders of personality is an attempt to apply to the various clinical conditions names that best encompass their distinguishing features. These names are not names of "disease entities" but terms that, in a brief way, describe the outstanding characteristics of a total personality dysfunction. To this day the nosology includes many names that are not descriptive terms— these were originally intended to be names of disease entities but are now part of our medical tradition. Those who use them, however, acknowledge that they are simply conveniences of professional language. No one who uses the term "hysteria," for example, really believes that there is a condition in which the uterus has wandered from its original site to the affected part of the body. But the word "hysteria" immediately brings to mind a certain disorder, requiring pages of descriptive detail to adequately depict the personality disorder involved.

The nomenclature as it is used, nevertheless, is more suited to persons in stages of development other than adolescence. It suggests a status quo, a quality of fixity, a clinical entity. This static quality, not true for any phase of development, is especially untrue for adolescence, in which both normal and abnormal personalities are still in the process of change. This is not to imply that there are no rigidities of character during adolescence, but the unique quality of such rigidity when it does exist makes it a special problem in pathology.

The adolescent personality is unsettled, for it is in the process of integration. Though it tends toward stability, it is not crystallized. Adolescent defenses are variable, unpredictable, and selected from the entire repertoire available from the individual's total history; thus, the adolescent personality often appears both extremely regressive and capable of mature, adult behavior. It is this complexity of personality formation in adolescence that makes static diagnostic labels seem inappropriate and the entire problem of diagnosis difficult.

It became necessary, nevertheless, to establish a diagnostic procedure for our study of school-leavers. Each adolescent personality has a certain "character direction"—a character in process of formation; it is this process that we wanted to describe. The pattern of character formation indicates the extant dynamic tendencies within the adolescent personality and suggests the quality of the future adult character structure. Individual designations for character formation describe the outstanding characteristic defenses or ego adaptations used by the adolescent and indicate the nature of the underlying processes. In spite of the inconstancy of the adolescent personality, the descriptive terminology of character formation takes into account that repetitive pattern of defenses making for uniqueness and differentiating one adolescent from another.[2]

Within the configuration of adolescent character formation, particular groupings of defenses create "syndromes" that stand out more than the character formation itself and are often the major concern of the individual and the most obvious criterion for clinical differentiation. These are the "neuroses," the most *immediate* major psychodynamic issue for all concerned. Otherwise, it is the character formation itself that is the major psychodynamic issue.

Diagnosis of adolescents is difficult for several reasons. Many defenses are transient, though unmistakably present, and are not truly characteristic of the individual. Often, modes of behavior are regressive, at least in terms of their origin, so that differentiation from pathological states is difficult to achieve, though extremely important. Finally, no matter how primitive or pathological a particular form of behavior may seem, from the point of view of ultimate synthesis of character these syndromes may be cores around which the total personality will integrate, often beneficially. For diagnosing our adolescent drop-outs we outlined a

2. Morris A. Sklansky, "Character Disorder in Adolescence," paper presented at the Fiftieth Anniversary Professional Meetings of the Scholarship and Guidance Association (Chicago, 1961).

threefold description: (a) the predominant observable complaint, (b) the major psychodynamic issue, and (c) the character formation.

THE PREDOMINANT OBSERVABLE COMPLAINT

The predominant observable complaint is the caseworker's assessment of the main problem to which counseling should be addressed. Multiple complaints usually bring the client to the agency. They may be complaints made by the school authorities, parents, or the client himself. As stated by the lay person, the complaints may be repetitious, diffuse, or vague and may range from specific physical symptoms to total life patterns. Therefore, the caseworker must summarize them or make them more exact. An adequate statement about the predominant observable complaint clarifies more precisely the nature of the disorder, and such a designation of the complaint is an important criterion in differential diagnosis. One may consider the total character formation the main current in the stream of life, the major psychodynamic issues as the eddies and countercurrents, and the complaints as the disturbances created by these eddies.

A complete list of the specific complaints is given by constellations in Appendix B-I. Here, we discuss only the major categories of constellations:

1. *Physical complaints* include functional somatizations such as headaches, fainting and so on. Except for a few hysterical girls who somatized, we had few physical complaints.

2. *Psychic complaints* relate to inner personal experiences and do not involve actual interaction with other persons. Some examples are anxieties and feelings of depression. About one-third of our students had such complaints.

3. *Social complaints* are those involving interactions with other people, such as provocativeness and passivity. About half of the students had social complaints.

4. *School complaints* run the gamut from learning difficulties to attendance problems. Ninety-three per cent of our students had such symptoms, but usually another complaint was found to be more descriptive or more dynamic.

5. *Environmental problems* are difficulties that impinge on the adolescent from the outside and over which he has little or no control. Such difficulties as economic need and negative parental management are classified here. Fifteen of the students had environmental problems as a predominant complaint.

THE MAJOR PSYCHODYNAMIC ISSUE

The major psychodynamic issue is the second part of the diagnostic formulation used in this project. This is the disorder underlying the predominant observable complaints. The character formation, a neurosis, or a psychosis causes the difficulty. When the disorder is a neurosis, we name the dynamically active forces, predominantly unconscious, that create the conflicts. To name the psychodynamic issues we use the extant psychiatric terminology as described in the Standard Diagnostic Nomenclature of the American Psychiatric Association.[3] While much of its terminology suits this phase of our diagnostic formulation, it is necessary to use some terminology that, though appearing frequently in psychoanalytic writings, is not listed in the Standard Nomenclature.

In the treatment group of seventy students (those with four or more interviews), all but two of whom we were able to diagnose, the major psychodynamic issue for sixteen students was a neurosis and a character disturbance for the remaining fifty-two students.

THE CHARACTER FORMATION

As we indicated earlier, the normal adolescent character is in the process of formation. Consequently, in our work with adolescents we prefer to indicate the direction of the character formation, and we use the phrase "character formation" rather than "character disorder" in describing the ordinary adolescent. When a premature crystallization of character has taken place, it is a condition similar to that of the adult, and we use the label "character disorder" advisedly. We think this differentiation is

3. *Diagnostic and Statistical Manual, Mental Disorders* (Washington, D.C.: American Psychiatric Association, 1952).

highly significant in work with adolescents: (1) it makes specific whether or not a crystallized character disorder already exists; (2) it indicates whether the client will be more or less subject to change; (3) it may suggest the nature of treatment necessary; (4) it influences the prognosis (adolescent character disorders are particularly difficult to influence therapeutically); and (5) the description of the direction of character formation indicates what the adult character may be when it is finally formed—with or without therapy.[4]

Ego Mechanisms and Defenses

In describing the adolescents who drop out of school, we found it of value to pinpoint the outstanding defenses. We look upon all manifest behavior as being, broadly speaking, ego adaptation—the outcome of the ego's work with the id impulses, the demands of the superego, and external reality. The concept "defense" is implicitly narrower, suggesting the ego's effort to protect itself against those impulses, affects, and so on, productive of distress or disorganization. But defense is also an adaptive mechanism of the ego.

Ego adaptations may be autoplastic (the dynamics are totally within the individual), or they may be alloplastic [5] (the ego tries to discharge tensions through an act altering the environment). Thus, a depressive reaction is autoplastic, a fight with the teacher is alloplastic.

In this adaptation to the pressure for discharge of the id impulses the ego may, depending on the requirements of the superego and reality, (1) permit direct discharge of the impulse, (2) attempt to keep the impulse repressed, maintaining the pent-up energy, (3) modify the mode (manner) of discharge, or (4) modify the goal or the object of the impulse.[6]

4. Sklansky, *op. cit.*
5. Franz Alexander, *Fundamentals of Psychoanalysis* (New York: W. W. Norton, 1948), pp. 235–236.
6. Sigmund Freud, "Instincts and Their Vicissitudes," in *Collected Papers,* IV (London: The Hogarth Press, 1925).

When the adolescent ego permits the direct discharge of impulse, as often happens, the frequent result is unacceptable behavior. Usually, the ego makes efforts to prevent such direct discharge. When these efforts attempt to keep impulses repressed, familiar defense mechanisms operate.[7] But not only may the adolescent defend himself against the impulse, he may also modify the way in which an impulse is satisfied or may direct the impulses toward goals and persons other than those originally and unconsciously intended. Many a teacher has been the scapegoat for hostility meant for a mother. Such modifications of modes of discharge and goals are the basis of sublimations extensively developed during adolescence.

DEFENSES AGAINST THE SOURCE OF THE IMPULSE

Ego defenses against the source of the impulse are efforts to prevent conscious awareness of the actual physiological source. The source cannot be altered, of course; but the individual may be totally unaware of the origin of his impulses (repression), and he may allow the impulses to come to consciousness only in the guise of belonging to another part of the body—one that usually symbolizes the original source (displacement). Thus, in conversion reactions of a hysterical girl the tingling sensation of the lips may serve as a displacement of the erotic sensations in the genitals. Conversion is a covert defense in that only the outcome is manifest. The defense operates unconsciously.

DEFENSES AGAINST THE MODE OF IMPULSE DISCHARGE

Defenses in this category are ego maneuvers for survival and acceptance in society; they are the ego adaptations making for success or failure. The demands of the instinct life are intense. It is a biological necessity to discharge needs for dependence, aggression, sexuality, and so on, but the ego must alter or modify the manner of satisfying these needs, since direct discharge may in-

7. Anna Freud, *The Ego and the Mechanisms of Defense* (New York: International Universities Press, Inc., 1946).

fringe upon the rights of others and bring retaliatory action. As repression is usually directed toward preventing discharge of the impulse, it may be considered a defense against mode as well as against source.

DEFENSES AGAINST THE OBJECT
OF THE IMPULSE

Defenses against the object of an impulse occur when recognition of its original nature produces anxiety or guilt. Since parents are objects of sexual as well as aggressive impulses, the adolescent defends against recognizing them as objects of his impulses and displaces his impulses onto persons or situations representing the parents. These objects are disguised, but usually have representative elements of the original object. As indicated above, teachers become identified with the parents, or the parental characteristics are projected onto the teacher. The adolescent may also use the new objects as he originally used his parents and may introject their characteristics or incorporate their personality into his own.

DEFENSES AGAINST AFFECT

Defenses exist not only against simple impulses but against the affective states that are their outcome. These affects may arouse conflict, anxiety, superego and ego-ideal edicts, and ego attitudes. One may defend oneself against affects covertly or overtly. Thus, guilt may be felt in association with a hostile thought; the individual can defend himself against it by isolation or deal with it by a counterphobic defense—as in the member of a gang who dares to cheat because he would be considered "chicken" if he did not. He denies his guilt by acting in a way opposite to his original inclination.

CONSCIOUS DEFENSES

Although we usually think of defense mechanisms as operating unconsciously, we know from our experience that adolescents are prone to conscious and deliberate alterations of the content of their minds and that they can communicate these alterations.

Thus, an adolescent may deny or suppress ideas and information of which he is fully aware. He may also quite consciously turn to fantasies as defenses against unpleasant facts and feelings. For this reason we have considered these conscious ego adaptations as defenses.

When the ego is unable to make an adaptation within its repertoire of techniques, there may be ego disintegration in which one observes partialized ego functions, disorganization, disorientation, failure in even ordinary perceptual functions, and total incapacity to cope with inner and outer pressures. Such ego disintegrations are seen in "identity diffusion" and the psychotic breaks of adolescents.[8] Primitive attempts at recovery and restitution follow, resulting in the chronic psychoses and psychotic character disorders clinically familiar to us.

COVERT VERSUS OVERT DEFENSES

Defenses may be mechanisms whose operations are not directly manifest but can only be inferred; these we have labeled covert. Those defenses whose operations are seen directly in behavior are called overt. Moreover, defenses, although given a single designation, may be complex ego integrations of simpler defenses, but it is a matter of convenience to use a unitary designation for them, recognizing at the same time their complexity.

For example, that repression takes place can only be inferred, and so it is considered covert—an unconscious mechanism. Furthermore, since it cannot be reduced to simpler mechanisms, we consider it a simple defense. On the other hand, passivity may be an overt defense, the effect of which is observed directly in passive, inactive behavior. But passivity is the unitary outcome of a chain of dynamics: fear of aggression, repression of such aggression, then indirect, aggressive discharge in disguise.

A brief discussion of some adolescent defenses serves as a series of profiles of the students. *Provocation*, the most frequent overt defense among the girls, is a defense against the adolescent's guilt over hostility. It allays guilt by provoking others to treat the

8. Erik H. Erikson, "The Problem of Ego Identity," *Journal of the American Psychoanalytic Association*, 4:1 (1956), 56–121.

adolescent punitively and thus relieve her of her guilt. *Acting out* is an ego adaptation allowing an impuse to be discharged in the context of the conflict over the impulse and its re-enactment. The whole constellation in its original form is unconscious and is re-enacted in real life in forms rationally acceptable to the adolescent's conscious mind. Much acting out involves provocation as a subsidiary defense. We consider *random activity* of a diffuse nature defensive, since it makes possible the release of anxiety or other disturbing affect. The conflicts remain unconscious, and the random activity serves to prevent their recognition, while draining off some of the tensions.

Turning to the overt defenses most frequent among the boys, we find, among others, passivity. *Passivity* reveals itself in inactivity, inertia, reluctance, nonchalance, ennui, and so on. In school passive adolescents are uncooperative, inattentive, uninterested, with poor study habits and failing grades. This defense is a difficult one to cope with in life and also in treatment. *Withdrawal* shows itself in nonparticipation in the ordinary adolescent social group activities. It, too, is a complex defense mechanism, for it is the outcome of various anxieties related to the impulses aroused in a group: shame, feelings of inferiority, fear of aggression or revelation of sexual impulses, and so forth. Most adolescents who withdraw do not isolate themselves as do schizophrenics, in whom there is no interest in others. They actually long for peer and object relationships. The withdrawal is secondary to a conflict that they would rather not have aroused or publicized. *Overcompensation* among adolescent boys is a defense almost characteristic of this age and sex group. It is a defense against feelings of inferiority or inadequacy, and its purpose is to heighten self-esteem or estimation by others. The need to be manly, competent, and vigorous has a high premium placed upon it in our culture. When personality development lacks these characteristics, overcompensation comes to the fore to help save face.

The girls' most frequent covert defense was *repression*. It can be recognized by its effects and especially by the absence from consciousness of that which, from a study of the case material, we know should be there. Repression can be shown to have existed when the repressed content later becomes conscious.

Somatization is a term used to describe the substitution of physical symptoms and bodily changes for psychic phenomena. The concept includes psychosomatic as well as hysterical symptoms, for it is not always clear how close to conversion certain physical complaints actually are. *Reaction formation* is a common defense in which an impulse is denied through the manifestation of attitudes and behavior opposite to those originally intended.

Identification was the most frequent covert defense used by the boys. Although the word "defense" seems an inaccurate description, identification is an ego adaptive mechanism serving defensive functions. It is a mental mechanism describing the tendency of one individual to take on the characteristics of another. As a defense it may serve to disguise ego-dystonic aspects of personality—feelings of inadequacy, inferiority, shame, guilt, and so on. Later identifications defend against earlier identifications. In the therapy of adolescents, identification with the therapist becomes an important basic catalyst for improvement.

Fantasy is also a mental process that cannot be looked upon as completely defensive. It is the inner psychic elaboration of a sequence of related details and serves to satisfy needs, resolve conflicts, and solve problems. When it takes conscious form, the fantasy is usually visual, although the other senses may be involved. Although the fantasies may be or may induce memories, they may also be constructed around phenomena never actually experienced. Fantasy may lead to beneficial or detrimental actions, depending on the ego's capacity to judge reality and to act in terms of its requirements. Fantasy may itself be a source of gratification and tension reduction and may be indulged in only for that purpose. It is defensive when it deters the ego from perceiving immediate events or outer realities that must be dealt with for adequate adaptation. An example is the drop-out boy who indulges in the fantasy that he is successful while sitting at home, avoiding school, and not looking for a job. Fantasy helps him avoid both the recognition of the inner conflict and the demands of outer reality for mature behavior.

DIAGNOSTIC DESCRIPTIONS

IN THIS PRESENTATION OF OUR nomenclature, we describe only the diagnostic entities observed among the drop-out students.

The Neuroses

Since we had only one student with a phobic reaction and one with a depressive reaction, and since these disorders in adolescence differ little from the adult counterparts, we do not repeat the descriptions here.

ANXIETY REACTION (ANXIETY NEUROSIS)

Anxiety occurs during the course of development of any clinical disorder. When it is continual, diffuse, and not warded off through the development of defenses, we describe it as an entity —"anxiety reaction." Anxiety is experienced as fear, and in an anxiety reaction the source of fear is neither specific nor subjectively known, differentiating it from ordinary fear.

A wide variety of physical sensations is experienced in anxiety: chills, tremulousness, blushing, sweating, scalp-tightening dryness of mouth, excessive perspiration in the palms, "butter-flies in the stomach," peristaltic motions, frequency of urination, and urgency in defecation. But all of these are accompanied by the awareness of a vague, dreadful, anticipated danger. Anxiety is so unpleasant that the adolescent almost immediately defends himself against it, but in an anxiety reaction his defenses do not maintain themselves and change frequently. Adolescents easily become temporarily anxious, but the adolescent with an anxiety neurosis suffers from unrelieved anxiety.

The situations precipitating anxiety are many and usually symbolically represent fear of the impulses themselves or fear of the consequences of acting on such impulses. These forbidden impulses may be sexual, aggressive, or both. Almost any circumstance that could permit such impulses to become conscious arouses anxiety. Many adolescents develop anxiety over the breakthrough of anal sadistic impulses, but their most common anxiety reactions occur over sexual impulses.

The stronger the ego of the individual, the more capacity he has to sustain anxiety without the development of defenses, though usually a wide variety of transitory defenses are brought to bear on the anxiety. Anxiety reactions respond well to therapy when the ego is strong and the stimulating causes are removed. In some cases the forbidden urges are eventually expressed to the caseworker, with consequent relief. More frequently, adequate defenses are established to prevent the breakthrough of the unacceptable impulses. Great care must be exercised in treatment lest regressive defenses set in, creating a greater degree of pathology than previously existed. With adolescents in acute anxiety states, support and reassurance are more helpful than "uncovering."

In those cases diagnosed as anxiety reaction or anxiety neurosis, we find a strongly organized ego, a punitive superego, a good capacity for object relationships, and special concern over tabooed sexual and aggressive impulses. The caseworker should be as much concerned with the nature of the defenses as with the anxiety itself, for these defenses will determine the ensuing pathology upon relief of the anxiety, and the defensive structure may produce a disorder less responsive to treatment and more severe than the anxiety reaction.

ANXIETY REACTION (HANDLED BY OVERT ACTION)

Since the experience of anxiety is extremely disturbing, the ego makes every effort to rid itself of the feeling and its accompanying ideation. The adolescent, more than the adult, cannot tolerate anxiety; his ego seeks defenses quickly. Adolescents are more prone than adults to actively manipulate the environment as a defense against anxiety. During an anxiety reaction these manipulations frequently are varied, diffuse, inconsistent, and disorganized. There is a helter-skelter quality to the adolescent's behavior as he seeks to do something to relieve the anxiety. Such diffuse overt activities should be recognized as an anxiety reaction when it is known that the stress is actually internal.

ADOLESCENT ADJUSTMENT REACTION

A diagnosis of "adolescent adjustment reaction" must be considered an inadequate diagnostic statement. It indicates that what is emphasized clinically is transient during adolescence and is related to the developmental process itself. Both of these qualifications are important, of course, but what is needed is a description of the specific behavior, the adjustment reaction itself. In making the diagnosis, it is necessary to indicate the kind of adjustment reaction—anxiety reaction, depressive reaction, and so forth—and to designate the character formation in which it is taking place. The diagnosis then indicates that the reaction occurs transiently and results from the phenomenon of adolescence itself acting as a specific stress on the personality.

The Character Formations [1]

EMOTIONALLY UNSTABLE CHARACTER FORMATION

Although the term describing this type of character formation seems unspecific, "emotional instability" is the most descriptive.

1. See Appendix B-II for outline.

single, predominant characteristic we find to paraphrase the whole character structure. These adolescents react primitively or childishly, with easy emotionality over minimal frustrations. The outstanding affect is rage aroused over a minor frustration. It is the ease with which the rage is aroused as well as its intensity that characterize this disorder. Moreover, the amount of rage seems disproportionate to its stimulus: a parental call to get up on time, a teacher's disapproval of classroom behavior, not being given money for movies, and so forth, are sufficient causes for angry outbursts. The rage is not controlled autoplastically (held in check by intrapsychic means) but is immediately discharged in angry verbalization, tears, physical abuse, destructiveness, and delinquent acting out. These adolescents are not psychotic. They perceive reality as others do; there is no bizarreness, seeming meaninglessness, and so forth. Yet they cannot withhold their emotional reaction to the frustrating stimulus. Although they sometimes seem impulse ridden, not every impulse demands satisfaction, but specific frustrations set off the reactions.

Although rage is the usual emotion expressed by emotionally unstable individuals, they show incapacity to control libidinal behavior as well. They may fall in love quickly or with little hesitation decide upon a course of potentially gratifying activity. Thus, they easily get involved in such delinquent acts as truanting and stealing.

The difference between emotionally unstable character formation and ordinary adolescent lability is one of degree. The "normal" adolescent is also unstable emotionally, but in the greater part of his daily existence there is adequate equilibrium, control of emotions, considered actions, and acceptable behavior. Emotionality is not his chief characteristic.

Emotionally unstable character formation is differentiated from impulse-ridden character formation by the latter's general yielding to all impulses; the emotionally unstable personality yields only to a specific impulse or impulses. Both of these character formations are infantile because of the incapacity of the individual to delay gratification and the relative insufficiency of ego integrated functions. Both are nonpsychotic types of character formation because the perceptual processes, thought functions, and orientation in interpersonal relationships remain determined by reality.

Therapy of the emotionally unstable individual is almost a redevelopment process. The caseworker helps the adolescent withhold his emotional intensity by building a supportive and rewarding relationship and by working toward an increase in ego capacity to delay reactions. The adolescent enlarges his ego by learning more facts, realizing all possibilities of action, and exercising better judgment.

SCHIZOID CHARACTER FORMATION

Traditionally, adolescence has been recognized as the developmental period when schizophrenia (dementia praecox) takes on its characteristic form as a clinical entity. Yet it is also a time when character formation may tend in the direction of psychosis but be arrested somewhat short of extreme ego disorganization. When such arrests occur, one may recognize syndromes, groupings of defensive functions, that have a similarity to schizophrenic reactions but are not psychoses. These are the "schizoid character formations."

Their outstanding characteristics are: unique and strange idiosyncrasies; lack of flexibility in affect and behavior; shallowness and persistence of whatever affect or apathy there may be; some bizarreness in thought, fantasy, and speech; noninvolvement in close personal relationships; tendency to social solitariness; lack of enthusiasm about most areas of ordinary interests; and unique interest in specialized hobbies or careers. In schizoid characters the ego is predominantly intact as far as perception of reality is concerned. Although the inner life is uniquely interpreted and logical thought processes are interfered with, there is adequate management of reality. Intellectual ability is not impaired and may even be outstanding.

These adolescents are frequently quiet and withdrawn; they attract attention only when some serious transgression or failure has taken place. Parents may wonder why the child does not "mingle" or show an interest in the opposite sex. The teacher may complain about nonparticipation in the class routine or extracurricular activities. The peers are the ones who, in their sensitivity to deviations, are quick to recognize the "queerness" and uniqueness of this type.

In treatment schizoid adolescents usually persist in a flatness or shallowness of affect that the caseworker finds he cannot alter. The interviews lack empathic resonance. Sometimes the persisting affect is irascibility rather than shallow nonchalance (these schizoid adolescents display paranoid suspicion—a constant vigilance in a persecutory world). Schizoid individuals often have odd mannerisms, inappropriate social behavior, and disorderly thought processes. Although these adolescents usually are social failures, they may follow a preoccupation with some field of interest to the extent of becoming experts. Occasionally they have successful careers. The contemporary adolescent world, however, is so intolerant of nonconformity or individual uniqueness that the schizoid individual becomes a social pariah. In actuality he prefers to be alone.

The differentiation of schizoid character formation from schizophrenic psychosis is primarily on the basis of the ego's intactness in perception, thought, speech, and hold on reality. The schizoid person may be queer, but he certainly is not insane; his life adjustment depends very much on finding the proper niche—a library, a laboratory, a workbench, or any place requiring few interpersonal contacts may be suitable. But pressures to conform to employee social routines or other rules and regulations may cause breakdowns.

The caseworker tries to do his best with the schizoid adolescent—emotional support, advice, education, and environmental manipulation are all necessary. Usually no efforts are made to give insight other than the recognition of manifest behavior.

ORAL-DEPENDENT CHARACTER FORMATION

Total personality structure may be organized around receiving satisfaction of an oral nature from the world. The oral-dependent adolescent is like an infant in his expectations from parents: he feels the need of being given to, cared for, protected, and guided. The feeling must, of course, be expressed in forms suitable to adolescence and with adequate rationalizations. Such an adolescent gives the impression of being soft, yielding, unaggressive, unambitious, lazy, uninterested, and even stupid. He is concerned with getting what he can out of life without too much exertion and certainly with the maximum avoidance of conflict. He is passive to his environment.

At home he is a late riser and must usually be awakened. He avoids chores, but is eager for meals, sleep, and entertainment. He enjoys television and movies, but dislikes the activity required in athletics, group play, or even reading (unless the comics are at hand).

In his peer group he is a follower and usually easily led if some gratification is promised. He clings to relationships, fears separation, and shuns being alone. At school he is not an ambitious student, volunteering little and making few efforts to do his work. He may attempt "apple polishing" to charm the teacher into acting maternally, but is rarely persistent if he does not meet with success.

The oral-dependent character formations include an aggressive as well as a passive type. The aggressive type is distinguished from his passive counterpart by a marked degree of clinging—an almost desperate holding on to relationships and situations in which the individual may be dependent. For both types dependency needs are urgent. These conditions, usually chronic, may be traced to trauma in the earliest infantile dependency on the mother: there may have been severe oral deprivation or an overly gratifying oral period in an otherwise difficult development.

The genital drives of the oral-dependent adolescent are expressed in pregenital modes. Heterosexual experience is used as another medium for obtaining dependent gratification. The intensity of the longing is, of course, greater during adolescence. Since the infantile nature of the character structure is incompatible with the values of the adolescent world, the oral-dependent individual suffers from some feelings of inferiority.

Treatment of this condition is difficult. The caseworker becomes another mother and in the context of this relationship may lead the adolescent to alter some behavior, but the inertia makes a significant change of personality extremely hard to achieve.

ORAL–AGGRESSIVE CHARACTER FORMATION— INFANTILE–DEMANDING TYPE

The adolescent with an oral-aggressive character formation is oriented toward obtaining maximum personal gratification with minimal discomfort. Unlike the oral-dependent adolescent he makes active efforts to obtain gratification, but the gratification is far more important than the effort. This kind of adolescent arouses the hostility of his parents and teachers because he is demanding. He insists on having his way, and he persists in trying to get it. Being adolescent, he may have poor judgment, and his "foolish" efforts may cause him difficulty. His expectations for gratification are inordinate and infantile, and the limits set by his particular reality do not alter his expectations.

Like the infant, he is easily frustrated and brooks no delay in getting what he wants. Grasping and insatiable, he makes use of every device within his ken. The more intelligent, creative, and experienced he is, the more devices there will be available to him. He frequently uses people, conniving against, controlling, and "selling" them to get his way. When the devices used are asocial, he becomes a "psychopathic" type.

The fantasies of the infantile-demanding individual, in keeping with his personality structure, are dreams of easy money, glory without work, and creation without application. Set on a path of achieving some fantasy goals, he often exerts himself; but when the bubble bursts, the fantasy continues without effort. Sometimes depression ensues.

The history of the infantile-demanding adolescent indicates early infantile frustrations with periodic opportunities for excessive gratification. The relationships to early objects are traumatic. Inconsistent indulgence in childhood may also be a factor in this character formation. The possibilities of deprivation and hunger have always loomed large in the unconscious.

Prognosis is better for the infantile-demanding person than for the oral-dependent, for in contrast to the latter, he does exert effort. The fact that he is an aggressive type is to his advantage, for if his aggression can be directed into acceptable forms and toward realistic goals, an adequate adjustment is possible. Relationships are important to him, and he attaches himself to the caseworker, hoping to use him for his own end. The caseworker takes advantage of this need to redirect the efforts and modify the goals of the client.

DEPRESSIVE CHARACTER FORMATION

Adolescents whose character formation arises from defensive and adaptive structuring around oral-aggressive impulses may manifest chronic depressive tendencies.

Such adolescents are often moody and introspective. Sadness, an air of thoughtful resignation, some bitterness, and even hopelessness seem to envelop them. They are serious, slow, or indecisive. Their social expressions are not always sad, but when not actively aroused to laughter or gaiety, they look serious or unhappy.

The depressive character is not an isolated person. Although he is often alone and lonely, he longs for relationships. He is drawn to others as others are drawn to him. Because he is capable of deep ties of affection, he is likable and good company when his mood permits. His relationships may be deeply binding and he takes love seriously; often he measures each date in terms of its depth and abiding quality. Rejection is painful to him and leads to deeper depressive moods.

The depressive individual's self-concept is one of self-depreciation, inadequacy, inferiority, and unworthiness. He underestimates his true abilities and longs painfully for superiority and uniqueness. With typical adolescent inconstancy he has periods of improved self-esteem and successful behavior alternating with the depressive mood. Schooling is serious business, but satisfactory work may be interfered with because of the special involvement of schooling in the emotional conflict. Good work enhances his self-esteem; poor work or low grades lead to further self-depreciation and pessimistic predictions of his own failure.

When these adolescents have intellectual interests, they are often "philosophical" and drawn to pessimistic literature and readings in existential philosophy or, in another mood, to nihilism or hedonism. When intellectual interests or talents are less significant, the youngsters are preoccupied with difficult relationships and life's hardships.

The dynamics of depressive character formation show certain consistencies. Usually this formation becomes more obvious with pubescence and is an attempt to resolve the intensified instincts of this period. This does not mean, however, that depressive character formation is a disorder of adolescence, but rather that the reawakened oedipal impulses and conflicts evoke infantile, regressive tendencies. Depressive character formation as a resolution of the oedipal conflict is an adolescent developmental phenomenon.

Orality is a prominent feature of the depressive character. A constant, aggressive demanding for narcissistic satiation reveals itself in chronic discontent and dissatisfaction. Bitterness, generalized hostility toward the world, and fantasies of destruction and sadism testify to the angry reaction to frustrated demands. But the more obvious defense against the aggression is self-directed and introverted: self-blame, self-depreciation, and in extreme cases, suicidal fantasies and acts. Accompanying these characteristics is the air of hopelessness and resignation—the expression of lost hope of getting the longed-for object or narcissistic gratification, and the simultaneous self-castigation for the hostile reaction to frustration.

The superego of the depressive character type is severe, primitive in its origin, and all-consuming in quality. It is in a great portion an "oral" superego. Its retaliatory mechanisms are biting, devouring, gnawing, destroying, and annihilating by incorporation. Depressive individuals have in their superegos a large quantity of anality, too. Sadistic impulses are both oral and anal in origin, and the superego's retaliation is likewise orally and anally sadistic. The adolescent's guilt over his hostility motivates the self-directed defenses, and the depressive structure then becomes the way of life.

The oedipal conflict is especially difficult for the adolescent with a depressive character formation to handle. He desires the

longed-for parent with all the unfulfilled hunger of the oral child
for his mother. The rival parent is seen as an intruder upon the
source of life itself and is intensely hated and feared—castration
being looked upon less as an attack upon the genitals than as
deprivation of life. Guilt accompanies the attitude toward the
rival parent and adds to the tendency toward atonement and
self-castigation.

The chief therapeutic problems are the redirection of the
hostilities, the alleviation of the severe superego, and the establishment of hope for gratification through more real and attain-
able means.

MASOCHISTIC CHARACTER FORMATION

The masochistic adolescent seems to be intent on finding suffering and defeat in life: he seeks out those aspects in his sur-
roundings producing pain and also provokes situations creating
pain for himself. He wears a mantle of suffering and is preoccupied with hardship. The masochistic adolescent usually presents
himself as having an unhappy life—misunderstood by his parents,
less preferred than his siblings, rejected by his classmates, and un-
wanted by members of the opposite sex. In school his work seems
an unmanageable burden. He has no interest in his studies, his
excuse being that they are boring, poorly presented, or require
too much homework. He complains that his teachers are un-
skilled, uninterested, and cruel. If he is actually a capable student,
parents and teachers expect achievement from him and are an-
noyed or exasperated by his pitiful lack of effort and tendency
to fail.

The masochistic individual often brings about his own failures
and then suffers from them. He may provoke his parents to mis-
treat him, his teachers to scold him, and his friends to reject him.
Through all of this, one senses his sufferings include a vengeful-
ness and a stubborn, resisting passivity as imperturbable as it is
exasperating. This passive resistance is a disguise for hostility.

The dynamics of masochism may take several forms, often
within the same individual. The self-defeat and suffering may be
self-punishment for guilt over hostility to parents. They may be

a way of relating to parents (perhaps required by the parents)—as if only suffering can evoke interest, attention, and love. They may be a pattern of submission to a hostile parent as the outcome of identification with a masochistic pattern. This suffering-and-failure complex has an erotic quality about it. Phenomenologically, it is dramatic and romantic, or at least effective in arousing the pity and sympathy of others, thus becoming a pleasurable end in itself; but it is also effective in its destructiveness, since it causes annoyance, irritation, frustration, and defeat to parents and teachers. Dynamically, the superego is strong and punitive, allowing the ego to express hostility only in disguised form and through techniques that are also punitive toward the self.

Masochistic character formation is to be differentiated from masochistic perversion, the achievement of orgastic relief during some painful sexual act. In masochistic character disorders the entire life is full of suffering and defeat, whereas in perversion the suffering is confined to the sexual act.

Depression and depressive character formation have much in common with the masochistic character formation, but the differences are important. The masochistic adolescent is not continuously sad and depressed. The pace of the mental activities does not alter, but mood varies. The depressed adolescent is not so much searching for defeat; he is already defeated. He is less active in provoking abuse: the ego has already submitted to the superego.

For several reasons, masochistic character formations are difficult to treat in adolescence. If the condition is only the character direction, the prognosis is better; but if rigidity of defenses has set in, the casework experience is, like the life of the client, full of suffering, pain, passivity, immobility, and provocation of frustration and hostility. The adolescent does not and cannot see his life pattern as inappropriate, but justifies and rationalizes it on a reality basis. A large amount of adolescent energy is invested in the defenses, and secondary gratification to the ego from the success of the defenses, from the revenge attained, and from the sympathy and pity aroused is also great.

There is extreme reluctance to any altering of these defenses.

The superego is strong, and fear of hostile impulses is intense. The reality of the therapeutic situation as a pain-producing situation is enough to convince the client that he is suffering there as everywhere else. The continuing parent-child interaction counteracts even the minimal effect of therapy.

COMPULSIVE CHARACTER FORMATION

Compulsive character formation is related to the anal phase of development. Although the character structure of adolescents has not yet crystallized, it is extremely difficult to detect this when the character formation involves compulsive defenses. The muscular power and the defiant stubbornness of anality are nowhere so evident as in this condition.

The adolescent with compulsive character formation who comes to treatment is one whose defenses have led him into some unsuccessful struggle with authority. Refusal to study, inability to concentrate, inattention to the teacher, unwillingness to cooperate, slowness to learn, and procrastination are common complaints of the school. Often there is recognition by the complainant that the adolescent has superior intelligence.

The compulsive adolescent gives the immediate impression of being superior and haughty. He seems excessively mature, highly organized, and proper. His bearing is stiff, his dress may be meticulous, and he is very careful to behave in accordance with the rules of propriety that he considers appropriate to an interview. His speech is controlled, his words often carefully chosen, his vocabulary excellent. He is excessively sensitive to preciseness of meaning and verbal exchanges, but he may speak slowly and only when spoken to, so that one feels he communicates only what he wants to say.

Because of the excessive control of affect, this adolescent seems to communicate no warmth during his verbalizations. Moreover, his descriptions of issues seem to carry an insufficient feeling tone: his nonchalance is more than it should be.

In his life the compulsive adolescent is a perfectionist, demanding of himself that he know all or do all perfectly, only to find he does not know enough and is doing little. He may be meticulous about his person, but ignore other areas of cleanliness, and the parental complaint of an untidy room is frequent. Although he gets joy out of seeing a job well done, for success is important, teachers and parents are shocked at his inconsistency and neglect.

In his relationships the compulsive adolescent seems distant, cold, even isolated at times. He may complain that in grade school he suffered from teasing about his "sissiness," excessive timidity, or prudishness, or that in high school other children do not consider him fun, although they may respect him for his intelligence. If he is successful in school, he is accused of being a grind, and since his manner is forbidding, his company is not sought out.

Many of these adolescents are among the most successful students, although the price they pay in energy and anxiety as they seek perfection is great. Among those who come to treatment, however, there is only sporadic success or the promise of success in treatment. They fail in school, unconsciously rebelling against their own perfectionistic standards by doing the opposite of what they expect of themselves and of what others expect of them.

The dynamics of the compulsive character formation revolve around the nature of the superego demands over the ego's adaptation of the anal impulses. The strict, primitive superego arises from the edicts of the parents during the toilet-training period. It requires production of a specific quantity or a certain quality at a certain place and at regular intervals. Moreover, the productions must be made at specific rates of speed and within certain periods of time. Some sort of effort must be made, and results are carefully evaluated. Reward is the outcome of good results, carrying with it the enhancement of self-esteem, show of affection, and promise of additional future rewards. But failure results in depreciation, loss of love, threat of punishment, or actual punishment.

In general, the ego's tendency is to comply with the demands of the superego and to feel anxiety or guilt when the demands are not fulfilled; but the ego also reacts with hostility because of the great pain felt, the amount of energy exerted, and the frustration experienced in attempting to force physiological functions to alter their natural rhythm to suit the superego's demands. This hostility, however, must be suppressed and can find discharge only in surreptitious, periodic manifestations of anger or in chronic, involuntary noncompliance, stubborn failure, and inertia.

As might be expected, treatment of compulsive character formation in adolescents is as difficult as it is in adults, if not more so. The obstinacy of the defenses in refusing to yield to therapy is as great as the obstinacy in the personality structure itself. The compulsiveness does not need as much alteration, however, as do the vicarious expressions of hostility leading the adolescent to make poor use of the school setting and the opportunities it offers. If the adolescent gains sufficient insight to attempt to counteract these tendencies in himself and to find outlets for his hostility in less self-destructive areas, he has achieved a great deal.

HYSTERICAL CHARACTER FORMATION

Among adolescents, especially girls, we find that the character structure may tend toward the integration of defenses that we describe as hysterical. Because individuals with this kind of personality structure are continually experiencing episodes of varying degrees of anxiety, we feel it might also be called the anxiety-ridden character formation. One might create two separate categories, but the difference is essentially quantitative: anxiety predominates in the anxiety-ridden character, and the defenses against anxiety predominate in the hysterical character. In either state both anxiety and typical defenses against the anxiety exist.

Numerous situations have emotional significance of dramatic intensity and quality for the hysterical adolescent. These adolescents are histrionic, but their behavior is not deliberate play-acting. They are highly sensitive and full of strong feelings. The situations arousing their reactions usually have to do with interpersonal contacts; love, sexuality, hatred, envy, and the like, are acutely felt. Although situations may be only symbolic of such "human drama," they nevertheless arouse the reactions of hysterical individuals. These adolescents frequently are avid readers of poetry, romantic novels, and plays. They are responsive to the well-known literary imagery of the moon, the weather, the sky, nature, and music. They fall in and out of love easily, hate intensely, suffer from loneliness, and have moods of self-pity.

Their bodily movements often portray their mood. Seductive in manner, they cause those about them to respond to their appeal. Their profuse fantasies are usually romantic, though not always conscious.

The hysterical adolescent defends himself against anxiety through the development of transitory phobias, dissociated states such as fainting spells, and somatic conversion symptoms. As in all phallic disorders, repression, displacement, symbolization, conversion, inhibition, and overcompensation are common. But in this character disorder the defenses are only transitory and behavior is concerned predominantly with interpersonal relationships. "Having someone to love" is important, and forms of behavior unconsciously calculated to win such love are most frequent. On the other hand, sexuality is feared and repressed, though it breaks through and manifests itself in shyness, easy blushing, preoccupation with romantic objects or situations, and dating problems.

Often these adolescents are involved in an intense struggle with their parents, whom they both love and hate. This mixture of feelings is manifested in deliberate avoidance of the parents, yet fear of separation from them. Teachers too are loved, hated, feared, idolized, as if they were intimately involved with the student. The hysterical individual is introspective and readily "psychologizes" about his way of life, his motives, and the motives of others. The affective life is intense and meaningful, though often one emotion is used to avoid another. The intensity is another factor used to attract a love object.

As in all psychodynamic issues that are primarily related to the phallic (oedipal) phase of development, the sexual longings for the parent of the opposite sex are prohibited and repressed. Even though he may be idolized, the parent of the same sex is hated and feared. This character formation is an integrative attempt to solve these conflicts and to keep them repressed.

Most hysterical adolescents have adequately developed egos and superegos. Hysterical adolescents readily attach themselves to the caseworker, who can, therefore, easily influence them. Their anxiety is great, however, and their defenses shift among those typical for phallic disorders. Although they develop helpful insights in therapy, insight cannot be pressed upon them without risk of excess anxiety and its consequences.

Adolescent boys in this category differ from girls in several surface manifestations. They feel it inappropriate to express their inner emotionality and attempt to suppress these tendencies. They are also more concerned with competitive masculine strivings, aggression, achievement, and the like, than are the girls. But oedipal conflicts are common to both sexes.

Hysterical character formation must be differentiated from anxiety reactions, conversion reactions, phobias, dissociated states, manic behavior, schizoid and schizophrenic reactions, and infantile character disorders. In anxiety reactions (anxiety neurosis) no characteristic defenses persist and anxiety is always present. It stands out above any other feature of the disorder. Although the hysterical character formation itself in adolescence may include conversion reactions, phobias, even dissociations, none of these are the predominant feature of the disorder. A symptom disorder, however, may be the major psychodynamic issue at some period in the life of the hysterical character.

Although the affective experiences of the hysterical character formation are profuse and intense and moods are a salient feature, no single affective state dominates it, as is true of hypomanic and depressive character formations.

Furthermore, the affect is appropriate to the situation that arouses it. In schizoid character formation and in schizophrenia, the affect, when present, seems inappropriate in content as well as in degree. It has a strong bizarre quality and it is not immediately comprehended by others. Hysterical character formation always arouses empathic reactions in both normal and neurotic persons. The hysterical adolescent may appear infantile in his behavior, and it is often difficult to distinguish this character formation from immature character disorders in which "acting out" is the dominant feature. In time, however, the sexual issue and the competition for love reveal themselves as the major psychodynamic issues in this condition, whereas in the infantile personality insistence on infantile gratification stands out and few genital interests develop.

INHIBITED CHARACTER FORMATION

One solution of the reawakened oedipal strivings during adolescence is the development of the character structure in which there is a generalized inhibition of impulse. Such adolescents are recognized by their excessive suppression of sexuality and aggression. They are reluctant to engage in either actual or symbolic sexual and aggressive activities. They are shy and reticent in social situations, yielding to others more out of timidity and embarrassment than out of lack of personal desire or of energy.

Inhibited individuals are usually good children, close to their parents, compliant, and highly moral in their behavior. The parents complain that they are bookish, introverted stay-at-homes. They keep urging them to go out, "mix with people," date, and attend parties, mostly with little success. It is not that the inhibited adolescent does not want to do these things—he longs to do them—but social activities mean contact with the opposite sex, display and revelation of one's impulses and interests, competition, and aggression, all of which are feared.

School is a situation symbolizing sexuality and aggression, too, and the inhibited adolescent reacts accordingly. He is quiet in the classroom and participates openly as little as possible. He may be bright, but does not exhibit his intelligence. Since he feels aggression and destruction are necessary to succeed, inhibition may keep him from doing well in his studies. Inhibited adolescents, however, can also be excellent students when the energies that would otherwise be directed to social activities are channeled into studies or intellectual interests. They are failures in the usual high school extracurricular activities, and in the presence of the opposite sex, they find themselves shy, tongue-tied, and clumsy. Stiff and tense in their bodily movements, they are sensitive about being observed in embarrassing activities. Their speech is hesitant, and they restrain any show of enthusiasm or emotion.

The inhibited character formation, like others in the phallic group, is primarily a defensive maneuver against the sexuality and aggression of the oedipal conflict. Both the ego and id energies are strong, and the superego is consistent and internalized to a great degree. Because these adolescents desire object relationships and have a good potential for developing them, they respond well to a nonthreatening, nonseductive, unpressured casework relationship.

The inhibited character formation is differentiated from passive, dependent character formation by the major psychodynamic issue involved. There is no bizarreness or inappropriateness of action as in the schizoid condition. The degree of withdrawal from social activities is less, and it is not out of conscious preference, as in the schizoid condition. The general maturation is far beyond that of the infantile character formation. Although the frustration resulting from the inhibition causes these persons to be unhappy, the sad affect is not as profound as that of the depressed adolescent.

If therapy is instituted early enough, the prognosis for response to treatment of adolescents with inhibited character formation is good.

OVERCOMPENSATED CHARACTER FORMATION

We use the adjective "overcompensated" to describe a character formation whose chief defensive maneuver in the personality organization is an obvious overcompensation. This is the adolescent whose very "strutting" bespeaks the need to be bigger, more powerful, more manly than he actually is. He brags and shows off a great deal and is full of fantasies about his prowess or his sexual successes. He is aggressive and tough in competition and gets into fights with authorities or peers larger than himself. He often has a chip on his shoulder and is highly defensive about his status. If he is overly proud, boasting, and lying, peers, parents, and teachers readily see through him; but he has no insight into his overcompensatory behavior.

Strong, unconscious feelings of inadequacy and inferiority underlie the overcompensation. This adolescent both consciously and unconsciously compares himself to others, always to find himself the loser in the comparison. Then he defends himself against the painful discovery. Unconsciously, he feels inadequate about his sex organ. A girl associates sexual inadequacy with the whole body; it is not desirable enough. A boy feels his penis is too small.

The dynamic struggle of this character formation relates to the phallic phase of development and centers on the oedipal conflict. In comparing himself with his father, the boy finds he is inferior. Sometimes he cannot use the father as an admirable model for his budding masculinity and finds himself inadequate on this account. A similar problem exists for the girl and her relationship with her mother. In both boys and girls sexual concerns are strong. The boy has a deep affection for his mother, with sexual attractions often coming to consciousness. Frequently, the mother encourages the boy's expectations of being sexually preferred to the father. For the girl, too, being loved in a sexual or romantic way is important; since she feels she is a failure in the competition for love, she employs overcompensatory defenses.

Adolescents notoriously use overcompensation as a defense. To diagnose a character formation in adolescence as overcompensated, therefore, one must recognize the pervasiveness of this defense and determine that the oedipal conflict is the major psychodynamic issue. The overcompensating adolescent usually has a good ego. The superego is not so much a problem as the ego-ideal which this type of adolescent feels he cannot attain.

Therapy makes use of the adolescent's need for a more adequate ego-ideal. The caseworker tries to represent a new ego-ideal or helps to mitigate the feelings of inadequacy resulting from comparison with the existing ego-ideal. In casework therapy the adolescent also comes to recognize the nature of his overcompensatory defenses and their fruitlessness.

PSYCHODYNAMIC FRAMEWORK

FOR DIAGNOSING

SCHOOL PROBLEMS

The Specific Psychodynamic Involvement in School—Students

WE SPECULATED THAT FOR MANY drop-outs as well as others with serious school problems, school takes on some special psychodynamic meaning and that this particular meaning plays a major role in the child's school difficulties. Such a youngster no longer reacts realistically to school as a place to get an education, but sees school in a subjectively modified way and uses it to meet his own needs and to work out conflicts not connected solely with his education. Such psychodynamic involvement may be preconscious or conscious on the part of the youngster, but often is at an unconscious level, with the child totally unaware of the dynamic forces at work.

When a student is driven to utilize school for emotional needs of his own, the school has not created his problem, and remedial educational measures will be ineffectual as long as his conflicts persist and are untreated.

Multiple psychodynamic factors determine drop-out. Among these multiple determinants, however, there are certain emphases —factors more heavily weighted in their effect. If these students are to be helped and their drop-out to be prevented, it is essential to understand the psychodynamic determinants and to work in the direction of modifying them. In our study we could not encompass all the determinants, so we directed our efforts toward a consideration of the most important psychodynamic forces.

Five categories of major psychodynamic uses of school resulting in difficulty were sufficient for classification of the students:

a. School difficulty resulting from unsuccessful handling of impulse or need
b. School difficulty resulting from maladaptive superego reactions
c. School difficulty resulting from the student's attempt to use school to resolve a conflict belonging to another area of life
d. School difficulty only one manifestation of a general personality problem
e. School difficulty resulting from reality problems.

For each student we saw, we sought to determine the basic category to which he belonged. In classifying any case we did not intend to imply that the student's dynamic involvement in school was the sole cause of his maladjustment. We recognized that problems related to school, like any aspect of human behavior, are highly complicated; school difficulties and drop-out are the final outcome of a long chain of unique, individual events. Nor did we mean to imply that the school dynamic selected was the only one operating: a student could use school psychodynamically in several different ways. Our categories overlap somewhat, as in practice there are no mutually exclusive divisions in psychodynamics. To have attempted multiple checking, however, would have muddied any attempt to group and draw out larger comparisons. From our knowledge of each case we evaluated where the emphasis lay and classified the case according to the predominant school dynamic. We attempted to do the same for the parents of the drop-outs, since we believed they might also show some special psychodynamic involvement in the child's school life.

SCHOOL DIFFICULTY RESULTING FROM
UNSUCCESSFUL HANDLING OF IMPULSE
OR NEED

In this impulse-need category are the children whose school difficulty is the ultimate result of unconscious conflict over specific impulses or needs unacceptable to them. School symbolizes their unacceptable impulses or needs, and they react to school as a whole or to any of its detailed aspects—achievement, teachers, relationships, and the like—as if these are the impulses themselves. The impulse is displaced onto the school situation. Such symbolization and displacement are common in adolescence, but in the disturbed adolescent we observe a relative failure of defenses with a consequent yielding to impulses or an exaggeration of defenses in the struggle to keep impulses from breaking through.

In this category we expect to find a youngster with an essentially well-developed ego and a previously satisfactory school record. His history may be fairly calm and untroubled, except for the school problem and such other conflicts that specifically result from the same unconscious struggle. He has anxiety or guilt about the school trouble, and this anxiety or guilt in turn plays a large part in the school difficulty. If there is rebellion, it is the outward manifestation of inner guilt and anxiety, for school and education are part of the adolescent's value system.

The individual feature of this category, however, is the unconscious nature of the conflict over the inner impulse or need for which school becomes a symbol. Some of these impulses or needs are sexuality, competitive aggression, hostile aggression, and dependency.

Sexuality. The sexual impulse is the main unconscious concern of the adolescent. Many elements of this concern are present in consciousness as well. Through displacement school replaces sexuality as the center of conflict or becomes the arena for free indulgence in sexual fantasies or sexual acting out.

Sexuality and heterosexual interests emerge in adolescence, and the emotional atmosphere of high school life is laden with sexuality. If the adolescent has conflict over his sexual impulses, he cannot tolerate their unceasing intensity in school. He reacts with neurotic defenses or by yielding counterphobically to the impulse. Either of these reactions may lead to additional difficulties and drop-out from school.

As an example, one boy was struggling with reawakened oedipal feelings toward his seductive mother. Her overinvestment in school combined with other elements in his life to make school a symbol for the close relationship that he was frantically trying to escape. His sudden truanting and failure in high school, following an excellent grammar school record, were defensive attempts to handle his unconscious struggle.

Another youngster, highly fearful of what he regarded as his homosexual propensities, became so anxious in school that he dropped out. As treatment brought out later, the basis of his anxiety was the sexual stimulation aroused by the necessary close association with other boys.

Competitive aggression. The youngster in this category has not been able to come to terms with normal competition. Because of an oedipal conflict involving castration anxieties, boys may be deeply afraid of their aggressive, competitive impulses and set up defenses against them. One solution is to withdraw from competitive struggle, nonachievement becoming the defense itself. Such boys are fearful and assailed by doubts and feelings of inferiority. Although they may seem infantile or passive, they can be distinguished from youngsters in whom infantilism or passivity is part of the total character structure—their past histories show areas of accomplishment before the current neurotic conflict took over. On the surface, they appear to lack energy because most of the energy is channeled into the defense of nonachievement.

Competition and comparison are important issues in our culture. Most adolescents are competitive in relationships with each other, with their parents, and in school, where aggressive traits are highly regarded. Although school life affords normal channels for sublimation of competitive aggression, boys fearful of these impulses become fearful of school itself. The youngsters in this group are both puzzling and irritating to school personnel. Many of them have good or superior intelligence, and teachers invest much effort in them, often to no avail. Schools describe them as the "if only" students: "If only they would try; if only they would let us help." Psychologically, such children cannot be helped to learn and succeed as long as learning and succeeding unconsciously represent serious threats.

Hostile aggression. This type of aggression differs from competitive aggression in having as its nucleus destructive, angry impulses. The youngsters in this category have problems over unconscious hostility, which causes them anxiety and guilt. They displace their hostile aggression onto the school, which in the unconscious becomes the object of the hostile impulses. Depending on the child's particular defensive structure, school may either symbolize a perilous place where he can be harmed or provide an outlet where he can vent his destructive urges on others. In the former, the youngster unconsciously fears that he will express his destructive urges. Another child, repressing a hostile impulse originally felt toward a parental figure, may yield to the impulse in the school setting and act out his anger on teachers and peers. A third child may not initiate aggressive behavior himself, but vicariously satisfy his hostility by enjoying or joining in the disruptive acts of his classmates.

Dependency. School lends itself to being a symbol of dependency, since by its nature it can yield dependency satisfactions and take on the role of a supporting parent. School offers a certain amount of protection to the child. It is generally a more benevolent milieu than the adult working world and by its functions tacitly signifies that students are not yet equipped to fend entirely for themselves. Such dependency gratification is the proper function of school and is a growth-inducing medium for the student who can use it appropriately. But, like most parents, the school expects something in return: the student must work and produce.

The youngster in this category reacts to school primarily as a symbol of the receptive, supportive aspects of a parent-child relationship. Being in school is equated with remaining dependent.

The immature child who gives in to his unconscious dependency needs will be content to remain in school if he is allowed to sit and do little. The difficulty arises when the school makes its inevitable demands for study and preparation of assignments, which he resists because such work on his part represents the maturation he cannot face. School difficulties ensue. Another student defends himself against his dependency by consciously rejecting it, and leaving school is a symbolic leaving of his parents.

SCHOOL DIFFICULTY RESULTING FROM MALADAPTIVE SUPEREGO REACTIONS

For the purpose of this study we include in our concept of the superego all the internalized values, mores, codes, edicts, and regulations directing the individual's behavior. The source of the superego is at first external—the parents and other persons in the environment—but the process of internalization makes the superego no longer dependent on these agents, and the individual becomes self-directed. To act against the superego creates feelings of anxiety, guilt, fear of punishment, inferiority, or shame. Our concept of superego also includes the ego-ideal—the values and goals that the individual sets up for himself. Failure to "live up to" the ego-ideal creates feelings of inferiority or shame. The representation of school as a superego control is the basis of this category. What kind of control it represents for the student is determined by the type of superego he has already developed.

The distinguishing characteristic of all youngsters in this group is their preoccupation with authority: their current functioning emphasizes a struggle with images of authority—teachers, principals, or phases of school structure. There may be problems of impulse or need, but these are not of prime concern. In contrast to the preceding category, there is generally less use of repression and, consequently, less need for unconscious displacement or symbolization. With impulses more in the open and the authority struggle prominent, these adolescents have a greater tendency either to act directly on the impulses or to suppress them out of guilt. The adolescents in the impulse-need category also have superego problems, since, dynamically, most impulse or need difficulties are related to superego problems, for example, a fear of being punished or losing love. Because rebellion in adolescence is a common phenomenon, we wished to isolate those cases whose main feature was rebellion against school as an authority figure.

Maladaptive superego reactions have their roots in an overrigid or a lacunate [1] superego. The rigid superego is inflexible and makes demands upon the individual, allowing for no qualifications or abrogations of its rules without creating painful affect. The lacunate superego permits unacceptable behavior in some areas, but is rigid in others.

Rigid superego. An adolescent can handle his reaction to a basically severe superego by submission or by revolt. The youngster taking the path of submission continues his earlier pattern of compliance and conformity. We had no youngsters of this type among our drop-out cases. Orderly, achieving adolescents may have other problems, but rarely do they have the kind of school difficulties leading to drop-out.

The adolescent who revolts is in rebellion either against his own internalized severe superego or against the externalized superego that represents his strict parents. He looks upon the school system consciously or unconsciously as a punitive authority against whom he must rebel. While refractory school behavior is also manifest in lacunate superego problems, there is a different quality in superego revolt—a sharper element of fighting, acute rebellion, and struggle. The child with a lacunate superego who is quarrelsome and breaks rules has much less emotional investment in the situation. The youngster who revolts has good standards; his value system approves the need for control and limits. However severely he may be acting out, he does have guilt about it at some level. Superego revolt is further characterized by the periodic nature of the rebellion. The adolescent functions satisfactorily at times; but as the tensions accumulate, his defenses weaken and an outburst may occur, often over some minor authority issue. With the tensions discharged, he pulls himself together again and may have guilt and shame reactions about the acting-out episode.

Superego lacunae. The adolescent classified here does not ac-

1. Adelaide M. Johnson and S. A. Szurek, "Genesis of Antisocial Acting Out in Children and Adults," *Psychoanalytic Quarterly*, 21:3 (1952) 323–343.

cept the usual school superego values of good performance, attendance, behavior, and so on. Such a student can see nothing wrong with truanting, creating trouble in class, and not studying. His parents may also lack the conventional superego toward school and, overtly or covertly, encourage the youngster's undesirable behavior. This type of child is difficult to deal with in the classroom and is hard to handle in treatment because he does not have the motivation that comes from regulation of the superego. Abrogation of school values creates no distressing affect for him.

SCHOOL DIFFICULTY RESULTING FROM THE STUDENT'S ATTEMPT TO USE THE SCHOOL TO RESOLVE A CONFLICT BELONGING TO ANOTHER AREA OF LIFE

So far we have discussed youngsters whose school malfunctioning is a unconscious displacement of emotional problems. They see school itself as their chief difficulty, and their complaints are centered around it.

In contrast, another group of adolescents utilize school quite consciously in an effort to resolve a conflict existing in another area of their life. Ordinarily, this conflict is quite obvious from the case material and is an open struggle between the student and his parents. The adolescent uses school to effect some change in his relationship with his parents.

Many of these youngsters can be distinguished by the fact that they are aware or soon become aware of the true cause of their difficulty. After they develop sufficient trust in the casework relationship, they tell the counselor that their problem is not with the school but with some aspect of family life—if only this could be straightened out, all would be well. Generally, they can describe the purpose of their deliberate behavior in school.

Cases in this category included a boy who was a truant out of anger at his domineering father. The boy himself revealed that he was truant because he wanted to retaliate against his father. Another example is that of a girl hungry for affection from her parents. Her experience with them had been that she received attention only when in difficulty. On quite a conscious level, she created disturbances in school to obtain that attention. Students grouped under this section do not have any unique clinical psychopathology. The school problems are simply reactions to external forces in the environment. Since the school problem is simply a means to an end, casework treatment with such youngsters must be directed toward the "end"—the basic struggle engaging the student. When this is worked out, the school difficulties should be alleviated, as they no longer serve a purpose.

SCHOOL DIFFICULTY ONLY ONE MANIFESTATION OF A GENERAL PERSONALITY PROBLEM

The students in this category suffer from a total personality problem, and their school difficulty is only one of its manifestations. School does not stand out as a specific area of trouble; problems in other areas frequently may be of graver import. The pathology in these cases as a rule tends to be more serious, pervasive, and chronic than in the classifications previously described.

For example, consider a boy with a deeply entrenched schizoid character structure. Because of the nature of his pathology he cannot tolerate close human relationships of any kind. At best he functions on a minimally adequate social level, and then only as long as he can remain withdrawn and isolated from people. School difficulties ensue because of his inability to accommodate to the ordinary relationship demands inherent in the school-group setting. His problems at school may be manifold and run the gamut from apathy in class to open disobedience. But these surface symptoms mask the deep and widespread character difficulty that is the source of his classroom trouble.

The oral-aggressive, passive adolescent is another type whose poor school adjustment stems from a general personality disturbance. Individuals in this diagnostic category use stubbornness as a major defense and display a highly tenacious, though often quiet, negativism. A child with such traits may create great difficulty in school, but his basic problem is the character disorder. He reacts to school as he reacts to most other aspects of his life experience.

Common-sense approaches such as reasoning, exhortation, or

threats of punishment, which may be effective for a relatively normal student, will not work with the youngster presenting generalized personality difficulties. The elements creating this kind of character operate at an unconscious level outside the child's voluntary control, and an appeal to logic may make the situation worse. For example, if a youngster's chief characteristic is a masochistic, passive, resistive stubbornness, punishment or pleading may give him pathological satisfaction, play into the structure of his defense, and intensify it.

SCHOOL DIFFICULTY RESULTING FROM REALITY PROBLEMS

Not all school difficulties stem from psychological problems of the student. Since there are environmental circumstances that can interfere with a youngster's school adjustment, a category covering reality problems is included in our assessment of school difficulties. It follows that students with such problems should function satisfactorily in school once the environmental trouble is resolved. Our grouping of reality problems considered three major kinds: economic need, physical illness, and education not a value in the student's environment. This list does not encompass every conceivable reality problem, but we discovered no others in the analysis of our cases.

Economic need. Although tuition free secondary education is provided in this country, there are other expenses a student faces if he is to feel comfortable at school. They range from adequate clothing to personal spending money for the school paper. An adolescent who cannot afford the cost of participating in normal school routines may become unhappy and develop school problems. Under such circumstances, the temptation to drop out to earn money on a job may be very great.

The classification of economic need also applies to those students who find it necessary to leave school to work and aid their families financially.

Physical illness. This heading includes situations in which physical illness, either of the student or some member of his family, causes school difficulties. The way in which a student's personal health problems can reflect themselves in school maladjustment is self-evident. Illness within his family also can impinge seriously on his school life. An adolescent may have excessive home demands made upon him for the care of the sick person and be too fatigued to study properly. Another student may be so preoccupied and worried over family illness that he cannot concentrate on his school work.

Education not a value in the student's environment. Through identification a child tends to absorb the values prevailing in his own milieu, primarily those of his immediate family, secondarily those of the wider environment in which he lives. High school graduation is the minimal educational standard for most people in the United States. But certain segments of the population—sometimes particular families and occasionally a broader socioeconomic grouping—do not hold such an educational standard.

An adolescent from this type of family or setting may have little interest in school and quite comfortably drop out. His leaving school need not be caused by any emotional problems or any external factors such as financial strain or illness. It can occur simply because he and his family and the culture in which he lives place little or no value on education.

Some youngsters in this category may be relatively free from personality difficulties and be able to function quite well as long as they remain in their own socioeconomic environment and engage only in those vocational activities where education is unimportant. Other adolescents may have emotional problems, but to be properly classified here their emotional problems must not be related to school or school-leaving.

This category (education not a value in the student's environment) has been included under the heading of reality problems for two reasons: (1) since it does not involve emotional problems concerning school, it needs to be differentiated from the general category called psychodynamic involvement in school; and (2) although the drop-out student and his family may see no problem in their indifference to education, the problem nevertheless exists from the point of view of the larger society in which the student lives. It is also a problem for the student himself. As our culture is constituted today, with effective participation in the culture usually restricted to educated people, a person with limited schooling has less opportunity, even though he may be naturally well endowed. The community and the nation lose his potential contribution. He himself loses, too, by being cut off from opportunities, not only in a material sense but in terms of meaningful and creative living.

The Dynamic Use of School—Parents

Parents react emotionally to their children's adolescence. It is a difficult developmental period for all, and the adult is glad to be beyond it and to have put his own adolescent conflicts to rest in some way. These conflicts are commonly repressed into the unconscious but may be reactivated under the right circumstances. Although the adult has almost an amnesia about his own adolescent emotional struggles, he reacts to the life of his adolescent child as if there were danger of his own conflicts being aroused.

Just as the student's symptomatic school behavior can result from his psychodynamic involvement in school, so can a parent's unresolved emotional problems become active again because of his child's schooling and reveal themselves in his attitudes, feelings, and behavior toward the child's school experience. Our concept of the parental psychodynamic involvement in the child's school life does not refer simply to the parents' reaction to the child's school problem when it occurs, but to the meaning of the child's total school life to the parents both at conscious and unconscious levels before as well as after the school difficulty.

In the main, with some additions and a few minor revisions, the classification for parents is similar to that for students. The major difference is that the parent is reacting to school one step removed—through his child. In this sense the parent is less directly involved, but he can be just as intensely involved as his child, and in some cases even more so. The general categories for parents are:

a. Student's school life exacerbating the parent's problem of impulse or need
b. Parent's involvement in the student's school life resulting from maladaptive reactions to the superego

c. Parent's involvement in the student's school life resulting from an overvalued school ego-ideal
d. Student's school life receiving no special focus; another element in the parent's generalized personality disturbance
e. Student's school life used by the parent in an attempt to resolve a personality conflict belonging to another area of life
f. Parent's reality problems affecting his involvement in the student's school life
g. No psychopathology nor reality-based problems influencing parent's involvement in the student's school life.

As with students, the classification for parents represents a casework assessment of the underlying dynamic forces at work rather than a description of surface symptoms. Overt attitudes and behavior may be only clues to deeper elements. For example, a parent pushing his child toward excessive independence at school may be doing so as a defense against his own dependency needs. Also, the dynamic selected for a particular parent is the one representing the most critical aspect of the picture.

STUDENT'S SCHOOL LIFE EXACERBATING THE PARENT'S PROBLEM OF IMPULSE OR NEED

For the parent in this category the student's school life—its activities, relationships, and structure—represents the parent's unacceptable and unconscious impulses and needs and exacerbates the parent's problem in his handling of them. He unconsciously reacts to the youngster's schooling by setting up defenses against or acting upon the reactivated unconscious impulses or needs. Neurotic parents with essentially good egos would probably be classified here as well as those who are anxious and guilt-ridden about the student's school life.

The distinguishing feature of the parent in this category is that his involvement is the result of unconscious conflicts. The relationship with the student may be relatively free from conflict except for the school issue and what it represents. Certain other areas of the student's life may also evoke the same reaction in the parent because they, too, have the same unconscious meaning.

School is an important value to this parent, and he would have no conflict over school were it not for its unconscious impulse or need significance.

Sexuality. The student's school life has sexual implications for the parent. For example, as her daughter enters high school, a mother with unresolved sexual impulses attempts vicarious sexual gratification by unduly pushing the daughter toward boys. Another mother with the same unresolved impulses may grow anxious about her daughter's contact with boys, become restrictive, and give suggestive warnings about sexual indulgence.

Competitive aggression. The student's school life unconsciously represents the parent's unresolved achievement impulses. It does not refer to a parent's competition with his child in the sense of rivalry with the child. If the parent's rivalry with the child is the more important issue, the case would belong in another category, depending on other factors in the case. The parent in this category is competitive with anyone, not just a specific person. Examples are: a parent presses his youngster to achievement, frequently comparing his child's work to that of other children, because the parent is concerned about comparing himself to others; another parent, fearful of his own competitive impulses, tries to have his child avoid competition and, by refusing assistance with homework, may unwittingly lead the child to failure.

Hostile aggression. Here the student's school life unconsciously represents hostile aggression to the parent. He reacts to it with anxiety, guilt, or unconscious encouragement of the student's acting out. The latter kind of parent may foster the student's disruptive classroom behavior by approving, overtly or covertly, his youngster's quarreling with the teachers and students. Another parent, frightened by his own unconscious, hostile aggression, displaces it onto the child's school life by becoming overly fearful that his youngster will be hurt by his schoolmates. He may become overly protective and urge his child to come straight home and not to mix with "those tough boys."

Dependency. The child's school life can symbolize and evoke the parent's unresolved conflict over dependency needs. Some of these parents, giving in to their dependency needs, foster the student's dependency in relation to school. They may encourage a child to frequently and unnecessarily ask the teacher for special help. Other parents with dependency needs defend against them. A parent of this type may try to push his youngster out of school by telling him he is old enough to go to work.

PARENT'S INVOLVEMENT IN THE STUDENT'S SCHOOL LIFE RESULTING FROM MALADAPTIVE REACTIONS TO THE SUPEREGO

For this parent the student's school life represents the problem of superego control or lack of control. Emphasis is on the nature of the superego rather than on the impulse or need, which tends to be handled directly or inhibited in undisguised fashion. Specifically, emphasis is on authority issues involved in the student's relations with teachers, principal, and school structure. Parents may have rigid or inadequate superego development.

Rigid. Parents with a rigid superego either submit to it or revolt. In submission, the parent accepts the superego as the authority to which he must yield, and the school system unconsciously represents punitive authority figures to whom the parent must submit. His involvement in the student's school life centers around his need to have his child be excessively submissive in school. He may automatically assume the student is in the wrong when there has been some conflict with school authorities, or he may make an unnecessary issue of punctuality, regularity, and good behavior in school. For the parent with a rigid superego the school system may unconsciously represent punitive authority figures against whom he must rebel. He generally has a very strict superego in most areas of functioning, but shows periodic rebellion. He may overtly or covertly encourage the student's objections to school regulations or, believing the school demands too much work from his youngster, may go to school to assert this.

Inadequate. Parents with inadequate superego formation have either lacunate or inconsistent superegos. The parent with a lacunate superego has adequate standards except in specific areas of school functioning. Such a parent belongs to a cultural milieu that holds education as a positive value. Since the lacunate parent's inadequate values always concern some specific area or areas, he is differentiated from the parent with an inconsistent superego, whose behavior is variable. An example in the lacunate category would be the parent who wants an education for his child but is consistently unconcerned about the child's truanting.

A parent with an inconsistent superego development swings between strictness and overpermissiveness about the same school issue or issues. One time he vigorously prods his child to do homework; at another time he is completely unconcerned about it.

PARENTAL INVOLVEMENT IN THE STUDENT'S SCHOOL LIFE RESULTING FROM AN OVERVALUED SCHOOL EGO-IDEAL

This parent places exaggerated emphasis on the importance of school and education for a variety of dynamic reasons. This category overlaps others; if the dynamic basis for the parent's overevaluation of school was indicated by another category, the case was so classified. In this category is the parent who satisfies his own ego-ideal by insisting that his child continue in school, get good grades, and plan to go to college. The student's own needs are not considered. Another parent, not having had the ability to do well in school and hoping to accomplish this vicariously, presses his youngster to get A's in all courses.

STUDENT'S SCHOOL LIFE RECEIVING NO SPECIAL FOCUS; ANOTHER ELEMENT IN THE PARENT'S GENERALIZED PERSONALITY DISTURBANCE

The parent's problem involves the total personality, and the pathology tends to be serious and pervasive. For this parent the student's school life receives no special emphasis; there is widespread disruption in the parent-child relationship. Examples: a parent with a schizoid personality is withdrawn and detached, showing no interest in any of his child's activities, including his schooling; a parent with an infantile personality is unable to exercise the responsibility of rearing a child and seeing to it that the child attends school regularly.

STUDENT'S SCHOOL LIFE USED BY THE PARENT IN AN ATTEMPT TO RESOLVE A PERSONALITY CONFLICT BELONGING TO ANOTHER AREA OF LIFE

The personality conflict here is quite obvious from the case material and often tends to be revealed in an open struggle between the parent and student. The parent deliberately seems to use school as a weapon in his relationship with his child. He does this consciously or preconsciously, not disguising the conflict by repressive mechanisms. For example, he may press for achievement in school as a means of dominating his child. A second parent depreciates his youngster's school performance as a means of attaining a competitive victory over him. A third parent, preferring another sibling, compares the student's work unfavorably with the sibling's in order to express hostility.

PARENT'S REALITY PROBLEM AFFECTS HIS INVOLVEMENT IN THE STUDENT'S SCHOOL LIFE

The parent's over-all attitude toward the student's school life is the result of realistic and environmental problems. If these problems were resolved, the parent's attitude would probably not present difficulties.

Economic need. Economic stress influences the parent to act in ways unfavorable to the student's school life. For instance, a parent needing financial aid from his child might urge him to leave school for a job or expect him to work excessive hours on an after-school job.

Physical illness. The illness of the parent or some family member realistically preoccupies the parent and causes him to act in ways detrimental to the student. In this category would be the parent who because of his own illness makes excessive home demands on the student. Another parent, absorbed with the illness of a family member, has not enough energy to take a normal interest in the youngster's school life.

Education not a value in the environment. The parental value system does not include a desire for education beyond what the law demands for the child. The parent in this category may or may not be emotionally healthy. The differentiating factor for placing him in this category is that his emotional problems, if they exist, are not related to the student's school life. School is simply not important to him.

NO PSYCHOPATHOLOGY NOR REALITY-BASED PROBLEMS INFLUENCING PARENT'S INVOLVEMENT IN STUDENT'S SCHOOL LIFE

The parent, as far as school is concerned, has a normal relationship with his child. He desires the youngster to secure an education; is appropriately encouraging and facilitating of home study, regular attendance, and proper classroom behavior. He works cooperatively with school and agency personnel who are trying to resolve the youngster's difficulties, educational or emotional.

In this category, generally we would expect to find the more mature parent. The parent may have emotional problems of his own but they are neither impinging upon nor involved with the youngster's school life. If there are reality problems such as economic need or family illness, the parent exerts himself to minimize their effects on the child and his schooling.

STATISTICAL FINDINGS

AND DISCUSSION

Introduction

THIS STUDY WAS DESIGNED TO BE A systematic, clinical analysis of a group of intellectually capable high school students who were potential school-leavers. At our request, the schools referred students showing these two characteristics. We offered casework services to the students and their parents. Social histories were obtained and records of all interviews were kept.

The counselors who treated the youngsters analyzed the case material. They adopted certain statistical procedures to help order the vast number of facts contained in the case records and to remove the study from an exclusively impressionistic approach.

Generalizations about school-leavers at large on the basis of our findings must be made with care, since the group of students we studied was all white and relatively small in number. Appendix A describes the statistical procedures used in the study, and contains the statistical tables. Appendix B provides outlines of the conceptual framework of our study. The concepts are fully described in Chapters 2–4.

The Study Group

The study group consisted of 105 students, forty-five girls and sixty boys. Ninety-three of the students were referred by the public schools and the remaining twelve by social agencies. Selection criteria and our method of securing the sample are described in Chapter 1. Although we had expected to have a large number of Negro students because of their known high drop-out rate, only five were referred. Because of their small number these Negroes were not included among the 105.

Twelve girls and twenty-three boys had fewer than four interviews and are referred to as the Nontreatment Group. The remaining seventy, thirty-three girls and thirty-seven boys, who had four or more interviews, comprise the Treatment Group and are the subject of more intensive study.

Functioning in School

We started with an examination of how the student functioned in school because this area of breakdown had aroused concern. We needed to know the extent and the types of school difficulties. Reports from the schools were examined for evidence of malfunction in three areas: academic achievement, attendance, and classroom behavior.

Academic achievement problems consist of grade placement retardation in relation to chronological age, basic school skills markedly lower than I.Q. expectancy, major course failures in the presence of adequate tool skills, and erratic and/or inconsistent productiveness.

Attendance problems consist of class-cutting and truancy. We considered cutting a problem when the school reported it as a problem or when there had been five or more unexcused absences from some classes in one semester or an equivalent five month period. Truancy was considered a problem if so reported by the school or if there had been three or more unexcused all-day absences from school in one semester or an equivalent five month period.

Classroom behavior problems as reported by the school lend themselves to grouping under five main classifications. *Hostile social approach* includes hostile competitiveness, provocativeness, stubbornness, suspicion, distrust, mischief-making, disobedience, bullying, vandalism, and fighting. *Attention inadequacy* consists of distractibility, poor concentration, and daydreaming. Hyperactivity and impulsive behavior are labeled *Action control insufficiency*. Boasting, exhibitionism, and exaggeration are called *Self-overestimation*. And we designate dependency, helplessness, passivity, clinging, social withdrawal, lethargy, and inhibition as the *Inadequacy constellation*.

The boys' school problems started in elementary school.

Almost two-thirds of the boys, as compared with less than one-third of the girls, had histories of malfunctioning from grade school on (see Tables 2 and 3, Appendix A). For about half of the boys with school problems the first difficulty had manifested itself by the fourth grade, and for many, problems recurred or spread to other areas of school functioning during grade school. At high school entry these boys were handicapped because they were older than the usual freshmen and retarded in basic reading and computational skills.

Among the thirty-nine boys with grade school difficulties, 79 per cent were underachieving, 62 per cent were misbehaving in the classroom, and 40 per cent had problems in more than one area of school functioning. Attendance was not a frequent problem in elementary school and seldom consisted of cutting classes or truanting. Instead, recurrent absences due to vague illnesses, bad weather, and the like reflected the students' unwillingness to go to school.

Although in our culture it is more important for boys than for girls get an education and to achieve, boys are permitted to act out aggressive impulse more and there is more tolerance of their misbehavior. For a girl, this kind of acting out and fighting are not considered feminine and therefore not tolerated. For boys, there are certain expectations that they will act out aggressively—"boys will be boys." This is similar to the dual morality about sexual behavior in adolescence and adult life wherein boys and men are granted more latitude than girls and women. In addition, however, for males, the idea that achievement is ultimately very important makes school an area in which defiance of the parents and conflicts about male adequacy may be readily expressed. Learning is intellectual achievement, and for the male this capacity is aggressive and competitive. When boys have conflicts over these impulses, learning and school become involved because of their aggressive and competitive nature. We believe the reason why boys outnumber the girls in our project population, as well as in the drop-out population as a whole, is that for boys school provides a special culturally determined focus for rebellion and conflict formation.

> Serious and multiple school problems in high school are common characteristics of school-leavers.

Ninety-three per cent of our study group of 105 had school problems in high school, and 72 per cent were malfunctioning in more than one school area (see Tables 4 and 5, Appendix A). For 7 per cent (seven students) no school malfunctioning was observed. In four of these cases there was insufficient evidence in the records for rating this item, and in the other three, financial problems were interfering with continuance at school.

The girls' chief problem was school attendance—80 per cent. Seventy-six per cent were underfunctioning academically and 38 per cent had classroom behavior problems. Academic achievement continued to be the school problem of greatest frequency for boys—74 per cent. Fifty-three per cent had attendance problems and 34 per cent had behavior problems.

Almost all of the students with academic achievement problems had less than half the expected course credits for the length of time they had been attending high school. Such deficiencies pose a greater problem to the junior or senior than to the beginning student. Upper classmen were heard to say, "I'll be twenty-one before I graduate." This was grumbled stubbornly by some, flaunted rebelliously by others, and by still others, whispered despairingly.

Of the seventy-three students with attendance problems, eighteen cut classes only and were not truant. More often than not, the cutting occurred in relation to a particular class. Some students cut to avoid a disliked teacher or subject, or an activity causing some discomfort, such as the bodily exposure necessitated in swimming class. Still others gave up toward the end of the school day and usually cut the last class.

Fifty-five students had the problem of truancy. For a few, mostly girls, truanting seemed to provide an opportunity for flirting with expected detection by the attendance officers and another clash with authority figures. But more generally, truancy was not a purposeful running *to* something but a running *from* some aspect of the educative process. A small number of these students remained at home studying and preparing class assignments. In this way they avoided the interpersonal relationships or the social aspects of school. Others ran from the learning task itself. Some of the youngsters whose truancy was part of the picture of rebellion had careful schedules for visiting school hangouts during the staggered lunch periods in order to be with their friends. Where dependency was the core problem and learning in school was equated with the dreaded growing-up process, the truant spent the day at home watching TV, napping, and nibbling—taking in but not putting out.

The most frequently occurring classroom misbehavior was what we have termed "hostile social approach," that is, provocativeness, mischief-making, fighting, and the like. Second in frequency was "attention inadequacy," that is, distractibility, poor concentration, and daydreaming. Both types of behavior are frustrating to teachers: the former because it disrupts classroom discipline; the latter because it defies the attempts of the teacher to correct it, and nullifies her very *raison d'être*.

**The girls became troublemakers
at adolescence.**

We learned that, in contrast to the boys who had chronic school behavior difficulties, the girls managed relatively well in elementary school and became rebellious and aggressive about the time of high school entry. There is greater social pressure on girls in latency (roughly ages seven to twelve) to be good, and conformity brings them the gratification of acceptance and approval from adults. At pubescence, when libidinal needs and external stimulation become even greater, the problem of sexuality may tip the scales in favor of a breakdown. Not all girls react by rebelling; but in those who do, the intensity of the libidinal demands is great, and often a history of frustration, usually based on an essential lack of affection from the parents, is uncovered.

At adolescence the previously conforming girls of our group became acutely aware that there were other (heterosexual) sources of gratification and that the peer group condoned aggressive behavior to secure these gratifications. Close personal relationships were as important to them as they are to most adolescent girls. Already frustrated by receiving insufficient affection from their parents, they now found themselves in an impersonal high school setting where it was difficult to get the attention and other gratifications that had been forthcoming from their grade school teachers. Neither home nor school wanted to recognize their budding sexuality, and when they experimented with heterosexual relationships, the adult environment became more rigid and controlling. In contrast, not only is sexual activity of boys more likely to be tolerated but boys also have more nonsexual ways of handling their sexuality: athletics and other physical activities are outlets for this energy.

When girls reach puberty, they feel the values they have conformed to and accepted previously are not really worth keeping. Our culture continues to verbalize the importance of education, but most girls feel that heterosexual love and marriage are the really important goals. We believe, then, that the maturational processes of adolescence, in both their physiological and psychological aspects, precipitated the difficulties of the girls studied in the project and brought to light underlying personality problems that had remained hidden during the latency years.

By contrast, the boys continued to have the same problems as in elementary school because school remained an area for expression of conflict and rebellion. Twenty-five of the thirty-seven Treatment Group boys had attendance problems at the time of referral. In view of the passivity of the majority of these boys, their cutting and truanting were not so much a response to the additional physiological stresses of pubescence as a response to a school situation that had become increasingly difficult. When boys reach high school, parents and society expect greater achievement and put more pressures on them. These boys were unable to cope with this pressure and simply avoided school.

Schools often spotted the troubled youngster.

When a student's difficulty with school persisted in spite of the school's encouragement or application of simple disciplinary measures, the school's next move was to call in the parents for an interview. Some teachers, sensitive to the effects of home and environment on children, did gain from these interviews an understanding of the child's malfunctioning and then tried to modify the way they handled the child. Other teachers, lacking this understanding, merely became more punitive and less helpful. Actually, schools cannot be expected to deal therapeutically with disturbed children and disturbed parents. In the classroom the teachers lack the time to respond to the individual needs of a great many pupils, but more important, they have been trained as teachers and not as therapists. This is not to belittle the very important part they play in the treatment of a student in collaboration with a trained social worker, psychologist, or psychiatrist.

Some students had been referred for psychological evaluations. Often the psychological reports described children with histories of emotional deprivation who were currently manifesting personality problems. The recommendations in the reports usually focused on classroom management of the child. Sometimes this represented a lack of recognition of the severity of the disturbance, sometimes this was the best that could be planned, since the few available psychological treatment facilities had long waiting lists for their services.

For all of the project students the efforts of the school to cope with the problems were ineffectual in correcting them or halting the spread of their malfunctioning. As a last resort some of the students had been committed to social adjustment schools. Such commitments usually served only to aggravate their problems.

The fact that teachers did pick out the troubled youngsters should not be overlooked. But schools need to have more resources for psychological study and to use them immediately to determine the nature of a youngster's problems. Careful social studies and diagnoses can separate the children who need psychotherapy from those who could be expected to respond to school methods of motivation and discipline.

Some parents tried to get help.

The families of about a fourth of our student group had sought psychological help for the emotional problems of their children prior to referral to the project. Most often this consisted solely of a diagnostic procedure; only two girls and nine boys had any kind of therapy after diagnosis. The dearth of treatment resources for children may have played as important a role in this situation as lack of follow-through by parents or as poor or inadequate diagnosis. Many of the children, particularly the boys, who could have been more easily spotted, might have been spared a great deal of unhappiness and would have been more salvageable had psychotherapy been available while their emotional problems were relatively reactive and before crippling defenses became entrenched in their characters.

Home Life

Although unsatisfactory functioning in school and its concomitant discouragement were often used as excuses for leaving school, they were excuses only and not the real reasons for dropout by this group of intellectually capable students. Other factors were operating to cause the girls to begin to have school problems in high school and to cause the boys to arrive at secondary school with histories of chronic school problems.

In this section we consider other facts or factors in the students' lives (see Table 6, Appendix A). By design, all the students in our project were of average or better intelligence, and physical illness was not an important consideration.

Nor were financial pressures of any significant importance. Among the seventy Treatment Cases regular scholarships or grants of money were given to only four students (6 per cent). The general agency statistics for the month of December, 1956, at about midpoint in the project counseling period, showed that twenty-eight of 109 students in regular counseling (26 per cent) were receiving financial assistance. Although these figures are only relatively comparable, they do seem to indicate that for our study population, about 30 per cent of whom were classified as being of lower-class status, financial stress was not a significant factor among potential school-leavers. Actually, we did not get many complaints of this nature from our students and their families, even as a rationalization.

It appears that intellectually capable students who are motivated toward school somehow overcome financial obstacles. The schools may secure help for these students through resources such as our agency. We cannot say on the basis of our findings, however, that for subcultures and deprived minority groups lack of adequate income does not play a role in school-leaving.

The boys had more factors in their favor.

Forty-eight per cent of the boys, as contrasted with 31 per cent of the girls, had I.Q.'s of 110 or over. Thus the boys, intellectually at least, were better equipped to handle education. Many of the boys lived with their natural parents and with few siblings in a middle-class milieu, but many of the girls came from broken homes with a relatively larger group of siblings in a lower-class milieu. Fewer boys than girls had engaged in actionable antisocial offenses. Actionable antisocial offenses are misdeeds for which court action may be sought: stealing, violation of curfew, running away, destruction of property, and the like (see Table 6, Appendix A).

**During the latency years the girls
adjusted to poor circumstances.**

It seems important to consider the less favorable backgrounds of the girls. Although many of the girls lived in relatively poorer circumstances, fewer had problems prior to adolescence. It appears that girls make a better adjustment to difficult situations by conforming, pleasing, and acting in a socially acceptable manner. No matter how hard the task, girls seem to manage accomplishing it. Perhaps their ego capacity is better than that of the boys for mastering developmental tasks up to adolescence. They mature faster, learn easier, and therefore may be able to tolerate, accept, and adjust to the kinds of difficulties occurring in the latency years.

It may be easier for them to learn because they can more easily identify with the female teachers in elementary school. Some girls, deprived of emotional satisfactions at home, are sustained by the interest and approval of a warm teacher.

What happens to the really "sick" girls? The antisocial offenses of most girls consist of breaking curfew, drinking, and running away, which do not incur the same kind of authoritarian response as the boys' stealing and destructive acts. No girls whose acting out had resulted in pregnancy and no seriously delinquent girls were referred to our study, but otherwise we believe we did obtain a fair sampling of the main kinds of malfunctioning.

We believe we did not get girls from "good" homes because these girls make adequate adjustments during pubescence and adolescence by continuing to accept the cultural values. Neurotic girls are often good achievers. Their emotional problems frequently go undetected in high school and are hardly of the variety that lead to dropping out of school. The troublemakers were the girls referred for study. Twenty-one of our thirty-three Treatment Group girls were rebellious and acting out aggressively.

**Boys from poor environments
were not referred to the project.**

We might expect that boys coping with poor environments would create a great deal of difficulty at home, in school, and in the neighborhood. Yet no grossly delinquent boys were referred to our study. We suspect that boys with poor home milieus comprise a high percentage of the general drop-out population. They develop infantile character structures in response to adverse home circumstances and have little regard for people and laws. Getting immediate satisfaction of their wants is their most important value. Schooling, which means little to them except as an area for rebellion, is interrupted by trips to corrective schools and institutions, and basic educational skills remain at a low level. If they would wish to do an about-face at adolescence, their educational task would be difficult, indeed.

Although we did not get many "sick" boys who acted out in this rebellious way, the majority of our boys had been seriously malfunctioning in their personality and school adjustments from the early grades of elementary school on into their high school years. Girls appear better able to take the stresses occurring in a poor environment, boys less able to meet the stresses of a more favorable environment. The difference seems not to be the quality of the environment but rather the more difficult time boys have in making adjustments to any kind of environment.

Treatment Group versus Nontreatment Group

Such then were the pictures that the 105 students presented at the point of their referral to the project. Some factors differentiating the Treatment Group of seventy students (four or more interviews) from the Nontreatment Group of thirty-five students (three or fewer interviews) are mentioned below.

**Students whose school problems
began early stayed in treatment.**

Although almost all of the students had school problems in high school, the presence of *elementary school problems* was a differentiating factor. Eleven of thirteen girls and twenty-eight of twenty-nine boys whose school problems started before high school entry remained in counseling. Many of the parents of these children were concerned about the academic problems and desired action toward correcting them. When parental concern was weak or nonexistent, the schools stepped in to demand that something be done. Hence, environmental pressures were put on these students to participate in a counseling program. Later in this chapter we report our finding that elementary school problems were associated with lack of improvement in personality functioning.

Higher than average intelligence played no special role.

Our instruction to the schools for the referral of intellectually capable students accounted for the skewed distribution of intelligence. There was no special relationship between higher intelligence and remaining in counseling, nor did intelligence appear to play a particular role in personality improvement in treatment. Fourteen of twenty-eight students with I.Q.'s of 90 to 109 (50 per cent) improved in personality functioning, and seventeen of thirty-three students with I.Q.'s of 110 or over (52 per cent) improved. This indicates that, given at least average intelligence, a higher degree of mental ability does not make the counseling process more successful.

The lawbreakers were forced to come for treatment.

As compared to the Nontreatment Group, there were relatively more students in the Treatment Group who had histories of actionable antisocial offenses: double the number of girls and four times the number of boys. We do not believe that such misbehavior motivated the students themselves to come for treatment (indeed, some of those students were the most recalcitrant in therapy) but rather that it motivated their parents and their schools to insist that they keep coming for weekly interviews.

In addition, for the girls, remaining in counseling was associated with broken homes, larger sibling groups, and to a lesser degree, lower social status. We believe that the higher occurrence of actionable antisocial offenses in the Treatment Group girls put environmental pressures on them to continue in treatment, and we speculate that the more stable families of the Nontreatment girls had personal strengths and other resources for coping with the problems without outside help.

The Nature of the Emotional Problems

From this point we shall consider only the Treatment Group of seventy students. In very few cases were we able to arrive at a dynamic understanding of the student who had fewer than four interviews, but in the Treatment Group we were able to completely diagnose all but two students. It is the Treatment Group that we know the most about, and it now becomes the focus of the study.

Predominant Observable Complaints

First, we shall examine the reasons or symptoms for which the students required treatment. Almost any of the symptoms we will talk about may occur to a degree or temporarily in normal adolescents. They become reasons for therapy when they are excessive or persistent. In our method of diagnosing adolescents these symptoms are called Predominant Observable Complaints. They are the reality or personality factors standing in the way of better functioning. It is toward these elements that we direct the casework treatment.

The study schedule provided for checking at least one and not more than two complaints for each student. Fifty-nine of the seventy Treatment Group students had two complaints checked. Appendix B-I gives a complete list of the eighty-three individual complaints grouped into twenty-two constellations. After the tabulations the constellations were grouped into three major categories: (1) *Ego-Dystonic Category*, containing the Anxiety and Negative Self-Image constellations; (2) *Alloplastic Category*, containing the constellations of Immature Activity, Hostile Social Approach, Minor Social Misbehavior, and Actionable Antisocial

Offenses; and (3) *Poor Coping Ability Category*, containing the Dependency and Passivity constellations.

A third of the students showed symptoms of personal discomfort.

Thirty-three per cent of the girls and 38 per cent of the boys had Predominant Observable Complaints of the type we categorize as Ego-Dystonic—unpleasurable psychic states (see Table 7, Appendix A). These students were burdened with apprehensions, fears, and anxieties, or with a negative self-image shown in self-depreciation, lack of self-confidence, and inferiority feelings.

The girls were stirring up their environments by their activity.

Forty-nine per cent of the girls were draining off their tensions on the motor and/or verbal levels. Adolescent stresses had broken down their earlier defenses of conformity or internalization, and through their symptoms they were giving some kind of immediate and overt expression to the stresses. Their symptoms fell into the Alloplastic Category. Specifically, each had at least one of the following as a predominant response: impulsive behavior or restlessness, provocativeness or stubbornness, disobedience or untruthfulness, or breaking curfew, drinking, and/or running away. In addition to the 49 per cent of the girls with alloplastic complaints, another 15 per cent were demonstrating the same kind of overt, irritating behavior, but other complaint categories described them more dynamically.

The boys were causing concern in their environments by their inactivity.

In contrast to the girls, 49 per cent of the boys were "unmasculine" in that they did not meet the social expectation for independence and aggressiveness. Although the symptoms of these boys were also directly observable, they were extremely different in nature and fell into the category of Poor Coping Ability. Those whose Predominant Observable Complaint was dependency were helpless, clinging, or demanding; and those whose Predominant Complaint was passivity were characterized as unmotivated, procrastinating, or resistant to normal reality demands. As we shall see later, these were not traits of recent origin; the lack of independence had long been characteristic.

In summary, only a small group of boys and girls displayed reactions appropriate to their age in their personality symptoms. The most significant finding was that of the sex difference: formerly conforming girls were rebelliously acting out in many areas in response to the new adolescent stresses; and boys who were inhibited or passive before stood out now because of their nonmasculinity.

Neuroses versus Character Disturbances

The second phase of the diagnosis indicates the psychodynamic issue about which there is a conflict. The issue may be a neurotic or a character disturbance.

Less than a fourth of the students were suffering from a specific neurosis.

Thirty-six per cent of the girls and 11 per cent of the boys were diagnosed as neurotic. These students had, in most cases, some type of anxiety reaction. As we shall see, the neurotics showed a significantly higher rate of improvement in treatment than those suffering from character disturbances. Since their egos are usually better developed and since their problems are acute rather than chronic, they are more accessible to treatment. Character disturbances, too, begin with anxiety and if treated at this early stage, offer a better prognosis.

The majority of the students
were suffering from budding
character disorders.

Sixty-four per cent of the girls and 89 per cent of the boys had
problems because of their character formation. Only a few were
actually prematurely synthesized and therefore full-blown character disorders; but for all, the system of defenses did not allow
smooth functioning, and the character formation itself was the
major psychodynamic issue of their personality problems. That
we had so few neurotics and so many character disturbances shows
that for the greater number of our students difficulty in school
was not a simple problem. It was not a matter of laziness, poor
study habits, inadequate parental control, faulty teacher discipline, poor school curricula, or even a specific neurosis like
learning impotence. Rather, the problems were entrenched in the
entire character formation and were related to the total personality development. Such problems do not respond to the usual
inducements of the school or to the efforts of parents to correct
them. Moreover, they do not respond quickly, if at all, to
therapeutic counseling.

Character Formation

Under character formation we consider not only the students
with character disturbances but the neurotics as well (see Table
8, Appendix A). The symptoms of the latter, after all, occurred
within the framework of a basic character structure. The eighteen
different types of character formation are listed in Appendix
B-II. We purposely devised many specific classifications in order
to be able to catch any associations between school drop-out and
particular diagnoses if such did in fact exist. The seventy Treatment students fell into thirteen of the eighteen designations.
Further reduction of categories was necessary for statistical purposes, so the character formations were grouped around the de-

velopmental issues at their core. Another major grouping was made on the degree of ego differentiation. Ego differentiation does not occur until the ego has mastered the oral feeding phase and has come to grips with the anal training phase of development. Thus, Early Ego Phase includes preoral, oral-dependent, and oral-aggressive character formations; Later Ego Phase includes anal and phallic character formations. The phallic character type is one who has mastered the training phase and has moved on to the task of integrating sexual and oedipal issues.

Less than one-third of the students were ready to deal with sexuality.

Twenty-one Treatment Group students had phallic character structures. We know that in the development of both girls and boys sexuality constitutes a difficult area. For the boys, the task is aggressive masculine achievement; for the girls, it is feminine love and object relationships. The integration of sexuality into the personality, beginning in adolescence, is one of the later development tasks. Only about 30 per cent of our students were well equipped to undertake the task. These students had solved earlier developmental problems without recourse to seriously maladaptive defenses and were relatively free to apply themselves directly to the problems aroused by sexuality.

The girls in the phallic classification were predominantly hysterical, that is, they were having difficulty in the final resolution of the family triangle situation. The inhibited and over-compensating boys were struggling with the problem of masculine, competitive aggression. The schools, in considering phallic character formations, looked upon aggressive girls as being "bad" and inhibited boys as being "sick."

Few drop-outs had compulsive characters.

Only five students (7 per cent) had characters formed around anal or training issues. The conflict over anality is usually resolved in our culture by compliance and achievement, and the school system makes use of these motives. Students for whom anality is a strong negative issue may drop out of school, but not many of this kind were referred to us.

> Almost two-thirds of the adolescents had failed to master their dependent and aggressive impulses.

For 60 per cent of the children the task of accepting and integrating sexuality into their personalities just added another problem to already burdened psyches. Nine students had been traumatized so early and severely that they had ego defects. They were indeed handicapped adolescents. Five of these students had Distortion of Reality as one of their Predominant Observable Complaints, and counseling did not alleviate this complaint for any of them. Of these nine children, we were able to help one girl with a financial problem and to decrease the self-defeating activities of two boys.

Ten students had oral-dependent, and twenty-three had oral-aggressive, character formations.

> The boys were passive—the girls aggressive.

The problem in oral-dependency is that the person stays dependent and cannot or may not even desire to become independent. Such a person is typically passive. Eight of the ten oral-dependent students were boys.

In oral-aggression the main problem is conflict over the earliest aggressive impulses, which are frequently interpreted as being, and actually may be, destructive and hostile. The dependent and needy infant is acceptable to the parents, but once he becomes aggressive and exhibits hostile behavior, the parents attempt to control or socialize his aggressive impulses.

Eight of the twelve girls but only three of the eleven boys in the oral-aggressive category had character formations of the infantile-demanding type. Normal aggressive techniques during the feeding phase had not resulted in the satisfactions enabling them to move along the developmental scale, so they had responded to their frustration by being doubly aggressive. At adolescence, infantile-demanding girls are still in conflict over needing the "good" mother and they become more rebellious in their acting out. At the conscious level they may think they are looking for a love object for sexual gratification, but unconsciously they are still searching for a maternal object for dependency gratification.

Of the remaining eight boys in the oral-aggressive category, four were masochistic, two depressive, and two passive oral-aggressive character types. Thus, more boys than girls used a passive type of management of their early aggressive and hostile impulses.

Defenses

The schedule provided codes for sixty-three different defenses. These were divided into major categories of Covert or Autoplastic Defenses, in which the dynamics are predominantly within the individual, as in repression; and Overt or Alloplastic Defenses, in which tensions are discharged through acts altering the environment, as in provocation. An explanation of our system of classifying defenses appears in Chapter 2, and a list of defenses by categories is found in Appendix B-III.

There was no preference for overt versus covert types of defenses by either boys or girls. The basic difference in behavior between the girls and boys, however, shows very strikingly in their different choices among the overt defenses. The two overt defenses used most often by the girls were *provocation* and aggressive or rebellious *acting out;* by the boys, *passivity* and *withdrawal* (see Tables 9 and 10, Appendix A).

Defenses around the mode or manner of impulse discharge occurred most frequently for both sexes. Seventy-two per cent of the girls' defenses and 53 per cent of the boys' defenses were so classified. Stubbornness, overcompensation, provocation, and passivity are examples of *overt* defenses around the mode of impulse discharge; repression, reaction formation, inhibition, and fantasy are examples of the *covert* variety. A preponderance of defenses around the mode of impulse discharge probably would be characteristic of a general population of adults, since all people have to become reconciled to the "live and let live" principle. It is certainly to be expected in an adolescent group where impulses at a high level of intensity are clamoring for discharge.

Only the boys had a category of secondary importance: defenses related to the object of the impulse. Some of the specific defenses were identification, projection, withdrawal, and avoidance. Admission of the need for close relationships, especially in relation to mothers, is less acceptable for males than for females. Our society encourages boys to cut the apron strings, but it is all right for girls to maintain closeness to their mothers. Therefore, a boy builds up defenses against close relationships. This category of defenses probably would appear frequently in any population of boys and men; it cannot be considered distinctive of the project boys.

In summary, diagnosis of the youngsters showed a high degree of pathology of early origin. Most had disturbances due to character formations that were in the process of crystallizing around issues of dependency and hostility. The girls were relatively "healthier" than the boys in that they at least actively rebelled.

Diagnosis of the Parents

In diagnosing the parents of our students we focused on character formation (see Tables 11 and 12, Appendix A). Because of lack of information we were able to diagnose only forty-nine mothers and twenty-seven fathers of the seventy Treatment Group students. Two-thirds of the forty-nine mothers diagnosed had immature or early ego phase types of character structure: ten had ego defects and twenty-three were still involved with dependency issues. Nine mothers had compulsive character structures, and seven had phallic character structures.

Like the majority of the mothers, half of the twenty-seven

fathers were oral character types, but ego defects were not prominent in the group of fathers diagnosed. Nine (33 per cent) had compulsive character structures, compared with 19 per cent of the mothers. Seven boys, but only two girls, had fathers in this category. Only three fathers (11 per cent) were phallic character types.

Like parent, like child.

In view of the fact that so many of the parents were themselves immature in their character formation, it is to be expected that their children, through identification, would also use defenses of an early or immature nature. Issues important to parents as developmental struggles become issues for the children. This is also true for the general population.

For twenty-three students, nine girls and fourteen boys, we had diagnoses on all three family members. For this group there is a very strong similarity between character formations of parents and children (see Tables 13 and 14, Appendix A). This small population of twenty-three families provides additional statistical evidence for what has long been clinical impression. Identification is a normal, universal ego adaptation beginning in childhood and continuing until, in late adolescence, the child establishes an identity of his own. In earliest childhood, the most impressionable and helpless period, the parents are the chief objects for a child's identification.

In summary of the diagnostic material, we found that our group of potential school-leavers was composed of seriously emotionally disturbed adolescents. The majority of the fathers and mothers we were able to diagnose had immature character structures that created difficulties for their children, not the least of which were problems in identification.

The Dynamic Use of School

Many students with personality problems are able to function in school. Some use intellectual overcompensation as a defense and are notable for their achievements in school; others do not function well academically, but still are able to maintain passing grades. The majority of students in this study had serious and multiple school problems interfering with their education. We examined our cases to learn the chief dynamic of each student's difficulty in school. The conceptual framework within which we classified the dynamics has been presented earlier (see Chapter 4 and Appendixes B-IV and B-V).

To review them briefly, the dynamics could have an unconscious basis, when some aspect of the school setting symbolized or represented an impulse (dependency, competition, and so on) or a superego authority. On a conscious level, school could be used as a battleground for settling conflicts in the parent-child relationship that had nothing to do with school itself. School problems could be just part of a general personality problem causing malfunctioning in all or most areas of a youngster's life. And finally, reality factors such as financial need, family illness and the like, could interfere with school functioning.

Among the thirty-seven boys of the Treatment Group, the dynamic behind the school difficulty of seventeen was unsuccessful handling of impulse and need; in eleven of these seventeen the specific impulse was *competitive aggression*. The rest of the thirty-seven boys were about equally divided between those who were using school to resolve a conflict belonging to another area (nine cases) and those who had a total personality problem in which school was only one of many areas of trouble (ten cases). This latter category was the most common among the thirty-three girls; nineteen made no special or particular use of the school as distinguished from other areas of functioning. The other fourteen girls scattered fairly evenly among the four remaining categories.

Among the students with immature character development, the school dynamic was most frequently part of a general personality problem. It is to be expected that children whose early traumatization centers around the gratification of basic needs would have problems in all areas of their lives and not just school-focused problems.

Among the more mature students, the girls with phallic character structure also had a general personality problem as the dynamic of their school problem, showing the widespread disruption in their functioning. But for the inhibited and overcompensating boys, unsuccessful handling of competitive-aggressive impulses was the school dynamic.

It is interesting that not a single girl was classified as having a problem in competitive aggression. Despite numerous feminine advances toward greater equality with men, our society still holds the most esteemed female role to be marriage and motherhood. The attributes necessary for successful fulfillment of this role are not dependent on achievement in the academic or vocational sense. For most women, such achievement and the competitive aggressive strivings associated with it are not major psychological issues.

Believing we might uncover interlocking parent-student school problems, we tried to determine the special meaning school had for the parents. We were able to determine the school dynamic for forty-seven mothers and twenty-two fathers. There was some slight coincidence of parent and student on the dynamics of *general personality problem* and *conflict belonging to another area*. The former showed the extent of malfunctioning of both the parents and the child; the latter, the hostile and subversive interaction within the family. There was some tendency among the boys fearing *competitive aggression* to have mothers who *overvalued* school for their sons. In these cases the mothers were aggravating the boys' problems about competing by pressuring for higher achievement.

Reality factors were not frequent nor of primary importance.

Theoretically it is possible that reality and not personality problems could cause early school-leaving. One might expect that youngsters from the lower socioeconomic group where income-producing activity might be a necessity early in life would drop out for this reason.

We had only a few boys from underprivileged homes, but in no case was financial aid necessary. Monthly scholarships were given to four girls. One had no personality problem and no school problem and with financial assistance remained in school and was graduated. Two others likewise remained through graduation; but one was a schizoid and the other a depressive character type, and both had problems in school functioning. The fourth scholarship was given to a girl whose chief difficulty was a reality problem of a different nature. She developed an anxiety neurosis in response to her mother's long-term illness. That she was motivated to finish her secondary education was evidenced by her returning to school after each of three drop-outs. Her neurosis interfered with academic achievement, however, and she dropped out for a fourth and last time.

One girl had the reality problem of a mother pressuring her to leave school on the pretext of financial need. This girl had developed a compulsive character structure as a reaction against a low-standard home situation and was having difficulty in academic performance. When approached by the school authorities, the mother solved the problem by placing her daughter with a friend who gave her room and board in exchange for some light household duties.

Another girl's reality problem was that neither she nor her mother valued education. She dropped out of treatment after eleven interviews, and during that time her truancy problem increased. We later heard that she became pregnant and was forced to leave school.

Thus, although six of our students were having reality problems, for five of the six, personality disturbances were the more basic causes for the poor school functioning. In our group, reality problems, when they did exist, were complicating factors rather than the predominant causes for early school-leaving.

Parental Attitudes

Attitudes were examined in relation to: (1) the parent's predominant feeling toward his child; (2) the parent's predominant feeling toward the agency; (3) the parent's ability to make necessary changes in his own behavior; and (4) the parent's capacity to introspect about the student's problem and his own role in the problem. We rated parents as facilitating, supportive, neutral, impeding, or destructive in attitude. This scale was later reduced to positive and nonpositive attitudes, the latter including the neutral as well as the negative attitudes. We rated the situation as of the last interview with the parent.

In the Treatment Group of seventy we were able to rate fifty-seven mothers and thirty-one fathers. A special study was made of the fifty-seven mothers (see Table 15, Appendix A). There was no relationship between maternal attitude and sex of the student. We found a tendency for positive maternal attitude to be associated with student personality improvement in treatment. Mothers whose character structures were of the more mature type more often held positive attitudes. The mothers who had more than the median number of interviews (that is, more than five) tended to have a proportionally larger number of positive attitudes. We did not rate parents for personality change in treatment. Our work with them was often directed toward containment in the interest of the student rather than personal therapy. Counseling probably had a facilitating effect in the development of positive attitudes for some of the mothers who were seen more frequently, but since two-thirds of them had children who improved through therapy, it is difficult to isolate the predominant cause for the positive maternal attitude.

The Course of Therapy

With a treatment case being defined as one with four or more interviews, of the total group of 105 students, twelve girls and twenty-three boys (33 per cent in all) dropped out of counseling before there was much opportunity to begin a therapeutic relationship. In the Treatment Group of seventy students, the number of interviews ranged from four to 113 with the median at fifteen interviews for both girls and boys.

For these seventy students, 87 per cent of the sixty-nine available mothers and 64 per cent of the fifty-five available fathers were seen. For the sixty mothers the range was one through fifty-one interviews, with the median at five interviews; for the thirty-five fathers, the range was one through fifty-eight interviews, with the median at two interviews.

At the close of the treatment phase of the project, seven students were still in counseling. Termination for the remainder (thirty girls and thirty-three boys) had been planned or mutually agreed upon for ten girls and three boys; by the student alone, for twelve girls and twenty boys. The parent or parents had some involvement in a premature termination for eighteen of the students.

The drop-outs were difficult to engage and hold in treatment.

Early attrition and unplanned termination were very high for the project children: 33 per cent of the total group of 105 dropped out of treatment before the fourth interview,[1] and 71 per cent of the Treatment Group of seventy left treatment too soon. The children were seriously and pervasively maladjusted and were difficult to treat. Although we had hypothesized that emotional problems rather than educational problems per se were the real reasons why intellectually able children would consider leaving school, we had not anticipated the magnitude of the emotional problems. But it is logical to expect that adolescents who are failing in the major task of their age group—academic preparation for a lifetime vocation—would be seriously disturbed youngsters.

1. In 1959 (after the close of the counseling phase of the project) a survey was made of the agency's holding power. A check of the children admitted during a three month period showed that 88 per cent of the youngsters were still in treatment three months (approximately twelve interviews) later. This is in contrast to the Drop-out population where 67 per cent had four or more interviews and 57 per cent had twelve or more interviews.

Outcome of Treatment—Changes in Personality Functioning

We judged improvement in personality functioning by change in the Predominant Observable Complaint(s). A complaint was rated *improved* if there were a reduction in the severity of the original complaint and no substitution of another symptom, or if a substitution of lesser severity appeared; *no change* if there were no lessening or no increase in the original complaint, or if substitution of an equally serious symptom occurred; *worsened* if there were an increase in the severity of the original complaint or the substitution of a symptom of greater severity. Actually, only in the case of one boy did the situation get worse, so outcome will be considered simply in terms of improvement and nonimprovement. A student was placed in the improved group if he improved on at least one complaint. Nineteen students improved on two complaints and eleven students had no second complaint listed.

Personality Improvement Rates by Factor

	GIRLS Number Who Improved	Per Cent	BOYS Number Who Improved	Per Cent
Sex	17 of 33	52%	17 of 37	46%
Predominant Observable Complaints (Fifty-nine Students Had Two Complaints)				
Ego-Dystonic Category				
Anxiety	4 of 8	50	6 of 7	86
Negative Self-Image	2 of 8	25	6 of 11	54
Poor Coping Ability Category				
Dependency	0 of 2	0	3 of 8	38
Passivity	0 of 1	0	3 of 13	23
Alloplastic Category (Irritating Social Behavior)	8 of 20	40	4 of 9	44
Twelve Other Classifications	11 of 22	50	6 of 20	30
Psychodynamic Issue				
Neurotic Disturbance	9 of 12	75	3 of 3	100
Character Disturbance	8 of 21	38	14 of 34	41
Character Formation (One Girl and One Boy Not Determined)				
Mature	10 of 14	71	7 of 12	58
Immature	6 of 18	33	10 of 24	42

**Casework treatment contributed
to better functioning.**

As the tabulation shows, 52 per cent of the girls and 46 per cent of the boys improved in personality functioning, and for the combined groups 48 per cent improved.[2]

**The anxious, self-depreciating
boys had a good improvement
rate.**

In general, because of the accompanying personal discomfort, anxiety and negative self-image are factors predictive of continuance in treatment and of improvement in treatment. For our group this was truer of the boys than of the girls. Among the boys, 67 per cent of these complaints improved, and among the girls, 38 per cent improved. Possibly the rate of improvement was higher among the boys because anxiety and negative self-image run counter to the ego-ideal of being a man, whereas these symptoms are more acceptable in and to girls, as they do not make them less feminine. It is part of the self-image of women that they can be emotional, and their masochism can absorb self-depreciating attitudes.

**Those who coped poorly had a
poor improvement rate.**

Only six of the twenty-four poor coping ability complaints were alleviated. Predominantly a complaint among the boys, passivity was particularly hard to treat. This is true only for the

2. A conservative estimate of the improvement rate in the agency's general population is 70 to 75 per cent. Assessment of personality improvement in the project children was strict and was related to *actual* improvement in the Predominant Observable Complaints (limited to 2 per student). For example, had the six students who showed better school functioning been included, the improvement rate would have risen from 48 to 57 per cent. In some of the cases rated as unimproved there were minor favorable changes, and in others we were successful in stopping the momentum of a process that gave every indication of becoming more damaging.

passive boys who had this attitude ingrained in their character structures. Passivity as a defense of the inhibited boys, in whom the inhibitions developed later in life, was much more successfully treated.

The acting-out girls had a low improvement rate.

Complaints concerning interrelationships with the environment were of high frequency among the girls. The improvement rate was 40 per cent. It was difficult to get these girls to internalize their problems not only because this would have meant an increase in felt anxiety but also the acting out served a function in their rebellion. We were more successful in decreasing this behavior when it was coupled with anxiety as in the hysterical girls.

Personality improvement was cross-tabulated with other characteristics of the group. Findings related to improvement in school functioning and continuance in school will be discussed under those headings.

80 per cent of the neurotics improved.

As expected, there was a higher rate of improvement among the neurotics than among those with character disturbances because the problem of the neurotic, being of recent origin, is less entrenched and therefore responds better or is more amenable to treatment. Thirteen of sixteen neurotics (81 per cent), as compared with twenty of fifty-two adolescents with character disturbances (38 per cent), improved; and the difference is statistically significant (see Table 16, Appendix A).

Students with more mature character formation showed a higher improvement rate.

There is a relationship between improvement and more mature character formation, particularly among the girls (see Table 17,

Appendix A). Seventy-one per cent (ten of fourteen) of these girls improved, as contrasted with 33 per cent (six of eighteen) of the girls with immature characters. Improvement occurred in 58 per cent (seven of twelve) of the mature boys and 42 per cent (ten or twenty-four) of the less mature boys. Thus, casework had a higher corrective effect among the students whose problems began later in life. Their egos were more highly developed and they already were better equipped to profit from counseling.

The students who were in treatment longer had a higher improvement rate.

Improvement in treatment is highly correlated with the longer treatment period when the median of fifteen interviews is taken as the dividing line. Sixty-six per cent (twenty-two of thirty-three) of the students who stayed in treatment for more than fifteen interviews improved (see Table 18, Appendix A). Similarly, there is a high correlation between improvement and mutual termination of treatment. In 85 per cent (eleven of thirteen) of the cases with planned termination there was improvement (see Table 19, Appendix A). If children with severe school problems superimposed on severe emotional problems are to be helped by counseling, the solution appears to lie in the therapist's development of skills for lowering the resistance of these children to counseling, since keeping them in treatment is essential if objectively determined goals are to be achieved.

There was no correlation of personality improvement with age of the student at the start of treatment when the group was divided into those who were under sixteen or over sixteen years of age. This finding is consistent with our recommendation to get children into counseling early—we mean early in the history of the problem at whatever age it occurs. The recommendation gains further emphasis when we observe that the presence of academic problems in elementary school, a sign of problems of long duration, is associated negatively with improvement in personality functioning. Only two of eleven girls and eleven of twenty-three boys with grade school problems profited from casework (see Table 20, Appendix A).

Students with mature mothers improved.

Another significantly related variable is the character structure of the mothers (see Table 2, Appendix A). Ten of sixteen mothers with more mature character structures (62 per cent) had children who improved in personality functioning, as compared with twenty-one of thirty-three mothers with more primitive character structures (64 per cent) whose children remained unimproved. As mentioned earlier, positive maternal attitude toward treatment and the treatment plan was related to improvement in treatment, and the more mature mothers had the higher frequency of favorable attitudes.

Outcome of Treatment—Changes in School Functioning

We hypothesized that casework treatment would improve personality adjustment, leading in turn to better school functioning, and that the combination of the two would forestall school-leaving. At the close of the treatment phase of the project, twenty-three boys and thirteen girls were still in school and four girls had been graduated. We examined the school functioning of these forty students for changes in the school problem areas.

Improvement was more dramatic among the boys, possibly because more boys had school-focused problems. Five of seventeen girls and fifteen of twenty-three boys showed improvement in academic performance; five of eleven girls and eight of twelve boys with initial school attendance problems showed improvement; three of nine girls and six of eleven boys with initial classroom behavior problems showed improvement. In the over-all picture, six of seventeen girls (35 per cent) and sixteen of twenty-three boys (69 per cent) showed improvement in one or more of the school problem areas investigated (see Table 22, Appendix A).

Some students improved only in school functioning.

Most of the students who improved in school functioning were those who had made improvement in personality functioning. Of those who did not show a favorable personality change, however, one girl was graduated from high school, and one girl and four boys improved in academic performance and/or attendance. In these six cases, casework had contributed to better educational functioning. The girl who was graduated was a depressive character planning to leave school in her senior year because of financial need. A monthly scholarship check solved this problem, but sixteen interviews were not enough to lower her inhibition or bolster her self-image. The other girl was a schizoid character type. We were unable to reduce her suspiciousness and withdrawal, but supportive treatment did lead to improvement in school performance and attendance.

Three of the four boys had character formations of the more mature type, and their school problems were based on poor handling of competitive-aggressive impulses. Because of their better developed egos and the specific focus of their problems on school, it is not surprising that better school functioning was an early sign of improvement. It is unfortunate that all three left counseling prematurely because other mature boys with the same symptomatology who stayed in treatment made noticeable changes for the better in their over-all functioning. The remaining boy had an oral-dependent, passive character structure. A "feeding" type of therapy helped him to become more productive academically in order to please his therapist, but he was not able to become more independently motivated.

Personality improvement led to improved school functioning.

For the forty students who were in school at the close of treatment, personality improvement was very strongly associated with improved school functioning (see Table 22, Appendix A). All of the twelve improved boys had improved in academic achievement, six of eight with classroom behavior problems improved, and six of seven with attendance problems improved. Of the eight improved girls, three had been graduated from high school and three had improved in school functioning. This seems strong evidence that successful casework structured around understanding and treatment of emotional problems results in better school adjustment. If the underlying issue is not changed by treatment, the school functioning usually does not improve.

Outcome of Treatment—Continuation in School

In relation to the total Treatment Group, seventeen of thirty-three girls (52 per cent) and twenty-three of thirty-seven boys (62 per cent) remained in school. Four girls and ten boys, however, were under the legal school-leaving age. We made a special study of the fifty-six students, twenty-nine girls and twenty-seven boys, who were sixteen years of age or older at the close of treatment. In this group, thirteen girls and thirteen boys were still in school or had been graduated. To judge the effectiveness of counseling in forestalling premature school-leaving, it should be remembered that we were dealing with a group chosen because they were potential drop-outs. Because of the severity of the school problems alone, we believe that, untreated, a great majority of the students would have left school.[3] In this light the nearly 50 per cent success becomes more significant.

3. The City of New York's *Experiment in Guidance of Potential Early School Leavers* (New York: Board of Education of the City of New York, 1956), in describing the experimental group that received in-school counseling to prevent dropping out, states on p. 37: "Utilizing only those factors that show very significant differences between graduates and early school leavers (.001 level of significance), boys or girls most vulnerable to early school leaving tend to show excessive legal absence, cutting and truancy; non-conforming attitudes and behavior; poor work habits; under-achievement and unrealistic goals; hyperactivity, fighting and aggressive behavior; will be anxious and fearful; will show attention-getting behavior; and will have severe disturbance in relationships. The greater the number of factors, the more liable is the student to drop out before graduation."

For boys, personality improvement is associated with remaining in school.

Our thesis was that alleviation of emotional problems would cast the balance in favor of continuing in school. Remaining in school should correlate with improvement in personality functioning as implemented by casework. For the boys of legal school-leaving age this was true (see Table 24, Appendix A). Eight of eleven improved boys (73 per cent) continued their high school courses and functioned much better in school. One of the three who dropped out had enrolled for courses at a business college before signing out of high school. Not counted among these eleven boys were two who had dropped out of school prior to referral to the project. While in counseling, both decided to take up their education again at night school; one enrolled in a private, accredited high school, and the other attended a vocational high school.

Eight of fifteen improved girls (53 per cent), however, left school while in counseling. We believe the higher rate of continuation in school for boys is due partly to the fact that their problems were more school centered and therefore alleviation of the emotional problem resulted in quicker resolution of the school difficulty and partly to the fact that schooling is more important vocationally to boys than girls and coincides with their ego-ideals. Although education is less a positive value for girls and high school graduation is not as important an intermediate goal on their way to fulfilling their feminine roles of wife and mother, in actuality many of the girls dropped out of school early in the counseling period before personality improvement had occurred. In addition, the girls who were acting out rebelliously had a most difficult time living down their pasts. If finally motivated toward schooling, they found themselves unacceptable to the teachers and the "nice kids." Since personal relationships are particularly important to girls, school became a very ungratifying environment.

The variable of school status at close of treatment was cross-tabulated against twenty-eight other characteristics for these fifty-six students of legal school-leaving age. Seventy-eight per cent of the students engaging in actionable antisocial offenses were drop-outs, in contrast to the 64 per cent of students without this symptom who remained in school (see Table 25, Appendix A). When a student malfunctions in school and also breaks community laws, it is likely that he will not complete his schooling.

The level of character formation is also relevant (see Table 26, Appendix A). Sixty-eight per cent of the less mature students dropped out, whereas 61 per cent of the more mature students stayed in school. For the latter, this is probably due to their better ego capacities.

School attendance problems were high among the actual drop-outs.

Other studies have pinpointed truancy as one of the chief factors associated with dropping out of school, and nonattendance in school is an extreme form of school behavior problem. In our study group of fifty-six students of legal school-leaving age, twenty-seven of forty-four students who had attendance problems (61 per cent) dropped out of school, whereas only three of twelve students without attendance problems (25 per cent) left school (see Table 27, Appendix A).

Counseling can effect better school attendance.

Of the forty students who remained in school, twenty improved in personality functioning. Among these twenty students, eleven of the twelve with attendance problems (92 per cent) improved in school attendance. Of the twenty who did not improve in personality functioning, three of fourteen with attendance problems improved in attendance.

For this group of forty students the difference between improvement in attendance versus improvement in academic performance and/or classroom behavior is not statistically significant, but it does suggest that the problem of nonattendance in school may be the first to yield in therapy.

> A grave combination—attendance problems and actionable antisocial offenses.

We have previously spoken about the strong association between actionable antisocial offenses and dropping out of school: eighteen of twenty-three students with such behavior left school. Of these eighteen students, seventeen also had attendance problems. For the actual drop-out population of thirty students, actionable antisocial offenses and attendance problems tended to occur together (see Table 28, Appendix A). This combination of symptoms should be a forceful warning signal of drop-out to parents, teachers, and therapists.

Summary

Our population consisted of 105 white children, forty-five girls and sixty boys, of average or better intelligence who were considered potential or probable school leavers. The thirty-three girls and thirty-seven boys who had four or more interviews comprised the Treatment Group, and the bulk of the statistical findings apply to this group.

For the total population there were such marked differences between the girls and the boys that in most instances it was necessary to consider them separately. The girls were predominantly a rebelliously acting-out group, whereas the boys characteristically were quiet and passive. The boys had what appeared to be better homes and environments. Although we believe the girls were fairly representative of girl drop-outs at large, we feel we did not get the rebellious, delinquent boy drop-outs.

The boys' emotional problems revealed themselves chiefly in school difficulties that had started in elementary school, but the girls began having emotional and school problems about the time of high school entry. We believe it is culturally determined that boys' problems are more school focused than those of girls. About a third of the girls had reactive types of disturbances; 89 per cent of the boys had character problems.

The group ran the gamut of diagnostic classifications. Our categories for the various dynamic uses of school, although valuable in explanatory terms, did not produce a distinctive pattern for school-leavers. We did have a relatively large group of boys with problems resulting from competitive aggression, but for most of the students the school difficulty was part of a general personality problem—just one facet of widespread malfunctioning.

Most of the adverse circumstances, findings, and outcomes were more markedly present in that majority of the students with immature character formations. Since the students were highly disturbed youngsters whom it was difficult to involve and treat, even the fifty per cent improvement in personality functioning brought about by therapy implies the value and potential of casework treatment. For the students who made favorable personality changes, there was a high rate of improvement in school functioning for both girls and boys and a high rate of continuation in school for boys.

Actionable antisocial offenses, school problems in general, and school attendance problems in particular showed strong correlations with dropping out of school. These are only manifestations or symptoms of the deeper emotional problems.

In our population we found no special school dynamic, personality problem, character formation, or specific external factor that could be considered primarily or uniquely related to dropping out of school. We can say with surety, however, that the students had severe personality problems that interfered with academic achievement and, more often than not, with social functioning in the home, the classroom, and the community. When the emotional problems are not treated or are unsuccessfully treated, there is a real risk that these girls and boys will remain maladjusted individuals, ill-fitted to cope with life in the adult world.

THE PROBLEMS AND

THEIR TREATMENT

IN THIS CHAPTER WE FIRST DIS-
cuss some general and specific techniques for casework service
with adolescents.[1] Since school problems were a common characteristic of our group of students, we shall next describe the
process whereby such problems add complications leading to the
decision to leave school. We shall explain how the school problems are used to initiate treatment. And, finally, we shall consider
a group of youngsters for whom treatment was focused on the
school difficulties, with relatively speedy favorable results in
school functioning.

The treatment section proper, which considers the emotional
problems of the adolescents, is divided into discussion of treatment of the character disturbances and treatment of the reactive
disturbances.

1. The designations caseworker, counselor, and therapist are used inter-
changeably.

Casework Treatment of Adolescents

The technique of casework treatment of early school-leavers is essentially the same as that of adolescents in general. It requires a knowledge of the stresses of adolescence and of the characteristic ways in which the adolescent ego responds to these stresses. Working therapeutically with this age group requires the development of certain attitudes and skills.

First and of utmost importance, the caseworker must be flexible. The adolescent ego is highly changeable and as unpredictable in therapy as it is in other relationships. Therefore, the caseworker must be "prepared to be unprepared." His approach must be suited not only to a particular diagnosis and to an immediate issue but to the client's ego fluctuation. Although the adolescent's character formation is usually idiosyncratic enough so that after a few sessions the caseworker has an impression of the outstanding consistent characteristics, individual ego defenses may readily yield from session to session or seemingly new ones be taken on. The worker must be able to tolerate this change and meet whatever challenge the change presents.

The caseworker's flexibility should be in his techniques, not in his own character. He must provide a constancy in his own personality that will act as a bulwark for the fluctuations of the adolescent ego. Since the adolescent is unsettled in his adaptation, he needs the integrating strength that comes from identification with a mature, consistent worker.

The adolescent ego has abandoned or put in abeyance its previous organization of parental superego, ego-ideals, and object relationships; and the caseworker has the task of replacing these organizing factors. Rather, it is more accurate to say that the adolescent searches for them and puts the caseworker into that role. The latter has the professional responsibility to play the role in a way therapeutic for the adolescent. He must have maturity, integrity, and a sense of responsibility to guide the adolescent ego toward a wholesome character formation within the range of its own individual configuration of capabilities and shortcomings.

The personality and integrity of the caseworker must not be

threatened by the developmental deviations of the adolescent. Excessively punitive superego attitudes must be allayed, yet unacceptable impulses and actions must be contained by sufficient nondestructive guilt and a sense of the appropriateness of actions to reality. The adolescent must control his primitive impulses; at the same time he must develop awareness of instinctual needs and acceptable modes for their satisfaction. He must abandon antisocial values and gang mores and replace them with a system of meaningful and gratifying values. Along the road of therapy there are frequent abrogations of rules, yielding to impulse, abandoning of good sense, and forming of poor relationships. All these the caseworker has to "attend to," in both senses of the word—hear out and help with.

To say that the caseworker becomes a "substitute parent" is to lose the sense of the complexity of that role in the truism. The adolescent is still dependent on adults for education, guidance, and subsistence. In growing toward independence and striving for emancipation he denies this dependence. He fights his parents rather than admitting his need for them. The caseworker's objectiveness and separateness from the family milieu makes the adolescent comfortable enough to accept his support.

Out of his experience and knowledge the counselor is able to enlarge the scope of the adolescent ego by imparting knowledge about the world and how to live in a social group. Most adolescents need a great deal of such information, and although they often will not accept sound advice from parents and teachers, they may do so from the counselor. Thus, for the welfare of his client the caseworker often finds it necessary to give counsel and advice. Such direction is given with a knowledge of the dynamics of the individual. Very frequently the adolescent makes his own suggestions, requiring only support for his ideas.

Underlying all techniques of casework with adolescents is the support provided by the client-counselor relationship. Without it, maneuvers with a still "adolescing" individual are hollow. This support rarely has to be explicit in the interaction, but it must be there. The adolescent needs it, unconsciously seeks it, and if he cannot find it with his caseworker, will look elsewhere.

The counselor, tolerating this need for support and giving it appropriate fulfillment, uses his technical skills to determine the direction and "dosage."

As the adolescent shrugs off the support of his parents, so does he tend also to depreciate their goals, which are a part of his heritage. Reassessing and then rejecting the ego-ideal acquired in the family, the adolescent is left without solid values and a meaning for his life. The experience is at best anxiety provoking, at worst, soul shattering. Most adolescents cannot long tolerate the void of a valueless universe, and they search everywhere for meaning—at school, in church, in books, in television, in movies, in peer groups, and in their relationships with their therapists. The values discovered in this search are tested for their worthiness and individual fit for a new ego-ideal. The caseworker can help the adolescent toward a reacceptance of those aspects of his earlier ego-ideal that are good and toward modifications and additions to correct the harmful aspects. This integration of a different ego-ideal, though not a simple duplication and incorporation of the caseworker's own personal ego-ideal, is nevertheless accomplished through him. It gets his stamp of approval and is accepted because of the affective interaction in the client-counselor relationship.

Treatment of adolescents also rests on methods fundamental to casework with any age group. A diagnostic evaluation is made of the important aspects of the case. This includes identifying the problem for solution in treatment and arriving at an understanding of the total dynamics:

1. by studying and assessing the personality of the adolescent and significant family members for ego capacity, chief defenses, and clinical diagnostic categories

2. by investigating the adolescent's interpersonal relationships with key figures in his life

3. by examining the external milieu: school, peers, and cultural factors

4. by appraising the current level of functioning of the adolescent and his parents

5. by exploring the historical material for pertinent develop-

mental factors, significant traumas, precipitating elements in the current complaint, and the problem's chronicity.

An over-all evaluation must be made of the severity of the case to determine how much change can be expected and to set up treatment goals. In the broadest sense, the treatment goal is the one specific to the field of social casework—improved social functioning.

After the diagnostic study and the establishment of goals, the caseworker makes decisions about:

1. *The treatment method.* Whether, for example, the approach should be ego supportive or interpretive.

2. *The type of relationship.* For example, the therapeutic relationship a schizoid person may need—friendly and dependable but not too close—is different from the warm, giving relationship appropriate for the youngster who has been deprived of dependency gratification and longs for it.

3. *The degree of environmental manipulation.*

The Nature of the School Problems

Because of the research topic, a common thread running through our cases was the presence of school problems. Only one student did not have a school problem: financial need accounted for her wish to leave school. All the remaining sixty-nine students had at least one school difficulty, thirty-five had difficulties in two areas of school functioning, and twenty-one had difficulties in three areas. More specifically, 86 per cent of the students came to us with problems in academic performance; 77 per cent, with problems in school attendance; and 46 per cent, with problems in classroom behavior.

Severe school problems bring in their wake some very special difficulties for the child already suffering from emotional difficulties. The school problems add new stresses and aggravate the emotional ones, and as the snowball rolls, it increases in size and velocity. The children in our project generally presented multiple facets of maladjustment.

A conforming, achieving child may have serious emotional handicaps, but often these are hidden and operate mainly on an intrapsychic basis. School maladjustment, on the other hand, stands out for all to see. It creates additional trauma and anxiety for the youngster, strong feelings of shame, inferiority, and resentment. As a result he may redouble his efforts to handle these feelings of discomfort, intensifying the very defenses that have contributed to the difficulty in the first place.

It is also natural for parents to react strongly to school problems. Some feel the child's inadequacy at school is a blow to their own prestige and status. Others are afraid that the youngster is endangering his vocational future. Still others may be irritated that their child presents problems involving the parents with the school authorities. Whatever the parents' basic reaction, it complicates the parent-adolescent relationship.

School maladjustment affects not only the child and his parents but also his school. The school can tolerate some misbehavior in a child if he is achieving satisfactorily. When a capable youngster makes poor grades and the school's efforts to improve his performance have failed, the educators become understandably frustrated. Aside from the poor academic performance of our drop-out students, their defenses also provoked their teachers. The two defenses most often used by the boys were passivity and withdrawal, and by the girls, provocation and rebellious acting out. These defenses do not evoke a sense of sympathy, as do the defenses displayed by adolescents who are worried, anxious, and eager for approval and affection. The angry, attacking qualities implicit in provocation arouse retaliation from those toward whom it is directed. And since the educator's prime task is to impart knowledge, a teacher may feel baffled and exasperated when faced with the lack of responsiveness (often stubbornness) and immobility of the passive child.

A large portion of our adolescents were truanting from school, a late warning signal of trouble, as we discussed earlier. One of the mores of our society is that children attend school regularly and behave when they are there. It is easier for a child to be hostile in his home than in the more formal and structured school setting. Since a general cultural sanction surrounds school, it is an environment that tends to inhibit, and most children do conform.

Truancy represents an active form of aggression against school requirements. It signifies that a child is so pressed and finds school so unpalatable that he must escape it, even at the risk of severe penalties. Truancy is a logical forerunner of leaving school; both represent a running away, a technique of avoidance.

The negative counterreaction from the school, the parents, and other sources entrenches the youngster's defenses. His syndrome develops a self-perpetuating character making him progressively more unpleasant to the school and the school progressively more unpleasant to him. If this process persists, the adolescent may finally see drop-out as the only solution. School-leaving, like other human behavior, is essentially grounded in the pleasure-pain principle. When school problems have reached the point where school is predominantly ungratifying and an unhappy experience, leaving school is an escape hatch, and the wish to drop out is very strong. It assumes some of the aspects of the "magic answer" to the student's difficulties. Although most students realize the advantage of completing high school, such knowledge is of little avail against the complex internal and external forces pressing toward leaving school.

Many children find certain aspects of school ungratifying but nevertheless remain. For them, one of several circumstances exists:

1. The adolescent has attained sufficient personal maturity to forego present gratification for the future gain of high school graduation.

2. Some elements of school may be displeasing to the child, but others are satisfying and tip the balance toward remaining in school.

3. Positive experiences for the child are tied in with his continuing in school. For instance, he obtains satisfaction from pleasing his parents, his teachers, or his counselor.

We found that, characteristically, once the decision to leave school had been made it was very difficult to reverse it. A tremendous amount of energy went into the adolescent's determination to leave. The emotional basis of his wish to drop out was frequently bolstered by realistic problems growing out of the original school symptom. If past school failures had resulted in substantial grade retardation, it was exceedingly difficult to help the child remain in school. The sixteen year old who is still a freshman finds it hard to face the prospect of being graduated at the age of twenty. In addition, he is embarrassed at being left behind by his former classmates and having to associate with new and younger children. Or, if the emotionally disturbed adolescent is substantially retarded in reading and arithmetic, he is discouraged by the necessity of making up these deficiencies before he can perform at a high school level.

School Problems and Beginning Treatment

Though school malfunctioning was a primary problem of our adolescents, it was an area they often were reluctant to discuss. For some it assumed the proportions of a taboo topic: if the counselor attempted to explore it, he encountered a great deal of resistance. Pursuing it created an impasse in counseling or led to the adolescent's discontinuing treatment.

Such unwillingness to talk about school went beyond the recognized reluctance of many children to focus on their specific trouble area. Because school symptoms evoked their intense concern, parents and others who had responsibility for the child usually badgered a great deal about school. The children were bored with the topic and no longer wished to hear or think about it. Some youngsters developed a deaf ear and were evasive or noncommittal when the subject was mentioned. Others adopted the more active façade of a defiant "I don't care" attitude.

Matt [2] had failed all his subjects and was cutting classes. His school behavior difficulties, talking too much and refusing to obey the teacher, had been in evidence since the fifth grade. This is our caseworker's report of his first interview at the agency:

2. Identifying data in this and all other illustrative material have been disguised.

Matt is a carelessly dressed, untidy looking boy. Despite the indication in the school report that he is brighter than average, he makes a generally dull impression. There was no rapport between us during the interview.

I told him of his parents' concern and asked if he could tell me something about his view of the problem. Matt smiled and assured me there wasn't any problem. He wouldn't be here at all except that his parents made him come. When I asked about the difficulty at school, he smiled again and told me easily that he fools around, gets a kick out of teasing the teachers, and doesn't do his assignments. I asked what happened then. He assured me nothing happens—they might flunk him, but he doesn't care. He goes to school only because his mother makes him go.

Matt mentioned casually that his parents were worried that he would have to go to the social adjustment school. He grinned and told me he knows plenty of guys who are there already. He wouldn't mind it at all. For one thing, you don't even have to do schoolwork there. He knows there are some tough guys at the school, but he has his own friends and he doesn't think he would get hurt. His whole way of talking about the social adjustment school gave me the impression that Matt thinks he would gain status with his friends by going there.

Toward the end of the interview I observed that troubles of the sort he was having in school and with his parents were never easy for a boy, and I offered to see him on a regular basis to find out if there was some way of improving the situation. Matt shrugged, stating he doesn't want to come here. He is going to go home to try to talk his parents out of the whole business.

We have learned from experience that it is well to bring out in the initial interview our knowledge of the specific trouble in school leading to the referral to the agency. It is necessary and therapeutic to get the matter out in the open, since failure to do so sets up a false reality and an unfavorable basis for establishing a caseworker-client relationship. It leaves the youngster anxious about how much the counselor knows, what he plans to do, and what will happen in treatment.

The adolescent's reaction to the factual statement of the school problem gives essential clues about what procedure is most likely to lower defensiveness and lessen resistance. When a youngster does discuss school, his manner and the content of what he says often provide helpful insight into his psychological pattern. With many children there are striking similarities between their reaction to school or to specific school personnel and their reactions to important familial figures. Sometimes the adolescent will on his own consciously recognize that he is displacing onto school personnel a feeling actually directed toward his parents.

This report followed Alice's first visit to our office:

After a bit, when I inquired about her father, Alice said that he is very strict. He raised her brothers and sisters in a very stern manner and he has hit her frequently. Just last week he slapped her for saying, "oh, nuts," when she was talking to him. He keeps telling her, "I want respect." A few minutes later she quite spontaneously brought out her recognition that she takes out her anger against her father on the teachers at school. She gets angry with him when he hits her but cannot say anything because he will hit her again. When she reaches school, the anger is still there inside her, and so she talks back to the teacher.

Alice acknowledged her lack of interest in school, blushingly remarking that she doesn't do much homework and that her Chemistry teacher tells her that she is lazy. In the course of this discussion Alice again brought out that she resents the authority of the school because of her feelings about her parents. This was said not in a facile, intellectualized way but with a kind of groping feeling, as if she were genuinely looking for answers. Speaking of her truanting, she laughed apologetically; she was caught fewer times than she actually cut. Embarrassedly, she commented, "You must think I'm awful for telling you all these terrible things about myself." I indicated by my manner that criticism was not my aim, that I was interested in helping, and that the information she had given me would aid us in working together.

Discussion of the school problems sometimes was a way of getting closer to the underlying, more dynamic problems. Some of the neurotic adolescents, especially the girls, quickly moved on to an implicit recognition that their school malfunctioning was connected with more fundamental emotional difficulties. When this occurred, further exploration of school per se was no longer pertinent and the focus could shift to more basic matters.

Jane had been sent to us because of her truancy, poor school achievement, and association with a delinquent group. She was on the verge of being transferred to a social adjustment school. Jane lived with her father; her mother had deserted the family and later died. We met with the father a few days before Jane's initial interview at the agency. Jane's caseworker wrote the following report about the first interview:

Jane is a small, neatly dressed girl with a tiny, pretty face. Seemingly uncertain of me at first, she spoke in a rather sad, despairing tone. Nevertheless, her quiet sadness was not apathy, and she was responsive. She impressed me as having the capacity for insight and in the interview showed enough strength to be able to detach herself from her behavior and observe it.

I opened by asking if she had talked with the adjustment teacher about coming here. Jane replied that she had, but she didn't have any idea of what we do. I explained that we counsel high school boys and girls because they have things on their minds—sometimes about school, sometimes about other matters. I asked if her father had explained anything to her about this appointment. Jane said he hadn't said much but told her he thought we could help.

I remarked that her father had said she was unhappy. She laughed a little in an anxious manner and agreed this was certainly so. I said I also understood that there were some current school difficulties, and the possibility of her being transferred from her present school. Jane nodded in affirmation as if she were glad this was in the open.

Suddenly she broke in to say that all the trouble had started in high school. Things were fine in grade school. I asked what had occurred to make the difference. Jane said she didn't know, though she thinks grade school was better because things were more "personal." In grade school you had one teacher all day; in high school there are different teachers, different classes, and a much larger group.

Again Jane said quite suddenly that her real problems are not school problems. Her real problems are "inside her." I replied that in that case she had come to exactly the right place. School problems are not the only things for which we give help; we know how to help with "problems inside." Jane laughed and relaxed.

She said she had felt like crying as she rode down on the bus to the appointment, and her eyes now filled with tears. I gave her a tissue and said that she could cry here whenever she felt like it and that it's natural to cry when you feel bad. After Jane recovered her composure, I asked gently what she thought made her cry. She said she did not know but in the next breath mentioned her mother with warmth and much suppressed feeling. She knows people think her mother was bad, but she has feelings for her mother because after all "she was my mother." I said that it is natural for a girl to have good feelings toward her mother and that the very fact of her being her mother made her a special person for Jane.

After some further discussion about her mother Jane said to me that she was absolutely starved. I suggested that we better get something to eat, since no one can talk very well when hungry. She murmured something about not having enough money for lunch. I said I would take care of the bill; I didn't want her to be hungry. Jane was pleased, and I had a strong sense of her need to put me very quickly into a maternal role.

School Problems as a Focus for Treatment

There was one group of youngsters whose school problems could be dealt with quite actively and directly in treatment, resulting in relatively quick alleviation of the school malfunctioning. These were the adolescents who used school in an attempt to resolve a conflict belonging to another area of their lives. As mentioned in Chapter 4, several factors characterized this group. Their basic problems were not with the school but concerned their parents or some other aspect of family life. As a rule, the youngsters themselves were aware of this. They were also aware, or with the counselor's help could readily become aware, that their school malfunctioning had a deliberate purpose: generally, to effect some change in the relationship between the adolescent and his parents. The specific purpose varied with the individual.

Some adolescents created school problems in the hope of gaining gratification. Such a pattern could derive from a background where the child was the object of his parents' attention only when he was in trouble. It could also develop when parents had habitually held out bribes for academic achievement or good school behavior. The child might then come to believe that bartering was a good way of operating with his parents—"You give me a motor bike and I'll get better grades." In other cases school problems could represent a retaliation by which an angry adolescent attempted to punish his parents and obtain revenge.

Some adolescents brought about a school crisis as a dramatic way of communicating to their parents that they were unhappy and that something should be done—the "cry for help."

For some time emotional conflict had troubled Harry, but because there were no marked overt signs, his personality difficulties went unnoticed both by his family and the school. Though of superior intelligence and an outstanding student, he began to do poor work. The climax came when he submitted an examination paper containing some obscene four letter words. The school and the parents took immediate steps to secure casework service. Soon after referral Harry's academic performance improved, so there was no longer a school problem. Our treatment then focused on the primary issues, which had evolved around the parents' depreciation of Harry.

Other youngsters used school for the discharge of the hostile emotions they felt toward a parent. This was not an unconscious displacement because they were fully cognizant of the meaning of their school behavior.

The various types of adolescents cited above generally had parents with a high investment in their child's education. The youngster chose school as the battleground, recognizing that school problems above all else would distress his parents. As would be expected, the conflict already existing between the parents and child became intensified by the parents' anxiety over the school difficulty. Not understanding what really was going on, the parents often frantically persisted in their unavailing efforts to make the child do better.

The adolescents for whom school problems represented a conscious device could be discerned rather early. From the beginning their behavior in the counseling situation revealed special features. Other youngsters in the project often came in for their initial interview with resentment, suspicion, and reluctance to discuss their problems or to accept counseling. These adolescents, by contrast, were ready to talk about themselves and their problems once they had some notion of what counseling was and recognized the counselor as a trustworthy and interested person. With all adolescents it is of basic importance to create at the outset this atmosphere of emotional support in which the youngster feels understood, respected, and liked and where he senses that the counselor is someone who will try to make things better for him. Only from this support can the student talk about the conflictual issues.

Our next step was to determine the essential conflict. We needed to know what really troubled the child. Here again we could focus on the difficulty rather quickly with these adolescents. Since their conflict was on a conscious level, they knew fairly well what was bothering them and could communicate it. In this respect they differed greatly from the youngsters whose school difficulties were rooted in deeply unconscious problems.

After the adolescent had described his school difficulties, he generally moved on to discuss the conflict with his family. At about the same time he would reveal the deliberate nature of his school behavior and his own purpose in behaving that way. If he did not bring this out spontaneously, he was as a rule able to accept the counselor's pointing it out.

When the basic conflict and the purpose of the school difficulty were understood by both counselor and adolescent, the third step was to reduce the conflict. This involved separating the adolescent's difficulty with his family from his school behavior through a series of logical questions. What did the negative feelings about the parent, though perhaps justified, have to do with getting poor school grades? Our effort was directed toward the rational part of the adolescent's ego to help him look at his behavior more objectively. The self-damaging aspects of his school malfunctioning were brought up, and gradually he was helped to a recognition that he was acting against his own best interests. We pointed out that his school malfunctioning was an ineffectual device, since it had not brought him the gratification or produced the effect he wanted. If his problem was a restrictive parent and he was hoping for a more lenient parental attitude, we could show him that his actions had caused the parent to be even more restrictive. We reinforced this by the suggestion that improvement at school could better accomplish what he desired. Many repetitions of the theme were necessary.

If concurrent treatment of a parent was taking place, the adolescent knew that we were trying to help the parent change. This hope fortified the youngster as he progressed in counseling. When the parent could modify his own impeding attitudes, there were good prospects of fairly rapid mitigation of the interlocking struggles. Sometimes quick and dramatic changes occurred.

A different situation prevailed when the adolescent's needs in the struggle were not primarily reactive but had become an internalized self-generating mechanism or when his wish for retaliation was much greater than his hopes of gratification from education. Progress was similarly slow, sometimes impossible, if the parent could not alter his part in the conflict.

The approach we have discussed above was geared flexibly to the psychodynamics of the individual adolescent. Moreover, though the techniques are necessarily described in intellectual terms and the interviews cited contain educative elements, the vital force of the treatment process and the dynamic behind the changes taking place was the positive emotional experience the adolescent had with the counselor. Because of this emotional relationship the child was free to reason and to be reasonable.

We have stated that adolescents utilizing a school problem to handle another conflict are consciously aware of their actual problem. This is true only for the specific struggle the adolescent is trying to solve through the device of school difficulties. In addition, the adolescent may have deeper unconscious conflicts. The differential factor, however, is that these unconscious conflicts, if they exist, do not noticeably affect his school functioning. When the school problems have been alleviated, new treatment goals may be instituted.

In May's case (see Case Illustrations, Chapter 9) it was appropriate to terminate counseling after the school problem was solved.

Nature and Treatment of the Emotional Problems

Our discussion of the treatment of emotional problems will first focus on the character disturbances and then on the reactive disturbances. The differentiation between a character disturbance and a reactive or neurotic disturbance is that the latter is a maladaptive response to a specific stress of relatively recent onset, and the former is a maladaptive total way of life that has existed for some time.

GENERAL CONSIDERATION OF
CHARACTER DISTURBANCES

Treatment of character problems presents the following special complications: (1) a behavior pattern that has persisted for a considerable period of time; (2) ego-syntonic behavior which does not create much conscious discomfort; (3) behavior that is rigid, repetitive, and quite pervasive; and (4) a strong investment of energy in the defenses. At best, progress will be slow; modification of attitudes and functioning is hard to achieve. The counselor's task is complex and delicate. He must first induce an unmotivated adolescent to remain in treatment by establishing a strong, emotional relationship. If this can be accomplished at all, it is only the beginning. On the foundation of the relationship the counselor selects the particular therapeutic techniques that seem most applicable: advice, reality testing, exploration of day-to-day functioning, examination of selected feelings, clarification, and so on. Timing and "dosage" are also important considerations. The treatment task is ordinarily a strenuous undertaking, encountering resistance much of the way.

CHARACTER DISTURBANCES OF THE EARLY EGO PHASE

The developmental tasks of the early ego phase are mastery of the oral-dependent and oral-aggressive impulses in the mother-child relationship. Those of the later ego phase are mastery of the anal training period impulses and the integration of sexual and oedipal issues. This integration is the specific developmental task of adolescence.

In our group, 33 per cent of the girls and 27 per cent of the boys were trying to cope with heterosexual issues; 9 per cent of the girls and 5 per cent of the boys continued to be absorbed with training and authoritarian issues; and 54 per cent of the girls and 64 per cent of the boys were struggling with the dependency and hostility issues of the very earliest mother-child relationship.

The adolescent with a characteristic pattern of extreme dependency has suffered severe oral deprivations in the past. Since his dependency results from a very early developmental phase, his personality problems as well as his school problems have been chronic. He is immature, has low self-esteem (though it may not always appear so on the surface), and is generally ill able to cope with life. One reason for his maladaptation in school is that his basic needs for affection, mothering, and parental care have not been met. He is still engaged in his search for dependency gratification, and this absorbs most of his energy. If this all-important satisfaction is not forthcoming, he cannot function and produce. At times, when his dependency strivings were fulfilled by an interested teacher or some other meaningful person, he may have been able to achieve satisfactorily in school. Usually this occurs at the grade school level, where there is a closer relationship between teacher and pupil. The dependent adolescent, however, has not developed to the point where achievement for its own sake has any meaning, for he sees no value in being grown-up.

The dependent adolescent may not be aware of what is creating his school problem, or if he is aware, it is too painful for him to discuss. He may realize, however, that his dependent behavior is immature and inadequate in comparison to that of his age mates. His sense of shame and inferiority impairs his functioning even more.

The four clinical groups of dependent adolescents have been presented in the diagnostic section:

1. The oral-dependent, passive type is a helpless child who just "sits" and makes no effort on his own behalf.

2. The oral-dependent, aggressive youngster's only outgoing effort is clinging to the person he hopes will provide some gratification.

3. The oral-aggressive, passive adolescent's chief defense is silent, stubborn, insistent behavior.

4. The oral-aggressive, infantile-demanding type is the child who clamors very vigorously for dependency satisfaction from others but who, like the preceding types, is basically infantile in that he does not move ahead on his own.

In school all four types may be truanting, failing, or showing marked academic underachievement. Ordinarily, the oral-dependent types will not create any behavioral disturbances in class, but the two groups of youngsters in the oral-aggressive classification may be irritating to teachers and school personnel. The passive child is annoying because of his negative stubbornness, and the infantile-demanding adolescent can prove harassing if his insistence on "getting what he wants when he wants it" manifests itself in the schoolroom.

THE PASSIVE, DEPENDENT ADOLESCENT

In their beginning relationship to the counselor these dependent adolescents react in two essentially different ways. Some are relatively communicative, that is, they are at least willing to engage in conversation with the counselor. Some may be quite responsive, though they keep their school problems an excluded area.

Other youngsters are noncommunicative. If they talk at all, they answer briefly, noncommittally, and evasively, denying anything is wrong. Rarely do they volunteer a response or do something to keep the verbal exchange going. Dealing with these adolescents tests the counselor to the utmost. Since an individual brings to the therapeutic situation the same character structure he uses in the rest of his living, the passive youngster does not allow himself to become any more genuinely involved in treatment than in anything else.

In character problems, furthermore, the defense itself is often defended against. Thus, more passivity—indifference, resignation, defeatism, and the like—greets attempts by the counselor to engage the youngster on any level. Counselors who have had experience with adolescents know that overt rebellion is a much better prognostic sign. Particularly in adolescence, classically the rebellious period, deeply entrenched passivity is a grave and formidable signal, presenting as it does a smooth, impenetrable façade.

The counselor's difficulty in eliciting some response from a passive adolescent can be seen in the following case record excerpts:

Ted, with an above average I.Q. presented school problems of failure, truancy, and lack of ambition. The parents were people of considerable financial means. Distressed because of his trouble in school, they nagged him a great deal.

First interview: Ted is of average size but walks with a slight stoop to his shoulders. His face has a brooding expression. He has a somewhat apologetic manner and a "my parents are right" attitude. I told him of his mother's concern about his school difficulties. Ted assured me that school is O.K. now that he is going to summer school. I asked what he meant by school being "O.K." now. He explained that he had cut school a few times and had flunked as a result. I then asked why he had cut in the first place. Ted assured me there wasn't any reason, actually; he just did. I observed that since he never did it before this semester, there must have been a reason for his doing it at this time. He shrugged and said he couldn't "think of anything."

Fourth interview: This was a slow interview. Ted seems content with his life as it is. He talked quite a bit throughout the interview but said very little. He doesn't believe he wants to go to college. It is really his parents' idea that he go. He knows he won't be happy if he goes to college. He doesn't care much for his subjects; he's pretty bad in Spanish and doesn't understand some of the things discussed in Science. His father still pushes him a bit about getting good grades, but Ted will be content if he just passes.

Fifth interview: There was the same talking about trivial matters throughout today's interview. I tried to engage Ted in discussion of attitudes regarding his father and mother, but he moved quickly away from the topic or professed ignorance of his mother's and father's attitudes and activities. I observed it is somewhat unusual to have this lack of interest and knowledge with regard to one's parents, but Ted shrugged and went on to talk of inconsequential matters.

Seventh interview: This interview moved very slowly. Ted persisted in his passive "nothing is wrong" attitude. He assured me everything is going all right. When I asked if it could be running as smoothly as he said (actually, things are still very difficult), he attempted to prove it to me by pointing out that at school he is getting along O.K., and nothing is bothering him at all. I remarked on the length to which he went in defending himself against my simple question. Ted denied, however, that he was defending himself at all but reiterated it was a fact that he is doing all right.

The most important requisite for the counselor engaged in treating a passive, dependent, noncommunicative child is an understanding of his own feelings. The counselor must recognize his own inner mood and be fully conscious of his sense of futility as well as of inertia and boredom. Such conscious recognition will help alleviate the counselor's tendency to succumb in the face of the resistance of this hard to reach type of adolescent.

There are some specific techniques that may help keep the resistant child (and the counselor) interested. In the beginning of treatment silences of more than a few moments duration should be avoided. The counselor can ask questions that cannot be answered by a simple yes or no or a shrug. When nothing else works, however, such questions may have to be asked. The purpose in asking the questions is not so much to secure information but to help establish the relationship, the vital bridge between the counselor and the adolescent, that is the indispensable first step in treatment. The questions should require elaboration. The counselor may request examples or illustrations. When the child answers, he may give details that can be further elaborated or questioned. The kinds of questions should be those that can be answered from conscious knowledge or from introspection of a not too profound nature. They may range from anything one expects the adolescent to be acquainted with to those things of real interest to him: movies, hobbies, activities, and so forth. Questions about school can be introduced if the counselor does not concentrate on this area and is sensitive to those points the youngster is not ready to discuss. When conversational techniques are depleted (and this occurs mainly because the counselor is exhausted), one can try games and drawings about which the child can elaborate his fantasies.

Throughout, the counselor's attitude should be one of sincere and friendly interest. Although the counselor may be forced to resort to more questioning than he would ideally prefer, he should avoid as much as he can any probing or pressuring into emotionally loaded areas.

The entire process of attempting to keep the adolescent coming to the interviews so as to involve him in a therapeutic relationship may take months. Patience and fortitude are useful qualities, as the counselor finds himself expending much energy for meager results. Such children may frequently fail to keep appointments. If the failure is more than occasional, the counselor should follow up appropriately by writing or calling. If the counselor can remain aware of his own frustrations and remember that an adolescent's behavior is defensive and symptomatic, even if deliberately provocative, he may find the task easier. When an opportunity arises to do some favor for the youngster, it should be done. It may be an offer of aid in a specific situation troubling the child, for example, communicating with the teacher to help straighten out some school incident. Such concrete demonstrations of help are often the most telling way to convince the youngster of the counselor's genuine interest.

If all goes well, the youngster becomes more responsive, starts to keep appointments more regularly, and in other ways gives signs that he is beginning to participate in the treatment process. Such participation is evidence that the counselor has at least become meaningful to him. At this point treatment can gradually be directed toward the therapeutic issues. The passive adolescent now approaches that phase of relationship in treatment that more responsive types of dependent children attain much earlier.

With both types of dependent children, however, there is still a long treatment road ahead. Something must happen in the counselor-client relationship to make the dependent child want to grow up. The core of treatment must be geared to the fact that these are emotionally hungry children who can give only when they are given to. It usually involves the patient process of feeding (psychologically and sometimes literally), which provides the child with a kind of "reliving" experience in a corrective relationship. From this relationship he obtains the emotional nutrition of which he was deprived. The counselor should have a warm, giving, parental attitude, the essence of which is an interest in the adolescent as a person.

There are many ways in which the counselor may demonstrate his interest. He may encourage the adolescent to talk about the things important to him—his interests, his ideas, his skills and his hopes. Discussion of day-to-day activities, answering questions, advice, and guidance when indicated—all strengthen the adolescent's attachment to the counselor and provide him with further evidence of the counselor's concern. These measures also serve to increase the youngster's self-esteem by showing that the counselor regards him as having worth and value.

At first, such techniques result in making the child more dependent on the counselor. In a sense he is encouraged to "regress," but this regression is "in the service of the ego" and a means toward the accomplishment of a definite treatment aim. The purpose of providing increased dependency satisfaction is to enable the adolescent to function better and ultimately to reduce his dependency needs.

The increased dosage of dependency gratification is a transitional stage, however long it lasts. It cannot be an interminable process because too prolonged dependency can retard growth by making a child feel more inadequate. Therefore, it is necessary at a suitable time to indicate some reasonable expectations of growth. When school is the focus of trouble, the expectation may concern some aspect of school functioning. If an adolescent is truanting and also receiving poor grades, the counselor may feel that the youngster is at a point where he can end his truanting. The counselor may decide to defer the matter of improved academic performance because this is often a dynamically more complex matter and more difficult to achieve. If expectations are set too high and the adolescent cannot meet them, he regards himself as a double failure: he has failed both the task and the counselor. Anxiety and hostility may then arise and result in a deterioration of functioning.

There are many instances where the dependent adolescent begins to perform better of his own accord, without any explicit discussion in the interviews. One reason for the improvement may be the child's wish to please his counselor. As the counselor gives approval, either verbally or by implication, the youngster receives gratification and has a further incentive for progress. The better functioning, however, often provides its own gratification for the adolescent, since it makes him feel more adequate. This heightens his feeling of self-esteem and lessens his need for large quantities of dependent satisfaction. He has had the opportunity of experiencing gratification in real life, not alone by dependency on others but by his own efforts and accomplishments.

In certain instances the counselor may find it advisable to enter a new treatment phase where there is emphasis on helping the adolescent understand his dependent passivity as a defense. This stage must wait until the youngster is solidly engaged in his relationship with the counselor and is emotionally ready to tolerate some degree of self-examination.

The over-all task in this new phase is to make the adolescent aware of his passivity and see it as a symptom of an emotional problem. The subsequent exploration of the reason for the passive behavior aids the adolescent in discovering his own purpose in the defense. The major focus is upon drawing out the youngster's ideas about why he behaves as he does. At this point some adolescents may bring out their feelings of deprivation and begin to comprehend that their purpose was to attain the longed for gratification that they did not have.

The next procedure is to make the defense ego-dystonic, that is, unacceptable to the individual. The creation of an ego-dystonic affect is achieved through showing how the defense interferes with the adolescent's own welfare and is ultimately self-destructive. During treatment the counselor has the opportunity to point out various examples of the defense in the areas where it is manifested most clearly. For the youngsters in our study, school was the prime area of trouble, and the focus was on the ways in which the defense was operating in school life. This did not preclude attention to other significant areas hampered by the defense, such as family and peer relationships.

If hostility is a major component, the adolescent should be encouraged to "feel and think" his hostilities consciously. Through expressing them verbally to the counselor, his ego can learn to handle these feelings constructively rather than continue to defend against them through behavioral maladaptations. Or, if indicated, the counselor can work with the conflicts that develop during the interviews.

It should be stressed that when the adolescent's progress is slow, and his behavior both inside and outside the interview setting has irritating qualities, the keynote is "sympathy for the symptom." This helps the counselor to remain in command of his feelings, to contain his impatience, and to avoid acting out non-therapeutic feelings. The attitude has positive benefits for the adolescent as well because confronting the adolescent with his behavior by itself rarely helps. The confrontation must be accompanied by a sympathetic understanding that the child can sense and feel. "Sympathy for the symptom" does not mean acceptance of the pathological behavior per se. It means looking upon the behavior, no matter how distasteful, as a symptom—something arising out of inner conflict, part of a greater issue, and not maliciously intentioned. This is true even if the adolescent himself thinks that his conduct is willful. The child cannot be expected to have a knowledge of unconscious mechanisms.

The case illustration of Chuck (Chapter 9) tells something about the course of treatment with a passive, dependent boy.

THE INFANTILE-DEMANDING ADOLESCENT

A sizable group of adolescents in our study had infantile-demanding character structures; three-fourths of this group were girls. Like the boys we have just discussed, the infantile-demanding youngster's basic problem is dependency. He is a psychologically hungry child whose life pattern centers around his constant need to receive from other people. Whereas the passive adolescent sits helplessly waiting for gratification to come to him, the infantile-demanding adolescent, who has progressed one step higher in personality development, clamors loudly for satisfaction and reaches out aggressively to obtain it. But his efforts stop there. He will do little to earn the privileges he wants and will resist the demands placed upon him. He acts as if his primary aim is to get "something for nothing."

The relentless energy the demanding child devotes to seeking gratification can be an asset in treatment, but it also creates grave therapeutic problems. The complications arise in part from his propensity for antagonizing the people about him; as a result, he is usually embroiled in trouble at school, at home, and with other children.

Though a needy youngster, the infantile-demanding adolescent is not an appealing one; he is hard to like. In contrast to some dependent children, he does not have the soft helplessness that stirs people to protective compassion. Instead, he creates anxiety and irritation in others by his angry way of pressing his demands and his inability to wait for their fulfillment. Whatever he wants, he wants at once.

Simply providing what these youngsters ask neither solves their problems nor satisfies them for any length of time. New demands follow immediately, and one gets the impression of attempting to fill a bottomless well.

For some time Thelma had been receiving a scholarship from the agency for her personal and school expenses, including her clothing needs. Arrangements were being made to send her to summer camp, and the agency agreed to provide the clothes and equipment she would require. Thelma and her counselor talked over in detail what her needs would be, drew up a suitable (and sizable) list, and then went shopping together.

When Thelma entered the sports section, she grew very excited at the large array of merchandise. After the agreed-upon equipment was bought, she continued to wander about, fingering other articles and asking that these be purchased also. Among the things she fastened her wishes upon was an expensive compass.

The counselor's explanation that the compass was unnecessary and could not be included did not settle the issue for the girl. She wheedled, sulked, and exploded in turn, finally accusing the counselor of "never wanting to do anything" for her.

As this incident reveals, the infantile-demanding adolescent is not easily rebuffed and has little capacity to appreciate or remember past favors. His attitude resembles that of the stock character in the joke who says, "What have you done for me lately?"

These youngsters are concerned only with the present; they do not wish to think ahead or consider the consequences of their behavior. As one girl exclaimed when her counselor pointed out the possible aftermath of certain behavior, "I can't think of next month or next week. I can't even think of five minutes from now. All I can think of is right this minute."

In the classroom the infantile-demanding adolescent expects inordinate attention and special privilege from the teacher but is reluctant to do what is asked of him. He balks at classroom regulations when they do not suit him and puts the least possible effort into the preparation of his assignments. When he is angry or wishes to tease or to attract attention, he can be very provocative.

Ruth was chewing gum in class. When told by the teacher to stop, she discarded the gum but kept on making elaborate chewing motions. The teacher ignored this, remarking she knew Ruth was pretending. At the end of class Ruth deliberately passed in front of the teacher and laughingly removed a second wad of gum to show she had been chewing gum all the time.

The counselor, too, is subject to the hostile reactions these youngsters so easily arouse. The force of their onslaught may be intimidating and their knack of discerning any sign of weakness may make the counselor feel insecure and anxious, and if he feels outwitted, he may spend the interview protecting himself rather than focusing on treatment. Therefore, the counselor must be skilled as well as reasonably confident of his skill. It is also important that he recognize and be in command of his own feelings as they emerge. Otherwise he is liable to make two kinds of mistakes: he may withhold legitimate gratification from the youngster out of irritation or anger, or he may yield to the child's unrealistic demands out of anxiety or guilt.

Successful treatment of the infantile-demanding youngster requires giving ample gratification as often as is possible, since unsatisfied needs are at the root of his trouble. The giving (within realistic limits of course) should be provided freely, quickly, and to the maximum. The youngster's arrogant manner of asking for things must not prejudice a consideration of his demands on their own merits.

Material gratification is quite meaningful. The counselor can furnish gifts, food, or other treats when the occasion is fitting. At our agency it is common for the counselors to have a snack with these children during their interviews.

Just as important as material giving, however, are the counselor's personal attention and interest. Favors and services may take unusual and ingenious forms, but are appropriate if they provide the help the child actually needs.

Vera overslept and was habitually late for school. Her mother worked and was not on hand to call her. The counselor volunteered to phone Vera at 8 o'clock each morning to awaken her. This went on for several weeks until she had made sufficient progress to get up by herself and go to school.

Optimum and immediate giving has several therapeutic effects. It helps to keep the child in treatment. These youngsters do not relate to people out of a desire for human relationships as such; they are mainly interested in others for what they can get from them. If satisfaction is not forthcoming fully or quickly, they fail appointments or drop out of counseling. These children do not want help because of guilt, discomfort, or desire to change as do youngsters who are more mature.

Meeting the demanding youngster with a free and open hand also has the corrective effect of diminishing some of the motivating force behind his demands. His grasping tactics arise in part from his experience that this is the surest way to get things. Often his parents are reluctant givers with the habit of first saying "no" to every request. They may believe it is bad for a child to be given something as soon as he asks for it; prompt giving is equated with "giving in." Later, however, they yield to the same demands when the youngster's pleas have become louder or when they are worn out by his sheer persistence.

The child accustomed to this method of operating comes to enjoy the winning of his demands; the gratification is sweeter for having been gained by fighting for it. When the counselor gives freely and without argument, it takes the edge off the child's inclination to battle and paves the way toward the realization that such tactics are pointless and unnecessary. It also shows the child that the counselor's primary interest is in giving, not in withholding.

But readiness to give is only one part of the treatment process; the counselor should be equally ready to refuse what is undesirable or unreasonable. Refusals should be made with quiet firmness, without defensiveness or apology. It is best to be factual, neutral in emotional tone, and brief in indicating why it is impossible or inadvisable to do what the child asks. Lengthy explanations have a way of sounding defensive; they will not satisfy these youngsters and will be used only as openings for further argument.

These treatment techniques aim at helping the demanding adolescent to acquire a greater tolerance for frustration. The fact that he has received ample gratification in treatment may in itself increase his ability to bear frustration. Furthermore, a child who receives adequate satisfaction becomes less angry. He no longer needs to engage in acting-out behavior that creates hostility in his environment, and his social situation becomes more stable.

Appropriate giving and withholding also constitute an educative process. It is a corrective experience to learn that demands when reasonable will be met and, when unreasonable, will be refused. Such solid, consistent boundaries not only define socially acceptable behavior but demonstrate that such behavior nets the greatest benefits.

When the youngster has settled down sufficiently to listen to the counselor, a therapeutic appeal should be made to his self-interest. This appeal is necessarily on a narcissistic level because the child's chief concern is still, "What's in it for me?" If, for instance, the adolescent is angry over some frustration, the counselor should accept the feeling of anger but ask, "Where is it going to get you?" He can suggest alternative behavior "Wouldn't it be smarter to do it this way?"—and thus guide the child toward wiser actions. In all these approaches the counselor works toward a more constructive channeling of the youngster's large supply of energy.

Moralistic appeals or judgments should be avoided. These adolescents are touchy about criticism, and abstract considerations of right or wrong do not have much meaning for them. When counseling is successful, they may grow more capable of thinking in terms of the future, or at least better able to postpone immediate gratification for the sake of greater gratification later. To this extent judgment has improved and capacity for postponement has increased.

Counseling, however, does not bring quick results with infantile-demanding adolescents, and there are many relapses. Among the various diagnostic categories, the infantile-demanding adolescents were the most likely to drop out of school. Although about half of these youngsters in our study improved in personality functioning in treatment, virtually all those who were above the compulsory age limit left school. This outcome is understandable in the light of their personality characteristics.

School completion necessitates foregoing immediate pleasure for the sake of greater benefits in the future. The infantile-demanding adolescents find this hard to do. Their penchant for trouble and for arousing dislike, moreover, creates negative attitudes on the part of the school. Thus, school becomes a highly unpleasant place for them and they wish to escape it. Since progress in treatment is slow, they may decide to leave school before counseling can modify the factors causing them to drop out.

The intensity of conflict between the infantile-demanding adolescent and his parents was another serious impediment to successful treatment. The parents themselves were very immature, often presenting personality problems similar to those of the child. Aside from having little to give to the youngster, they were unable to restrain their anger at his demanding ways or to refrain from actions that aggravated the situation. Turbulence within the family was usual and sometimes culminated in a serious behavioral episode. Running away from home occurred most frequently in the infantile-demanding youngsters—especially the girls.

The combination of continuous turmoil and slow improvement made it hard to retain these adolescents and their parents in treatment. Unless the situation improved rather quickly, they grew restive in counseling and stopped coming. Therefore, the problem of stabilizing the environment is crucial.

After the counselor overcomes the hurdle of maintaining contact, his goal with the parents should be to help them deal more consistently and constructively with the youngster, to give more freely in some areas, and to limit in others. The parents need to become more patient and, ideally, more understanding. Even when the nature of the parents' own character problems precludes their gaining an understanding of the youngster, being told that he is troubled and unhappy may increase their patience. Additional treatment approaches are discussed in the chapter on parents.

Since the infantile-demanding adolescent is a harassing problem at school, close collaboration with school personnel is particularly important. Chapter 8 suggests ways in which such collaboration can be carried out.

Beth and Joe, whose histories appear in the Case Illustrations (Chapter 9), exemplify treatment efforts with infantile-demanding adolescents.

We have not devoted a section to the treatment of depressive or masochistic character formations because we had so few students with disturbances of this nature, but the report on Dan (see the Case Illustrations) does give an account of a masochistic character disturbance.

CHARACTER DISTURBANCES OF THE LATER EGO PHASE—THE INHIBITED BOYS

In our study, the boys with either inhibited or over-compensated character formations had problems due to mismanagement of their competitive-aggressive impulses. The etiology of this dynamic has been presented in Chapter 4. To restate it briefly, most often the unconscious determinant is an oedipal conflict involving castration anxiety. Achievement has become equated with surpassing the father and in the unconscious of these boys this superiority entails the risk of castration. It therefore becomes dangerous to achieve. The boys are deeply afraid of their competitive-aggressive impulses and in an effort to remain safe defend themselves by nonachievement.

The conflict over competitive-aggressive impulses need not necessarily manifest itself in school. On the contrary, some boys defend themselves against castration fears by pouring all their energy into academic achievement while restricting themselves in the more obvious masculine and heterosexual areas. Such boys, however, did not come within the purview of our project. We saw only those who were having some type of school problem. For these boys the competitive aspect of masculine sexuality had become involved with the competitive-achieving aspects of school.

The issue of competition is associated specifically with the phallic phase of a boy's development. Its resolution is one of the chief tasks of all adolescent boys: by the successful working through of the competitive oedipal struggle, adult masculinity is attained.

On the surface, boys with inhibited character formation convey an impression of passivity. They are quiet, submissive, and self-effacing. Since the inhibition is a generalized character trait, it can affect many areas of their functioning. In our study, however, the inhibition stood out most sharply in its effects on scholastic performance and attitudes toward school. In the classroom the inhibited boys were not the type to foment aggressive disturbances. Inattentive and uninterested in class, they usually had little to contribute to discussions. Often they did not complete assignments, and they skimmed over examinations. When the difficulties resulting from academic failure pyramided, absence from school followed.

Paul's I.Q. was in the superior range. During elementary school he managed to pass, though his marks were below average and far below his capacity. In high school his scholastic difficulties became more acute. He failed a number of courses, and in his junior year did not pass a single subject. He then transferred to a different school.

The new school soon noted his apathetic and uninterested attitude. When he began cutting and truanting he was referred for psychological study to determine whether he should continue in school since he was over compulsory school age.

The psychologist commented that Paul did not know what he wanted to do. He lacked the emotional and social maturity to profit from high school, yet he was afraid to leave school. Intensive counseling was recommended since there was nothing constructive the school could do within its own environment.

Despite the timid, fearful manner of the inhibited boy, one can sense that he possesses a great deal of energy. The energy is being constricted and "held in." This contrasts with many passive-dependent adolescents in whom one feels a definite lack of energy and motivation. Moreover, as with most phallic character types, the inhibited boy yearns for relationships and, if properly approached, can be engaged rather soon. This is unlike the passive-dependent adolescent, especially the stubborn type, who seems mainly intent on resisting the helping relationship.

Another prominent characteristic of inhibited boys is their pervading and painful sense of inferiority. This, too, often distinguishes them from the passive adolescents who are primarily dependent in orientation and fixated at earlier levels in their development. Although some dependent boys may consciously suffer from inferiority feelings, others may not experience much discernible conflict. The ego-dystonic nature of the inferiority feelings of inhibited boys shows that this conflict is actively operating. The resultant discomfort provides an important motivation and becomes a tool for treatment.

Paul was extremely self-depreciating and believed he had meager capacity. Tests confirmed his superior mental ability and revealed that he possessed considerable verbal skill. When pressed by the psychologist to talk about vocations, he did not think he could do the college work necessary for becoming an electrical engineer, the one profession that interested him. He thought he would be better at something where he used his hands—repairing electrical equipment or driving a bus.

The agency counselor observed the same self-negating manner. In the first interview "Paul adopted an attitude that he didn't know what counseling was all about even though he had talked to the school psychologist, adjustment teacher, and his parents about coming here. He did not say this in a hostile manner, but rather he attempted to give the impression of being slow and easily confused. Paul's face is generally impassive, and one might get an initial impression that he is slow-witted. However, as I talked with him, I sensed that there is a bright intelligence beneath his overlay."

The inhibited boy possesses many other strengths inherent in having reached the phallic period of character formation. He is in good contact with reality and can make appropriate judgments. His superego has been internalized. He has a strong need and capacity for relationships of many kinds, not only the one with the therapist. His ego-ideal is in the direction of achievement in spite of his defensive maneuvers against it. Just as the counselor of a hysterical girl perceives her real wish to be a mature woman, the counselor of the inhibited boy can detect the youngster's basic yearning to be an adequate man.

In his first interview Paul displayed some signs of reaching out for the counselor. He did this with reserve, waiting before he said very much and testing the counselor with the attitude of not understanding any reason for the referral. The counselor proceeded slowly and sensitively: "I indicated I understood from the psychologist and his parents that he was having some difficulty in school and said I would like to hear more about it from him. He stated he simply didn't do his work. He has quite a struggle with math and expects to fail science. He doesn't like his math teacher at all. When he started math, he didn't know what the homework was and didn't have any friends to ask, so he soon fell hopelessly behind. The teacher told him he might as well drop the course, since he was going to fail. I commented that this must have been a pretty tough thing to hear. Paul paused briefly, said I was right but that it really didn't make any difference because he didn't like the teacher and was glad to get out of the class.

"Earlier, I had interpreted counseling in terms of our getting together once a week. I gave him as a goal helping him find out what he wanted in life and also helping him to get it. I stated directly that this was more important than getting good grades in school. Later he gave his interpretation of my meaning, stating he thought counseling would be a way of helping him find a career for himself. I indicated that a choice of career was one goal of counseling."

In summary, the counselor wrote: "I feel Paul is a boy who has been frightened in his relationships and approaches every relationship with considerable caution. However, he does seem to have a good deal of capacity to relate, and I feel it will be possible to help this youngster." After the second interview the counselor said: "Paul seemed much more involved with me today, and I believe I am gradually reaching the point where a treatment relationship will develop."

Most inhibited boys manage well in elementary school; their academic problems first appear at adolescence. The fact of the previous good functioning has advantages in treatment. The adolescent, though now inhibited, has at one time experienced the gratification of personal achievement. This carries many implications for the raising of self-esteem. It also is useful in enabling the counselor to point up realistically the present discrepancy between ability and achievement and to give hope to the boy that he can again achieve satisfactorily.

The achievement of inhibited boys can improve but requires the alertness of a skillful therapist. These youngsters sense that their school failure is something beyond their control. They would like not to drop out of school, but they are pushed by forces beyond their control. When secondary complications ensue, they feel that they have no recourse but to drop out. They have some recognition that they are suffering from emotional problems and respond positively to the invitation to receive help for the problems.

The therapist has little difficulty in explaining the nature of treatment to these boys, who are usually intelligent and eager. They respond cooperatively in the first interview, describing their difficulties insofar as they are aware of them. They try to answer the counselor's questions as he attempts to elaborate the picture being presented to him. Under their passivity, timidity, or even affected indifference, these boys are anxious. The caseworker helps overcome their anxieties through the sincerity and warmth of his personality.

These students do not immediately believe in the success that therapy promises. They are accustomed to failure and are on the brink of it now. They are unconsciously strongly motivated to achieve success, however, and their hope is reawakened by the therapist.

A relationship with another person is significant to them. Although they fear aggressiveness, they long for the esteem of a parental figure, and the therapist becomes an important person in their life. As the therapist communicates his sincere interest in the student, the student finds it easier each time to reveal himself to his caseworker, who becomes an interested senior friend, a confidant, and an advisor.

During this phase of therapy the caseworker directs himself to the establishment of a relationship, the development of motivation for therapy, and an elaboration of information about the student's life. Much of the time together may be spent discussing interests, hobbies, and goals in life. This is not simply social chitchat. It is extremely important in the establishment of rapport and the discovery of interests that may perhaps be put to vocational use in the future. The potential drop-out, who is in conflict over competitive aggression, may have given up his interests and even his talents. He may have suppressed the hope of achieving goals that would satisfy these interests and talents. In this phase of the relationship these are reawakened, and the longing to achieve is stimulated.

Because of the inhibited boy's various ego assets, improvement might occur quickly. We were sometimes surprised by the rapidity with which favorable changes took place. These were "transference improvements," but they had much real value for the adolescent.

Chad's school work markedly improved after eight interviews. He is an interesting example of the great strides an inhibited boy may make even from one interview to the next. He also demonstrates that although an inhibited boy may sometimes adopt the defense of "not caring" about school performance, this defense yields easily with suitable handling because underneath there is a genuine desire to achieve.

Chad was sent to the agency because he was cutting school, was not doing well in his studies, and was noticeably inattentive in class. In the first interview he assured the counselor that he simply did not like school and that was why he didn't do the work. He then explained, with the air of tossing a bombshell, that he didn't care for books either. He didn't think he had read half a dozen books in his whole life. The counselor took this matter of factly, listening in a friendly manner, and asked the boy to expand his ideas. During the interview the counselor conveyed his genuine interest and imparted his hope of being able to help. Chad agreed to continue counseling. The following week the boy confided that he really wanted to go on to college, adding, "I guess what I actually need is some self-discipline about my homework." A little discussion followed, mostly concerned with Chad's thinking about the various meanings of self-discipline and its application to his homework. The third week Chad came in beaming: "I've been thinking a lot about our interviews, and I've got a new system for my homework. So far it's been working out swell, and all my assignments are up to date."

He next revealed his intense desire to achieve. "I want a good future for myself; and, you see, if I don't do well in high school, I won't be able to go to college. One of my friends quit high school, and, boy, did he mess up his future." In the fifth interview Chad gained a little more insight into his own feelings. In a very tangential way he touched on his conflict over competition and achievement. "I used to fool around in school a lot, and do you know why that was? It was because I was really scared I could never succeed. I was ambitious all right, but I didn't think I was going to make it, so I fooled around instead."

In his conscious thinking Chad reversed the order of things. Rather than recognizing that his past inability to succeed was due to fear, he attributed his fear to the thought that he might not succeed. Since his problem was unconscious, it was not to be expected that Chad would perceive it correctly at the conscious level without much more intensive treatment. But a correct perception of the basis of the unconscious conflict was not essential for this adolescent boy, and intensive uncovering could be bypassed. Through a medium that was ego directed, he was released from the constrictive defense he had erected against his unconscious fear, and his improvement continued.

Since the fear of competition and aggression leads to the repression of interests and the efforts required to fulfill them, the adolescent has a conflict. The work of resolving this conflict takes place next. The student discusses his difficulties at home, at school, and in social activities. All provide opportunity for insight, reassurance, and encouragement. An effort to attack the school problems directly or to concentrate on that area exclusively must be avoided. The adolescent would interpret this effort as pressure to achieve, and he has had a sufficient quantity of such pressure from all directions before.

Great benefit is derived from investigating other areas of the conflict over competitive aggression. Often these boys have been pushed to a level of achievement that they feel is beyond their capacity. They believe their fathers are hardworking, powerful, and unusually intelligent; and in comparing themselves, they feel they cannot be what their fathers are. They consider their fathers violent men with whom a competitive struggle would be physically disastrous. The neurotic resolution for these boys is to inhibit their own aggression and avoid competitive activity.

In treatment the inhibited boy must come to feel that his competitive impulses are "natural" and that his aggression is nondestructive. This means that the adolescent becomes unafraid of the rage and hostility within himself. These boys, inhibited and anxious though they are, find no dearth of subject matter once they are free to discuss their personal affairs.

Paul was soon able to talk about his angry feelings. He was the oldest of four children. His parents were involved in a marital conflict of long standing for which each blamed the other and for which neither would accept help. The mother was bitter, hostile, and depreciating. The father was a confused and inadequate man. He liked Paul and was proud of his intelligence but was so inconsistent in his relationship that the boy never knew what to expect. One moment the father was interested and close. The next time he would push Paul away and grow irritable and punitive if the boy continued to seek closeness. Because of the father's deficiency, the mother turned to Paul as a "little father," expecting him to shoulder a great deal of the responsibility for his younger brothers and sisters.

At first, Paul revealed no outward anger about his home and family situation. He was similarly submissive and uncomplaining in his relationships with his peers. Soon cracks began to appear in his armor of submissiveness and inhibition of anger. In his seventh interview Paul began to abandon the pretense that things were all right and spoke of his irritation at his mother's sickness and his many home responsibilities. He expressed anger at being expected to discipline the younger children and to help them with their homework. Moreover, he said that he had neither the place nor the privacy required for studying his lessons.

Paul next told about the situations at school that angered him. This verbalization of conscious hostility was followed by a change in his pattern of submission and compliance. He took a major step forward when he was able to defend himself by striking back at a schoolmate who had been in the habit of baiting and teasing him. Aside from the more positive self-image resulting from this demonstration of competence in relation to another male, there was a more subtle, dynamic gain. Paul unconsciously began to feel that masculinity and self-assertiveness would neither destroy him nor the person against whom they were directed.

The same inhibition reveals itself in school and sexual situations. The therapist, however, cannot expect a student to reveal early in therapy his conflict over sexuality. The competitive sexual striving with the father is unconscious and therefore can come to consciousness only with great anxiety. Proper timing, careful limitation of discussion, and reassuring handling of sexual anxieties require the counselor's sensitive skill. The goal is to free sexual interest of conflict and to permit its conscious expression in socially acceptable activities.

Paul grew able to talk about his dual feelings toward his father and to recognize that he both loved and feared him. Paul understood this fear only in its realistic aspects, connecting it with his father's punishments in the past. Although the counselor avoided any interpretation of the unconscious oedipal basis of Paul's fear, he did suggest that the youngster's fear of his father was displaced onto his contact with other boys. This interpretation contained much significance for Paul. He agreed it was true and in subsequent interviews elaborated on this theme. He said he could now understand why his schoolmates often picked on him or used him as the butt for their pranks: they sensed his fears and knew he would hesitate to defend himself. Reaching such understanding was a liberating experience for Paul, and he moved toward showing a more adequate amount of aggressiveness.

As the student's awareness of his conflicts widens, it becomes possible to relate them to his school activities. As he becomes less fearful of his impulses, his own motivation to be successful makes it possible for him to study his defenses and then to discard them so that he can participate in the required school activities.

Through some exploration of his father's inconsistent attitude toward him, Paul became able to realize how this had sensitized him in his relationships with other persons. For example, he disliked a certain teacher but did not know why. Following the discussion about his father's inconstancy, Paul indicated that the teacher was a changeable person given to different moods. He saw it was this quality he had reacted to, and he was now much more comfortable with the teacher.

The therapist is the new ego-ideal in the relationship. Through his reassurance and encouragement, he makes it possible for the adolescent to regard himself as successful in masculine strivings. Sometimes the adolescent tests out his aggression with the therapist. This role of the therapist as competitor or object of aggression is a transference reaction and occurs only periodically. Deftly handled, it can be put to great therapeutic advantage both in the expression of the released impulse and in gaining insight.

The student who overcomes his inhibition reports his achievement in school with great satisfaction and looks to his therapist to approve his gains and enhance his self-esteem. The therapist encourages further growth by expressing this approval. For these boys, "nothing succeeds like success."

In the Case Illustrations (Chapter 9) the report on George illustrates the treatment of problems of competitive aggression in an inhibited character type, that of Keith, in an overcompensated character type.

NEUROTIC DISTURBANCES IN HYSTERICAL CHARACTER FORMATION

The rebelliously acting-out girls with hysterical character formation were an interesting group to study and treat. We observed striking similarities in the histories of their behavior patterns. In preadolescent years they had been good, conforming little girls who did well at school, got along well with their parents, had suitable friends, and made no trouble.

Lois' father stated that until his daughter was twelve years old she had been a well-behaved child and received good grades in school. He referred nostalgically to the years between six and twelve, when she was extremely interested in paper dolls. Lois' mother reported it was a joy to have her in school until the onset of the present problem. She always received excellent report cards; and when the mother went to school, the teachers said they were glad to see her because they had only good things to say about Lois.

At approximately the onset of adolescence and particularly with their entry into high school, the girls erupted into an outburst of rebellion, defiance, and acting out. This behavior was not confined to one setting but occurred at home, in school, and often in the community. Any issue became explosive, setting off violent arguments with the parents.

Lois would never hang up her clothing and then wanted to add to the morning confusion in the kitchen by ironing a skirt she "just had to wear" that day. Her mother stated angrily, and with appropriate gestures, "I sometimes get so irritated by Lois I could shake her."

Academic work suffered and impertinent behavior often took place in the classroom. Lois refused to do her homework and would not recite in class. She seldom stayed in her seat but moved around talking, laughing, taking away the pencils of the other students. She had no consideration for the rights of others and in general kept the classroom in turmoil.

Some of the girls formed relationships with youngsters who, although they were not actually delinquent, had reputations of being "tough" or "hoody." Such attachments seemed to grow out of a need for excitement and stimulation in a diffused motoric effort to handle their intense feelings. Some of the girls rationalized these questionable relationships. Lois, for example, was going out with a delinquent boy in order to "reform" him. The activities of these girls, as they dashed about looking for they knew not what, contained an element of panic. One said, "The restlessness starts in my feet, goes to my head, and then I blow my top." But the girls' widespread rebellion was motivated by more than the need for discharge of tension. It also symbolized their urge to overthrow parental authority. Indeed, they rejected most of the current superego figures in their lives. The parents became especially concerned when the girls' activities and attitudes had a sexual coloration.

Lois provocatively kept her diary out in the open, and her mother was upset by the frank way in which she described her boy friend's physique and charms. The mother became really alarmed when a new entry openly hinted that Lois was planning sexual activity with him.

The psychodynamic issue with hysterical girls is conflict over sexuality. Their symptomatology, both intrapsychic and overt, is an effort to deal with oedipal problems—to keep repressed their sexual longings for the parent of the opposite sex and their hostility and rivalry toward the parent of the same sex. The sexual quality of their acting out was observed in their seductive attitudes, their provocative dress and make-up, their choice of boy friends, and their disregard of curfew. Such behavior frightened both the parents and the school. The parents were bewildered, being unable to account for what had happened to their previously well-behaved daughters. Some, in the past strict and controlling disciplinarians, became dazed and helpless. In the face of the revolt they surrendered their prerogatives as parents, and the adolescent assumed control of the situation. Other parents tried to intensify old methods of exacting obedience and became more rigid. But this, too, was unsuccessful and provided the girl with a rationalized justification for increasing her rebellion.

Outwardly, the symptoms of these girls looked very severe. The high pitch at which they flung themselves into their rebellious defiance, their apparent flirting with sexual experimentation, their general storminess, and their difficulties at school all made the situation look very grave.

Though the girls were flighty, impulsive, intense, and labile in mood, they were not impulse-ridden characters. Having progressed psychosexually to the phallic stage, they had achieved a fairly high level of ego development. Their basic problems were relatively mature having to do with love, womanhood, and identity formation. Although many of them also had residual conflicts over the dependency-independency issue, the oedipal struggle was predominant.

Aside from their relatively well-developed egos, the hysterical girls had other assets for treatment: (1) Since their acting-out behavior was ego-dystonic, they were motivated to accept help. (2) They had sufficient superego formation, and although they could not always control their behavior, they did feel guilt and shame because of their misbehavior. Their guilt and shame were not apparent to the people against whom they rebelled, since they were covered by a façade of defiance. (3) Their standards were fundamentally sound. They attached value to school, and most of them had a genuine wish to graduate, even though extraneous circumstances sometimes precipitated a decision to leave school. (4) Since the rebellion was relatively recent, it provided the treatment advantage of not being a chronic and entrenched character problem. The acting out was periodic and was followed by more adaptive behavior when the girl was, as one of them put it, "in a mood to be good." Hopeful parents and school personnel then heaved a sigh of relief, only to be engulfed in feelings of weary despair when the rebellion recurred. (5) They had a strong need and capacity for relationships. Although many dependent adolescents respond to helpful persons, the ties established by these hysterical girls were more intense, dramatic, and mature. Many of them formed a rapid identification with the counselor, developed a crush on her, and copied her clothes and her mannerisms. Attachment to the counselor, however, did not automatically end the undesirable behavior. Since it stemmed from an unconscious conflict, it was not immediately accessible to conscious control and could not be handled by an admonition to stop it.

The above assets distinguish the hysterical girls from the girls fixated at earlier levels of development. The most important point in differential diagnosis is that the underlying dynamic problem is conflict over sexual issues. Although it might take some time for the issues around sexuality and love to be revealed in the interviews, an experienced counselor picked up clues indicating the presence of predominantly phallic problems.

Since hysterical girls are fearful of sexuality, they do not, as a rule, engage in frank sexual acting out. Just as these girls tend to look "sicker than they are," they typically manage to act "more sexy than they are."

We consider it an important finding that the change from elementary school to high school was a contributing cause of the girls' rebellious acting-out behavior. The change in schools had occurred right at the time the girls were also required to adjust to inner physiological and psychological changes. Since the adolescent period itself brings new personality stresses requiring new adaptations, some adolescents react to the new school setting as "insult added to injury" or the last straw. In the high school setting there are vastly larger student bodies, appreciably fewer general rules and regulations, and many teachers and classrooms. Students are no longer guided from activity to activity but must proceed independently by relying on their own judgment and controlling their own behavior.

For many of the girls whose characters were formed around dependency issues the biggest trauma was the change in the teacher-pupil ratio and relationship. Their nurturing, succoring needs had not been and were not being adequately met in the home, and now they lost the satisfaction derived from winning approval and attention from a teacher-friend. They gave up their conforming ways and rebelled, feeling their only choice was between engaging in disapproved activity or becoming a non-entity.

The girls who had mastered the early developmental issues of dependency and hostility relatively well were ready to move on to heterosexual issues. For them the impersonality of the high school setting did not provide the firm, reasonable guidance that they required. In their attempt to establish their own identities as individuals and mature women, they trod on the teachers' toes and morals. Schools as well as parents became unduly alarmed about the adolescent girl's heterosexual activities and tended to assume a rigid, punitive attitude at a time when she needed acceptance and thoughtful, kindly direction. Since the old internalized controls were no longer adequate, and the meaningful adults in the environment not only failed to help but actually created new problems, the girls became almost frantic and increased their rebellious acting-out behavior. They were like frustrated two year olds who cannot end their own temper tantrums but must cry themselves to exhaustion.

Although the acting-out hysterical girls had a considerable amount of emotional health, they could not work out their problems by themselves. They were in urgent need of help because their behavior, if left to run its course, could spoil their lives. Their fringe delinquent behavior—violating curfew, drinking liquor in taverns, or associating with boys whom the police were currently questioning—occasioned brushes with legal authorities.

Their most immediate reality problem, however, usually was the conflict with the school and the serious consequences this forecast. Along with truancy and lack of academic application, the girls' defiance toward school authority, clashes with individual school personnel, and reputations as disruptive classroom influences and bad examples combined to make the schools reluctant to keep them. At the time of referral to the agency many of the girls were on the verge of being transferred out of their regular schools to special schools for students presenting severe disciplinary problems.

Because of a combination of factors peculiar to these cases, the counselor is liable to certain pitfalls, which only a high degree of professional skill and self-awareness can avert. At the outset of treatment there is often a series of crises involving the girl, her family, and the school. Stopping the acting out is an urgent goal in order to forestall even more serious reality problems. Since the girls are inherently likable and responsive and have adequate egos, one can slip into the error of using common-sense appeals to logic as a means of inhibiting their behavior. This "appeal to wisdom" may be used effectively at a later date, but it is usually premature in the opening phases of treatment, even when a positive relationship is under way. A moralistic tone, though it be unintentional, is another danger.

At the beginning of treatment the counselor must restrain a very human impulse to act like a fireman rushing in to put out a fire. The restraint is in the service of keeping the adolescent in counseling so that a meaningful relationship can develop. It is also necessary to enlist the active cooperative restraint of the parents and school, since they bear the major brunt of the tumult. They may be tempted toward hasty measures that will prove detrimental. A strong, positive relationship between the counselor and the girl is essential because the initial efforts to mitigate the acting out are usually achieved through the girl's need to please the counselor or to maintain her good opinion. Highly suggestible, these girls are apt to act upon suggestions coming from someone they like and respect.

The establishment of such a relationship is not ordinarily too difficult if a suitable counselor is chosen, since the hysterical girl wants the relationship. We believe a suitable counselor is one who, aside from general qualifications for therapy with adolescents, can readily serve as an ego-ideal for the particular adolescent client. Our experience has shown that "matching" is an important factor in keeping adolescents in treatment. For example, if a hysterical girl is an intellectual sophisticate who delights in verbal banter and enjoys shocking staid adults, it helps if the counselor is by nature a keen, verbal, fairly sophisticated person. This is not to say that such matching must be trait for trait or that counseling will fail without it. Competent counselors can undertake many roles, and therapists successfully treat adolescent clients whose personalities are very different from their own. But since retaining adolescent clients in treatment has been a weak point in the work with this age group, the selection of a therapist with the proper personality makes it more likely that the adolescent will continue in treatment.

There is no contradiction between the ability of hysterical girls to form a rapid attachment to a counselor and their general pattern of rebellion against adults. Although the hysterical, acting-out girl, like most adolescents, rarely seeks out treatment of her own accord and usually comes at the insistence or urging of some outside source, she ordinarily does not carry over her revolt to her continuing relationship with the counselor. This is because the counselor need not represent an authority symbol who must be resisted. Personally removed from the focus of the girl's dynamic conflicts, she can symbolize the sympathetic, thoughtful adult whose basic concern is for the adolescent and her best interest. The hysterical girl's inner yearning for a relationship will do the rest.

Since the establishment of a strong, supportive, and therapeutic relationship is vital to the treatment process, nothing should be done to weaken the relationship, even though anxious parents and schools understandably press for quick results and urge that tangible steps be taken. Fortunately, if everyone (including the counselor) can withstand the initial turbulence, there is ground for hope that there will be some improvement reasonably soon. This improvement, though it may be temporary, will be a sustaining support if later relapses occur. With treatment and progress, moreover, subsequent relapses may prove less severe.

Though hysterical girls have many engaging and charming qualities, they can also try to provoke the counselor. Even when the girl is not directly provocative in the treatment relationship, her recurring acting-out behavior may evoke a reaction of irritability, annoyance, anxiety, or even anger in the counselor. But it is the counselor's professional obligation to understand her own feelings and the nature of the adolescent's behavior that arouses them. Most important, it is her professional responsibility not to act out her anxiety, annoyance, or anger, or to let these negative reactions interfere with her therapeutic awareness.

Though the counselor in building the relationship should do nothing to drive the girl away from her, she should not ignore the girl's activities or be bland about them. Often the girl spontaneously will provide a flood of material about her feelings, questions, complaints, and hopes relating to parents, school, brothers, sisters, boy friends, and girl friends. This material will inevitably include her acting out, and the counselor should begin to deal with it at the earliest moment compatible with therapeutic management of the case.

The acting out of the hysterical girl or of any adolescent is not determined solely by intrapsychic conflict. It is the outcome of many circumstances and may in part be a reaction to some clash with the environment or to interpersonal or intrafamilial conflicts. Since the hysterical girl is not conscious of the inner forces behind her acting out, she vigorously uses these external elements that help set off her outbreaks to justify her behavior. She may dwell at length on a parent or a teacher who was "unfair" and whom she "had a right" to defy.

Lois, who had a reputation for being a bad influence in class, was trying to improve and for some time had behaved better in the classroom. Her teacher, in reprimanding another student during an incident in which Lois was in no way involved, remarked to the student in front of the class, "Now don't be like Lois Nelson." Lois blew up in a violent argument with the teacher and was suspended from class.

The girl's complaints and her high indignation concerning such occurrences may be quite valid. Although the counselor must be able to empathize with the girl's motivation, her aim in the early phase of treatment is to interpose a block between the impulse or motivation and the action. The acting-out youngster must be taught the difference between feeling and acting. She must be helped to understand that although it is natural for her to have these impulses, feelings, and motivations to behave in certain ways, she must refrain from such negative actions. The counsel to restrain action is put into terms of the adolescent's welfare by showing her how the action is to her detriment and diminishes her chances for ultimate gratification. If the adolescent can learn to restrain action no matter what her feelings may be, much has been accomplished.

Upon looking back at her past behavior, one girl who had reached this stage remarked, "You know how I used to be. When I got mad, whatever popped in my mind I said, and whatever I felt I just sort of went ahead and did. But after a while I remembered what you told me, and I started to think first. Believe me, things have worked out better since then."

In this initial endeavor to set up an inhibition between feeling and acting, the counselor's efforts are bolstered by the hysterical adolescent's innate ego capacity. These girls are not at the mercy of their impulses. Their adequate ego development has provided them with a good sense of reality, good standards, and basically good judgment. These faculties can operate when counseling, through appropriate handling of feelings, has helped the girls to "simmer down." Their level of ego integration, moreover, enables them to grasp the fact that their acting out has been damaging and unsatisfying. Their ability to identify with a counselor enables them to incorporate those aspects of the counselor's ego that they need for further character development and better control of impulses. Despite the vicissitudes of treatment, the counselor who works with these girls has a rewarding sense of being able to "communicate" with them.

Capacity for introspection is a special characteristic of the hysterical girl. She is sensitive to the nuances of emotional life

and is intrigued by the idea of thinking about feelings and motives, both her own and others. For this reason, the counselor's
offer to help her understand more about the meaning of her behavior will often be seized upon avidly. Her eagerness and ability
to introspect provide an important deterrent to impulsive acting
out. She will often respond favorably to the explanation that
there are underlying reasons for her behavior and to the suggestion that it would be wise to postpone or moderate certain activities until she understands more about their causes and motivation.
It can be pointed out that when she has a better understanding
of her feelings and drives, she will be able to deal with them more
comfortably and will have greater awareness of what she is really
seeking and how to obtain it. How intensive this understanding
should be depends on the girl herself and the over-all demands of
the case.

Though the dynamic conflict in the hysterical adolescent concerns sexuality, the treatment aim of improved functioning may
not require direct exploration of this central conflict. The sexual
material brought up by the girl may be no more than the usual
questions raised by adolescent girls in their interviews—how to
attract boys, how to behave on dates, how far one should go in
expressing affection, and so on. In some cases there may be somewhat more focus on problems around sexuality. For example, a
girl may come to reveal that she really fears sexuality, despite her
surface show of sexual daring and provocativeness. Considerable
help can be given as the girl feels free to air and discuss her sexual
impulses, to recognize that the feelings that engendered shame and
fright are accepted by the counselor as natural and good and are
part of the normal heritage of women. This verbalization and
working through make it possible for the girl to handle her sexual
drives in a healthier way and to relinquish her defenses of overly
seductive or aggressive sexual activity.

With other girls there will be very little concentration on
sexuality per se; the major emphasis will be on school, the family,
and the meaning of the rebellious behavior. A girl may finally
see her rebellion against the parent mainly in terms of her wish
to emancipate herself and become an adult. She may see her
recalcitrant behavior at school as a displacement of her feelings

about her parents. And she may come to view her total defiance as a misguided and childish means of self-assertion, in contrast to the more appropriate and rewarding ways of demonstrating maturity. This kind of understanding, though in no sense a comprehension of the basic dynamic struggle, may set in motion a swing toward improvement, and no more is necessary. Improvement in such situations is achieved through treatment techniques primarily of the ego supportive type.

In the Case Illustrations (Chapter 9) Ellen, Fern, and Laura demonstrate treatment of hysterical girls.

Environmental Services

Since emotional problems were chiefly responsible for the difficulties of the adolescents, our general presentation has focused on the treatment of the emotional issues. It should be made clear, however, that casework service was not confined to help for emotional problems; many of our youngsters also needed help with environmental difficulties. In particular, work with the parents and the schools was important and will be discussed in subsequent chapters.

In the diagnostic evaluation of every case, the adolescent's concrete needs were examined and the necessary service provided. The range of services covered many areas. They included, among other things, arranging for hospitalization, medical and dental care, psychological testing for vocational planning, finding appropriate jobs, providing scholarships for incidental school expenses, paying tuition fees or making loans to enable a child to attend a private school, and expediting camp or other recreational experiences. In a few cases, it became advisable for the adolescent to be placed outside his home and we collaborated with child placement agencies to effect this plan.

Environmental help was given as an integral part of the total treatment program. In addition to filling a realistic need in the adolescent's life, important as that was, provision of a concrete service often enabled the youngster to move forward in handling his emotional difficulties.

The extent to which external issues were significant varied, of course, in specific instances. Fern, whose situation is described in the Case Illustrations, urgently needed many kinds of environmental assistance and providing such aid became one of the paramount tasks of the caseworker.

THE PARENTS

IT IS THE POLICY IN OUR AGENCY
to have the first or application interview with the parents. Concurrent work with parents is often essential or at least highly desirable if the child is to receive optimal help. An adolescent's problems do not exist in a vacuum. He depends on his parents for material subsistence; his emotional ties are very much alive despite the emancipatory process that should be under way; and since he lives with his parents, his interaction with them plays a role in the continuance, if not in the etiology, of his emotional problems.

There is another essential reason for counseling the parents of a youngster in trouble. Whether or not the parents have a predominant part in the dynamics of the child's difficulty, they are usually affected by his problems. So they, too, are human beings in trouble and have a claim to help. They should not be looked upon simply as adjuncts to the treatment of a youngster.

In treatment philosophy and methods our agency belongs to the tradition of family casework. We accept the needs of the total situation as our treatment responsibility; and we attempt to meet these needs whether they are environmental, psychological, or both. In keeping with this concept, we do not limit parental counseling to problems connected with the adolescent or the parent-adolescent relationship. If the situation warrants, we provide treatment for problems concerning the parents as individuals, whether or not these problems impinge upon the adolescent. On occasion, we have continued casework service to parents for their own problems after the child's difficulties have cleared up and his counseling has terminated. In general, however, parents who come to an adolescent treatment agency are mainly interested in receiving help related to the problems of their child and do not wish to involve themselves beyond this.

EXTENT OF CONTACT WITH PARENTS

In the early days of the Drop-Out Project we altered our practice of seeing parents first and devoted the initial interview to the adolescent. We anticipated that this particular group of youngsters would be in severe conflict with their parents and might resist coming to the agency if the parents were first to tell "their side of the story." We also felt that older adolescents might be treatable without parental participation. Initial treatment emphasis, therefore, focused on the child himself. Our thought was that we could bring in the parents after we had established a working relationship with the youngster.

It gradually became clear that the method of beginning with the adolescent was unsatisfactory. Lack of knowledge of the child's developmental history slowed up the diagnostic process. The one-sided view of the family interaction impeded our understanding; we were handicapped by not knowing an important part of the child's reality. Most seriously, we found that when we wanted to involve the parents of the students already in counseling, the adolescents were suspicious about our reasons and opposed calling in their parents. Moreover, many of the parents themselves were reluctant to enter treatment. Their resistance had many causes, but for some, one element seemed to be displeasure and distrust at having been bypassed in the original planning stage of the child's treatment.

As we became aware of these facts, we changed our procedure

and saw parents first. We were quite successful in arranging initial interviews with parents but less successful in engaging them in further treatment. In many cases the lack of participation was due to the parents' narcissistic character structure.

In the Treatment Group, sixty-nine of the students had mothers who were readily available; and fifty-five students had fathers who could reasonably be expected to come for interviews. For eight students no parent was seen, and for nine, one parent was seen only once. Thus, for one-fourth of the students, parental participation was very meager. If, for classification purposes, we designate the first two interviews with parents as the application process and appointments beyond that number as treatment, then 60 per cent of the mothers and 25 per cent of the fathers could be considered treatment cases.

DIAGNOSES OF THE PARENTS

We had sufficient information to diagnose two-thirds of the available mothers (forty-nine of sixty-nine) and one-half of the available fathers (twenty-seven of fifty-five). Like the drop-out youngsters, a large proportion of the parents suffered from serious personality problems. None of the parents had neuroses—all had character disorders with the attendant implication of repetitive entrenched behavior that does not arouse much personal discomfort and is very difficult to alter.

Ten mothers and one father had preoral character formations; four of the ten mothers were psychotic. Thirty-seven parents had oral character structures. Therefore, 63 per cent of the diagnosed parents were immature; most of them had been greatly deprived in their childhood, and their basic orientation was directed to their own needs and concerns. They did not have the capacity to constructively meet the needs of their children. Whereas about half of the immature mothers were aggressive types, 86 per cent of the immature fathers were dependent types. Such men are usually weak, helpless figures—poor husbands and even poorer fathers.

Twenty-six per cent of the parents had compulsive character structures, and 12 per cent had phallic (mainly hysterical) character structures. Both of these structures are considered more mature types because they permit better personal functioning. Compulsive parents, however, with their qualities of rigid orderliness, need to control others, and meticulous concern for appearances, present complications for their children. Complications are especially apt to arise when the children malfunction in school because such behavior not only thwarts the compulsive parents but shames them. The hysterical parent, though presenting problems, affords his child a more favorable opportunity to develop because such a parent is usually a warm person with some capacity for good relationships. As the percentage figures indicate, however, few parents were in this group.

PARENT-CHILD RELATIONSHIPS

The kinds of relationships existing between the parents and their children were as varied as the individual personality structures of the people involved; but, as one would expect in a group of parents and children with serious personality problems, most of the relationships were unhealthy and distorted. A number of girls came from homes in which there was considerable disorganization.

Jean, though alert and intelligent, was a delinquent girl who shoplifted and rode in stolen cars. Her mother worked in a tavern and herself had a history of delinquency. After divorcing Jean's father she married a shiftless man with whom she fought physically. She housed and supported her first husband's father who drank heavily and had been married four times. A couple of hoodlum maternal uncles moved in and out of the household.

Another girl, Gail, had an inadequate, dependent mother and an alcoholic father. The family had moved so many times that Gail had attended eleven different elementary schools. In answer to a question from her counselor, Gail said she could not tell if she got along well with the girls at school. The family moved so frequently that the girl never had a real opportunity to make friends.

Some homes seemed organized and stable on the surface, but underneath, a parent's serious pathology affected the child.

Hank had a tyrannical father, a rigid, unyielding man who attempted to rule every area of his son's life. Hank worked each evening after school until 10:00 P.M. and all day Sunday in a drug store. When he arrived home from work on school nights the father would keep him up, requiring a minute account of every event that had occurred during the day.

Hank wished to spend Saturday evenings with his girl friend. The father accused him of neglecting his siblings and arranged many home chores to keep him busy. The boy banked his earnings but the account was in his parents' names and the father would not permit him to draw money to buy a small gift for his girl.

Hank emancipated himself by leaving home and joining the Air Force. This seemed the best of the alternatives open, since the father's behavior could not be modified, and our attempt to work with him was to no avail. If the boy had been subjected to his home situation much longer, the consequences would have been serious.

Hank's father and other compulsive parents were critical, nagging, and pushing the children to achieve. The infantilizing parents hampered their children's development in another way. Ben's mother fondled and pampered him and still was tucking him into bed at the age of fourteen. The mother of sixteen-year-old Dick hovered over the boy constantly; among other things, she forced him to go to bed at 9:00 P.M. Other examples of parent-child interaction will be found in the Case Illustrations.

PARENTS' REACTIONS TO THE
GIRLS' SCHOOL PROBLEMS

The distress of the girls' parents did not center as much on the daughters' maladjustment in school as it did on their general behavior problems. The parents' complaints mainly had to do with the girls' defiance of the family and their over-all rebellious behavior. Along with this, a major concern was the possible sexual misbehavior of their daughters. The parents did not always specifically state this to us; but their anxiety was constantly reflected in the peripheral issues about their daughters they brought up: the intense interest in boys, the late hours, the wearing of tight skirts and sweaters, and the flouting of parental edicts. One father captured the essence of many parents' apprehension when he said ruefully, "Life was a lot easier for us when Trudy was eleven and all she was interested in was horses and dogs."

The corollary is that many of the parents' conflicts about their own sexuality were reactivated by the heightened awareness of sexual impulses in their adolescent daughters. These unresolved, unconscious conflicts, as well as the justified, real concerns, aroused intense feelings in the parents and rendered them confused and uneasy in dealing with their daughters.

We were able to rate twenty-two of the thirty-three girls' mothers in regard to their psychodynamic involvement in the school problem. For two-thirds of these mothers, schooling took on no unique significance, and they reacted to their daughters' school difficulties in the same way they reacted to other facets of their relationships with their daughters. This attitude was similar to the one we found in the adolescent girls themselves (it will be recalled that the girls did not seem to attach a special psychodynamic meaning to school). The attitudes of the parents, like those of the daughters, are probably attributable to the cultural mores of a society in which educational and vocational achievement is not regarded as a major task for girls and is considered less important than it is for boys.

These comments do not mean that the school problems of the girls were of no concern to the parents. There was concern as well as irritation and a variety of other emotional overtones. But for the parents of the girls, school was not as likely to be an area fraught with special meaning as was the case with the boys' parents.

PARENTS' REACTIONS TO THE BOYS' SCHOOL PROBLEMS

For the boys, school difficulties took precedence over all other difficulties in their parents' eyes. Some situations almost had the aspect of a life and death struggle between parent and child in which everything in the parents' relationship to the child was colored by the school problem. Quite apart from real problems and difficulties, school seemed to supply a symbolic structure through which parents could act out their own internal needs and conflicts as well as their conflict with the child.

The greater and more special import of school to parents of boys as contrasted to parents of girls is seen from our data on the psychodynamic meaning of school to the boys' mothers. For the twenty-five mothers rated in the treatment population of thirty-seven boys, about one-half were focusing on their youngsters' school life in a specific way. Twenty-eight per cent were overidealizing education, that is, going beyond realistic considerations in attributing a major significance to school. Another 20 per cent were using their sons' school life in an attempt to work out a problem in a totally different area. Only fourteen fathers could be rated, but eight were also utilizing school for the purpose of resolving conflicts in another area.

These numbers are not large; but the clinical evidence is impressive in depth, as we observed the intensity with which parents focused on the school issue. One mother wept bitterly as she burst out, "I think it will just kill me if my son doesn't finish high school." Another related, choked with emotion, that some of the members of her club had been speaking with pride of their children's good grades in school. She had felt utterly humiliated that she could say nothing about her boy's accomplishments. When she returned home, she told her son how ashamed she had been and let him know this was his fault.

SPECIFIC MEANING OF THE CHILD'S SCHOOL LIFE TO HIS PARENTS

There are many ways in which parents may use their child's school life. The youngster's schooling may be used to dominate him. The desire of one father to control and dominate was so pervasive that he had difficulty with all of his children and several dropped out of school. Larry, the boy we were treating, was an extremely bright youngster with an I.Q. of 135. The father was constantly checking Larry's school work, questioning him minutely as to whether he was doing it properly, and going to school so frequently to discuss his son's progress with the teachers that he became an annoyance to them.

Somewhat similar driving behavior occurred in parents who

had an overinvestment in their child's school achievement because
they used the child as an extension of themselves. Whatever the
logic of their rationalizations, these parents needed to have their
youngster successful in school to bolster their own narcissism.

Dan, whose full story is told in the Case Illustrations, had a father
who tried to live out his needs through his son and behaved, almost
literally, as if the boy had no identity of his own. The father, a
precise, perfectionistic, driving man, had achieved some business success but suffered from inner feelings of inferiority because he had not
gone to college. Almost from the moment Dan was born, he decided
the child would be successful in school and go to college. The father's
relationship with his son overwhelmed and frightened the boy. It consisted mainly of pushing and prodding, perfectionistic expectations,
and carping criticism whenever the youngster's performance slipped
below standard. Dan's father tutored him and gave long lectures about
the value of education and the necessity for college training. Dan
developed a reaction of stubborn passivity, which made his father even
more frantic and pressuring.

A child's school problems may serve opposing needs in each
parent. Then the youngster is caught in a cross fire in which his
scholastic difficulties, serious as they are, become chiefly a
medium through which the parents express their hostility toward
each other.

Neil's father was both an ineffectual and depreciated man. Not
only was the mother the dominant figure but she was generally hostile
to men. She had been bitterly disappointed in the early years of her
marriage when, despite her insistence, her husband had not completed
a journalism course. In this atmosphere Neil grew up to be a dependent, inadequate boy. His serious retardation in school exacerbated
the specific emotional disturbances in the parents that had brought
on the boy's difficulty in the first place. Neil's inability to pass in
school deepened the mother's basic hostility to male figures and reawakened her old anger at her husband's academic failure. The father,
on the other hand, used Neil's school maladjustment to retaliate
against his wife and to reassure himself that his own school failure
was unimportant. Since he did not dare oppose the mother openly,
he formed a kind of conspiracy with Neil in which he supported the
boy's lack of interest in school by conveying the idea that achievement in school did not matter. The result of the vengeful interaction
of the parents was catastrophic for Neil in both his personality
development and his educational progress.

PARENTAL EFFORTS TO COPE
WITH SCHOOL PROBLEMS

School problems possess characteristics that induce strong reactions in parents and also provide a stage where parents may readily act out many complicated emotions and conflicts. One characteristic is "high visibility"—when a child is doing poorly in school, his failure is open to public view. It cannot be concealed and swept under the rug as is often possible if the child is suffering from some other type of emotional disability. Thus, shame and embarrassment are added to the other emotions the parent is experiencing.

It is normal for a parent both to want his child to succeed and to feel that his own prestige is enhanced by the child's accomplishments. Unconsciously, every parent sees his child as an extension of himself; what the child does necessarily reflects upon the parents. Pathology exists only when the situation becomes extreme—when the child is viewed solely as an extension of the parent and is used primarily for the satisfaction of the parent's needs, without regard for the child's separate identity and individual welfare.

It is also normal for a child's difficulty in school to have a sharp impact on his parents. Whatever the personality structure of the parent and whether the parent-child relationship is predominantly positive or negative, the parent usually has some concern for the child's well-being. He cannot help but be aware that persistent school problems may jeopardize the child's future. Society sanctions parental concern about a child's failure in school and regards it as desirable. It was easy for many of the parents in our study to rationalize that their attitudes about the child's difficulty in school were justified or to defend themselves against conscious awareness that their behavior was contrary to the child's interests. Most parents tended to feel quite self-righteous about their indignation and about whatever measures they were using to force the youngster to do better.

Inconsistency was a common failing in parental efforts to correct the poor school situation. Parents often alternated between punishment and bribery, praise and ridicule, strictness and over-permissiveness, and other variants. Chronic inconsistency can do greater damage in the personality development of children than almost any other kind of parental behavior except the grossest abuse and neglect. A child can make some kind of adjustment, even in a difficult situation, if he knows what to adjust to. But confusion, helplessness, or even disintegration may set in when shifting parental attitudes leave the child not knowing what to expect.

The inconsistency of the parents often stemmed from their inability to find some effective course of action. Punishment might keep the situation under control temporarily, but when it failed, the parent would resort to some other approach or discipline more severely than before for the same type of offense. Parents unwittingly summed up their inconsistent practices by a familiar and plaintive remark, "We tried everything, and nothing worked."

Even those parents who were not consciously or unconsciously hostile to the child often responded to his problems with school in unconstructive ways. They instituted complicated and handicapping systems of rewards and punishments and withheld expressions of affection at a time the child needed them most.

We found that parents tended to be openly angry with their youngster when his problem concerned school. They had little sympathy for the child in contrast to more tender feelings displayed toward a youngster who was shy or lacked friends. Thus, the child who functioned badly in school had his unfavorable position compounded. Not only was school an unhappy place for him but he had to contend with angry parents at home.

The parents' hostility and irritation were especially prone to emerge when an intellectually capable youngster was failing in academic achievement. It was difficult for the parents to comprehend underfunctioning. They assumed it was willful. The combination of irritation and lack of understanding in the parents was also a cause of confused, inconsistent handling that did more harm than good.

Alex was an only boy in a sibling group of four. He suffered considerable emotional and physical neglect in his infancy, and grew up to be a timid, clinging child. The father was a capable, vigorous man.

Underneath, he had some warm feelings for Alex, but his gruff manner intimidated the youngster.

When Alex began having trouble in school, his parents concocted a scheme to solve it. Through the help of a relative, they applied at Family Court to have Alex committed to the custodial residential institution set up in the Chicago school system as a last resort for severe problem students. Luckily, the court proceedings were dropped when Alex's school learned of the plan and intervened. The parents explained to us, with evident honesty, that they never had any intention of going through with the plan to send Alex away from home but had begun the procedure only as a ruse to "frighten" Alex into better behavior.

Sam's chief trait was a kind of sly manipulation by which he frustrated and fended off anyone who tried to come close to him. His need to provoke people so that he could keep his distance was the outcome of an unfavorable early life when he had been shifted about among a succession of parental figures.

Sam was deep in school trouble as a result of his provocativeness and lack of application. His mother tried to help by placing him on a rigorous schedule of study at home. But Sam then had more scope for acting out his manipulative provocation, and he usually won the battle of wits with his mother. Sitting with his books open for the allotted hours, he spent most of the time watching the clock. To counteract this, his mother insisted on going over the study assignments with him to be certain that he completed them. Sam went along with her demands but then would "forget" to hand in the completed assignments. On other occasions he made a "mistake" and studied the wrong lesson. Sam ultimately improved with treatment; but, aside from direct service to the boy, we had to help his mother to discontinue her unwise, though well-meant, tactics. She finally recognized how these had played directly into her son's defenses.

Deprivation of privileges, pressures to study, and similar devices are traditional methods that often are successful in clearing up transitory school difficulties. When a child's school problems stem from an emotional disturbance, however, such superficial measures do not reach the basic causes and can further aggravate the problem.

Some Treatment Considerations

As is true of all therapy, the type of treatment appropriate for a specific parent is determined by his individual diagnosis.

Selecting suitable helping techniques requires a knowledge of the basic therapeutic process. The general principles pertaining to treatment, however, are not restated here; they are already familiar to social workers and other specialists in counseling. Rather, our discussion will concern some special treatment issues relating to the presence of problems in school, the immature, defensive parents who comprised a majority of our clientele, and the approaches and modifications of treatment made necessary by these conditions.

WORK IN LIMITED CONTACTS

Though many of the parents studied in the Project came in for only a few interviews, even this limited contact had some benefit. We have already mentioned that this contact hastened diagnostic evaluation of the case. In addition, some of these parents, though unwilling to participate in intensive treatment, were helped to support their child's participation in treatment and to encourage him to keep his appointments. At times, the parents' tensions were relaxed simply by the knowledge that a helping factor had entered the situation, with the result that the acute conflict in the home was diminished (temporarily, at least) to provide a breathing space during which counseling could begin with the adolescent.

In many instances the parents came for widely spaced interviews. This gave a type of continuing, if tenuous, contact. Some parents, though resistant to regular interviews, communicated with us at times of crisis. Specific suggestions and help to resolve the crisis were provided. The interview also afforded an opportunity for comforting the parents and encouraging them to let treatment of the adolescent continue despite an apparent relapse in the youngster's behavior.

Because of the small number of interviews with most parents, we generally were forced to adopt the limited treatment goal of containment—preserving the status quo in the parents' behavior toward the adolescent and warding off further deterioration. Although these parents did not help treatment in an active way, at least they did not sabotage it.

Quite often, however, improvement of the adolescent helped to contain the parents. For example, when some of the more worrisome school symptoms diminished or disappeared, an equilibrium might be restored for the parents. The fundamental relationship might be no different, but the sources of friction created by the child's difficulty in school would be reduced. With the removal of these extra complications, parent and child might then arrive at a tenable way of living together. Some parents who had been coming for interviews quite regularly stopped coming at precisely this point. With the immediate crisis gone, they could not be persuaded to continue. It was as if their latent resistance to counseling could now emerge more freely. Strengthened by their reasoning that "since things are better, it is not necessary to come," they discontinued their own treatment.

THE SABOTAGING PARENT

A few parents seriously interfered with treatment and made progress with the adolescent impossible. Some of them needed to have an underachieving child, and when the school problem did not improve almost immediately, they used this as an excuse to withdraw the child from treatment.

Fifteen-year-old Pete had serious school problems dating back to the second grade. The problems stemmed primarily from a dependency conflict. The boy responded well to his counselor, who felt that treatment could be successful. After one month of counseling, however, Pete's mother decided that he should stop. Her stated reason was that counseling was not helping, since Pete's grades had not improved. The mother's underlying need to have a child who failed came out when, among other things, she said, "The Lord didn't intend him to be a brain and things won't change."

Sometimes a slight improvement in the child caused parents to terminate the youngster's treatment. This usually signified that the parent had been receiving unconscious gratification from the youngster's symptoms. Tim's mother illustrates this point and also the network of rationalization a parent may erect if he is determined to end treatment.

At seventeen, Tim was a keen, intelligent adolescent. He was failing all his subjects, however, and his schoolroom behavior was so unruly that he had been barred from all his classes. He also was engaging in some minor delinquencies. Tim used boastful aggressiveness to cover up his deep fears. The boy responded unusually quickly in treatment; he became genuinely involved with his counselor and in the marking period during counseling, he passed all his courses.

Tim's father, a cold, punitive man openly hostile toward the boy was seen twice. He would not return, asserting he was too busy but was willing to have Tim continue. The mother, an infantile, self-centered woman appeared four times. She related her pleasure at the improvement in her son yet chuckled with admiration as she recalled episodes of his former rebellious acting out. She canceled further interviews on various pretexts. Some time later, Tim dejectedly informed his counselor that his mother would not permit him to come again. She had told her son that we were not helping him and it was all a waste of time. The boy's own desire to remain in treatment was obvious.

In a telephone conversation with us, the mother could not declare openly her wish to discontinue treatment. Instead, she presented a series of reasons that became more confused and self-contradictory as she went on. She first stated that Tim no longer needed help because he was so much better. Then she let it slip that he had recently stayed out all night. Belatedly recognizing that this implied a need for further treatment, she shifted and asserted we could not alter Tim's difficulties by working with him alone. The whole trouble was the father's fault, and since he would not enter counseling, there was no way we could help.

When her counselor said we would work with Tim alone, she again shifted tactics saying Tim was losing too much school to keep his appointments here. When we offered an after-school hour she said her son felt ashamed about counseling and did not want to come. The mother acknowledged that Tim had not said this in so many words, but she "knew" it was how he felt.

In trying to help Tim's mother to allow the boy to continue, her counselor used various supportive methods to permit her to save face. An appeal was made to her primary self-interest by telling her how proud she would be to see her son graduate. As a last measure we made a strong attempt to stir up some guilt. She was told directly that Tim was headed for trouble if he did not receive therapy and that when this occurred, the responsibility would be squarely on her. The mother ended with a vague promise that Tim could continue, but as we expected, he did not come back. Some months later a report from Family Court indicated Tim had been sent there for destroying property in a downtown theater.

INITIATING A TREATMENT RELATIONSHIP

We were able to effect favorable treatment results with some parents, who were helped to achieve significant changes in attitudes and behavior toward their child. With other parents we were unsuccessful. At times this was due to their own resistance and personality attributes. At other times it was due to mistakes we made or our insufficient knowledge about the special meaning of school problems to parents.

Out of our distilled experience, both successful and unsuccessful, came some methods and cautions that may profitably be observed in working with parents of children who malfunction in school. These methods are especially applicable to parents whose conscious or unconscious involvement in the school situation makes them defensive, that is, prone to rationalize, to project responsibility for the difficulties, to be self-righteous, to be angry at the adolescent.

When a parent has a great emotional involvement in his child's school life, treatment could be directed toward helping the parent understand his involvement in the problem. The rationale would be that aiding the parent to become aware of his own feelings and the reasons for his behavior would assist him in modifying his attitudes and interaction with the child. At the start of the Project we anticipated that a number of parents might respond to this approach. But we had not fully appreciated the kinds of emotional reactions that school problems arouse in many parents, nor had we sufficiently understood how the presence of school difficulties can create special and unyielding resistances within parents. With many, an attempt to broach the matter of their own role increased their resistance, causing more rationalization, denial, and projection.

In retrospect, it is understandable that precisely when a parent has a strong involvement in the school issue and is bolstered in his overt attitudes by his culture, he will resist exploration of his part in the situation. He also refuses to recognize any connection between the problems in school and a personality disturbance in the child. The initial problem, then, is the parents' defensiveness, and the immediate task confronting the counselor is to lower this defensiveness. Until this is accomplished, there is no way to engage the parents in the essential treatment issue—their handling of the child.

When a youngster's problem in school has led to referral

to an agency for help, not only has the parent been disappointed and hurt by his child's difficulties in school, but quite likely he has received criticism, open or indirect, for the way in which he has dealt with the youngster. This may have occurred during interviews with school personnel, in speaking with friends whose advice was sought, or in arguments with his spouse.

Thus, the parent appears at the agency feeling attacked and misunderstood. He may believe that he has been criticized for a situation that he could not help or that he has been rebuked for doing things he thought were right. He comes in anticipating the same kind of attack and criticism. In maintenance of his defense against anxiety or to preserve his own self-esteem, the parent then blames the adolescent, the school, bad companions, or the other parent.

Avoid premature self-examination. Since the parent is already apprehensive, it is a mistake for the counselor to make the parent more anxious about what he has done or to raise questions that imply mishandling. Such tactics only heighten the defensiveness and create an impasse. The key in treatment of parents, as in treatment of adolescents, is "sympathy for the symptom." Even when the parent himself, out of guilt, shows a tendency to move too quickly into consideration of where he erred, it is safest to focus at first on what the parent did that was right and to hear his reasons for doing what he did. The parent's errors in handling may have come from desperation, from not knowing what alternatives were better, from having tried other methods that did not work, or simply from his assumption that his methods were correct and would pave the way for better school performance.

It may take some time to reduce the parent's defensiveness, for the parent to feel his difficulty and point of view are understood and appreciated. Counselors sometimes underestimate or become impatient about the number of interviews needed to accomplish this. Such underestimation and impatience may spring from a vague notion that "treatment" does not really begin until one is actively helping the parent to examine his part in the problem or is at least making suggestions for a better means of solving it. The preliminaries, however, constitute treatment just as much as any other phase of therapy.

Although the counselor should be cautious about prematurely bringing the parents to self-examination, this does not avert the need for obtaining material from which to gain a diagnostic understanding of the problem and of the parents. The school difficulty should also be discussed. Indeed, most parents wish to focus on this area, and if the counselor avoids it, they may feel he is evading their primary concern. In exploring the school problem, we generally found it safest to start with the facts, to ask the parent for information about such matters as the child's school history. Parents were usually receptive to discussing this kind of objective material, and we obtained information that, in any event, was necessary.

Avoid premature giving of advice. Aside from a premature examination of parental errors, the counselor should guard against another technical pitfall—giving advice too quickly. When it has become evident that the parent's handling of the adolescent is unsatisfactory, the counselor, in his zeal to correct the situation, may prematurely advise the parent to alter his methods. For example, we found many parents reacting to their child's school problems by pushing and nagging. Neither the parents nor the child were comfortable or satisfied with this procedure. Worst of all, the nagging behavior did not solve the problem but aggravated it. Observing this, we were tempted to stop the behavior quickly by suggesting that the parents give up their pressuring techniques. But the matter was not quite that simple. A technical consideration of timing was important.

Though nagging is ineffectual and often harmful in the long run, it may at the moment be the only way to keep the youngster functioning. Perhaps the child has come to depend on the parents' prodding for whatever school performance he has been able to achieve. If the parents abruptly reduce their pressures, there is danger that the youngster's functioning may deteriorate and that he will do even less. We have seen overprotective parents who, on receiving advice to stop the overprotection, suddenly relax their controls. Their previously inhibited child may respond with injurious acting out. In any case, a sudden parental change often makes the child feel that the parent has had no true change in attitude. "I know what he's thinking, even if he has stopped pushing me."

It is generally true that parents who have relied on nagging—or any other well-established pattern of behavior—and have gained some security from it will not easily relinquish their behavior. In the case of the nagging parent, the zealous counselor may be reduced to "nagging the parents to stop nagging."

Or, consider the angry and frustrated parents of a dependent child who is failing in school. Quite early in treatment they may be advised to give their child a great deal of love and attention. This may well be what the youngster needs; but at this early point, when the parents are still upset and irritated, they simply are not able to "give" a great deal. Perhaps they can manage to do a little more for the child, and if this is so, the counselor should encourage them. But in the beginning, the demands on the parents to change should be kept small, even though it is clear that change is needed. If the parents' relationship with the counselor deepens and provides them with a source of gratification, they may become able to give more to their child.

It was our further experience that many parents displayed an increased capacity for changing their attitudes and behavior toward the adolescent once the youngster himself had begun to show some progress in treatment. The child's improvement, among other things, made the parents more hopeful and therefore more ready to respond when the counselor suggested new and better ways to deal with the child.

A broad treatment principle underlies this matter of giving advice. It is a familiar concept and widely applicable but is sometimes forgotten when dealing with parents who mishandle their children: before attempting to change well-established patterns of behavior, one should thoroughly understand the meaning and purpose of the behavior, the individual's ability to change, and the consequences of the change.

One practical matter about counseling recommendations to parents remains to be considered. Before coming to the social agency, parents usually have been in touch with school personnel. They may have received suggestions from the school on methods of handling the child. It is well for the counselor to know what the school has advised and, if possible, to coordinate the suggestions from both school and social agency so that there is some general agreement on the course to be followed. Otherwise, the counselor may make recommendations conflicting with those offered by the school. The result is further confusion for the parents.

TREATMENT FOLLOWING THE BEGINNING PHASE

In view of our observation that most parents of children who had difficulty in school could not be treated by techniques of clarifying the parents' involvement in the problem or by exploring the causes of the child's trouble in school, we need to consider what methods were effective in ongoing treatment. The techniques we found most useful were those of ego supportive casework. These techniques fell broadly into two groups. The first could be called the use of benevolent authority, with *direct* advice as the major tool. The second also used guidance and advice but was more indirect in tone and approach.

Both methods were used within the framework of a good counselor-parent relationship and after the parents were open to suggestions about new ways of behaving. Both methods also utilized the elements that are an integral part of supportive therapy, such as encouragement, building of self-esteem, and ventilating of feelings.

When the therapist assumes the role of the benevolent authority figure, he gives advice and makes direct suggestions as a professionally competent and experienced person. It is best to keep the advice simple and uncluttered by psychological explanations. The counselor says in effect, "This is something I think it would be well for you to do." The parent may then go along, not necessarily out of conviction about the wisdom of the advice, but because he likes the counselor and wants his approval, because he respects the counselor as an expert, or because he feels comfortable in having rules of conduct laid down for him.

In the indirect approach, which is more permissive and requires the parent to involve himself to a greater degree, counselor and parent mutually consider the merits of plans brought forth by the parent or proposed by the counselor.

In addition to fostering more sound behavior in parents, the counselor's responsibility is to help the parent attain some consistency in his behavior so that the child is not further damaged by sharply veering attitudes. One reason for the inconsistency of parents is their impatience for results. They find it hard to wait long enough to give a new technique a chance to work. If through counseling they have embarked on a different course of behavior toward their child, they expect him to respond very quickly with marked improvement. Such expectations are not often realized. Although adolescents may occasionally respond with quick and dramatic changes, characteristically they take a long time to integrate new behavior.

Parents need help in maintaining themselves through this critical period so that they will not yield to their impulse to discard the new methods and reinstate the old. During this time of disappointment and frustration, the counselor can give support and encourage the parent to be patient. Though psychological explanations should be sparing, it is helpful to tell the parents that one axiom of human behavior is that people in general and adolescents in particular do not change quickly. Therefore, the youngster's failure to improve is due to this fact rather than to direct lack of response to the parents' new approach. This may clarify the basic dynamic issue in a meaningful way to the parents. It provides them with the reason behind the counselor's suggestion for continued patience—a suggestion that otherwise might strike the parents as opposing all common sense.

In their eagerness for far-reaching and rapid changes, parents tended to equate a small amount of improvement with no improvement. Though the adolescent showed a few signs of progress, for instance, passing with low grades where formerly he had failed, the parents might be dissatisfied because they thought advancement was too slight. They might react in detrimental ways, causing a setback in the child's progress. If parents can grasp the principle that change comes about slowly and that expectations must be moderate, there is less risk of jeopardizing the first weak sprouts of improvement in the adolescent.

If improvement of the emotional difficulty occurs first, there is a tendency on the part of parents to negate or not recognize this progress because their chief interest is in reduction of the school problem. This attitude can discourage the youngster who feels he is getting better. If he does not receive support from his parents, he may suffer a relapse. It is helpful to inform such parents that there is not simultaneous improvement in all areas and that, frequently, improvement in emotional problems must occur before the child can function more adequately in school.

In general, an important and effective counseling device is to give the parents hope. Unless they can look forward to the eventual improvement of their child, they cannot be expected to put forth effort in their own treatment. Conveying hope to parents either verbally or nonverbally is essential throughout therapy but is especially important during the period when they have altered their own behavior and have yet seen little or no change in the youngster.

DILUTING THE TOTALITY OF THE PROBLEM

There is a general therapeutic goal underlying the treatment of parents whose adolescent children have severe school problems. This aim may be described as "diluting the totality of the problem." When a child, particularly a boy, is doing poorly in school, the parents tend to see him in a distorted perspective. They may look upon him as a child who is failing everywhere, as someone totally bad. In reality, he may have many worthwhile qualities and may be managing well in a number of areas. The "black or white" viewpoint in which parents become entangled stems from their strong emotional reaction to school problems and the positive values that are attached to school achievement.

Sweeping parental disapproval can have a serious effect upon the adolescent. His feeling of worthlessness intensifies his anger or his discouragement. It reduces his ability to overcome his difficulties in school and undermines his capacities in areas where he has been successful. As his functioning grows poorer and his self-concept is increasingly damaged, his undersirable defenses and personality problems deepen.

Parents need help in attaining an accurate view of their child so that his school maladjustment does not overshadow their entire picture of him. Without minimizing the school difficulty, the counselor can remind the parents of areas where the youngster is adequate and can point out his assets and worthwhile qualities. Such comments are beneficial in many ways. They provide reassurance and hope; they may reduce the parents' feeling of failure and stigma; and most important of all, by separating the adolescent's problems related to school from his worth as a person, they may help the parents move toward better understanding and acceptance of him.

COLLABORATIVE WORK

WITH THE SCHOOLS

WHEN SCHOOL DIFFICULTIES ARE
the result of a child's emotional disturbance, the nucleus for casework treatment is the child and his parents. Nevertheless, collaborative work with the school is vital. The school, aside from
its educative function, exerts great influence on a child because
it is the place where he spends a large share of his day. Though
the educational problems of our youngsters were emotional in
origin, we found that the attitudes of the school were of great
importance in determining the course of the problem. Constructive management by the school can give a great impetus to the
treatment process and contribute toward a favorable outcome.
Both the school and the social agency have a stake in a common
goal—alleviating the youngster's educational problems and helping
him to become a happier and more productive student. When
counselor and school work together in a child's behalf, the efforts
of each are enhanced by the other. The school can provide

valuable information about the child, which helps the counselor to determine the nature of the difficulty and plan the casework treatment. Conversely, the counselor shares his understanding of the child with the school, which helps it plan a constructive way of handling the student.

How the School Can Help the Social Agency

Since the school observes its students for many hours a day in a critical area of functioning, it knows a great deal about them. Reports from teachers, administrative personnel, adjustment teachers, and school psychologists about a child's attitudes and behavior can provide significant information about his symptoms and personality.

TEACHERS' COMMENTS

The first school report generally came to the agency before we saw the adolescent and in many instances provided clues for planning the initial interview. The teachers' comments often gave hints about dynamic issues: "John is quite childish and will work only if he is given a great deal of attention. He sulks when he doesn't get it." "Jerry tries to please, but he is timid and lacks self-confidence. He is afraid to recite in class." "Eleanor is very touchy and always tense. I feel she is a really unhappy girl."

Sometimes evaluations by different teachers were in marked contrast to each other. Rita's five teachers described her: (1) upsets the room with her antics; (2) well behaved, friendly; (3) concentrates well, natural facility for Spanish; (4) day dreams, indolent; (5) fidgets and disorganizes the class.

From this surface picture the therapist was able to surmise that Rita was a girl with considerable fluidity, that her behavior was not rigidly fixed, that she had the capacity to respond positively, and that her conduct and learning patterns varied sharply, depending on the circumstances. One could not say whether Rita's favorable attitudes in certain classes arose because the subject matter intrigued her or because she liked the teachers. We found it advantageous to learn something about the personality of the teacher in whose classes a child functioned well. This knowledge affected the choice of therapist by the agency and gave clues to the best therapeutic approach.

CUMULATIVE RECORDS

In addition to giving a picture of the current school situation, the school can also provide from its cumulative records a history of the child's progress and behavior. The added knowledge about the chronicity and severity of a student's school problems and the changes in his adjustment expedites the counselor's understanding of the nature of the emotional problems.

TEST REPORTS

There are advantages in securing reports of intelligence and achievement tests from the school. The former estimates a child's potential learning ability, and the latter, his actual level of school functioning in basic learning skills. When these two scores are compared, they reveal the disparity between mental potential and actual mastery of important tool subjects. Severe retardation in basic subjects gives notice to the counselor that, aside from the counseling, special educational help may be required. If a youngster's achievement test level is satisfactory but his performance in his regular courses is poor, there is a different inference to be drawn about the nature of the problem than if the basic achievement level is also poor.

The pattern of grades in the various subjects over the years is also important. It tells whether the students' educational disability is bound up mainly with one topic or, as was the case with many of our youngsters, whether grades varied without regard to specific subjects and seemed connected mainly with the child's feelings about the teacher.

How the Social Agency Can Help the School

Casework service can provide help to the school in three vital ways. First, by treating a child's emotional problems, the agency can help him improve the way he functions in school so that he ceases to be a problem to the school. Second, the caseworker can give information about a child that will add to the school's understanding, thereby enabling them to deal with the child in a more helpful way. And third, the school's increased understanding and favorable attitudes and methods of handling extend to other students and other situations, producing an over-all beneficial effect.

THE STUDENT'S BEHAVIOR

It is usually inappropriate for the caseworker to present to the school a complete or technical dynamic formulation of the child's personality make-up and its etiology. This material should be expressed in concepts and language directly meaningful and useful to educators. It should give a clear picture of the child in common-sense terms that illuminate the puzzling aspects of his behavior.

The recognition that a youngster's behavior may be symptomatic of some problem can in itself make the teacher more comfortable and secure in her relationship with him. It can take the whole problem out of the area of personalities, so that the teacher need no longer feel that the misbehavior is a special reaction to her or is the direct result of mishandling on her part. If, for instance, she is told that a youngster is giving vent in the classroom to the anger and resentment felt toward his mother, she will be more comfortable because she no longer feels personally attacked. The way is then open for her to view the situation realistically and objectively and to utilize her new and fuller knowledge of the child to institute methods based on his needs.

MANAGEMENT OF SCHOOL LIFE

Our experience was that many teachers were eager for this type of understanding of their troublesome students. We also were gratified to note how such understanding frequently resulted in the school itself thinking of constructive methods of handling the child. In any event, it paved the way for collaborative planning.

The suitable structuring of the school setting, along with a program of direct treatment by the agency, sometimes produced dramatic improvement.

At the time sixteen-year-old Linda was referred to our project, she had been suspended from school because of her extreme defiance and flouting of school regulations. The school was reluctant to have her return, since they could no longer tolerate her behavior.

Linda was an energetic, intelligent, and articulate girl, but her aggressive and domineering manner had antagonized both her teachers and classmates. She argued with the teachers over their interpretations of course material, attempted to rule dictatorially any activity she entered, and ignored school edicts with the air of a person of special privilege.

The school first sought to get Linda to conform by stern reprimands, then by punishment of various kinds. But the effect was to make Linda feel justified in her supposed grievances, so that more than ever she unloosed biting verbal attacks on the school staff. The situation came to a deadlock: the school reacted hostilely to Linda's hostility. The teachers regarded her as arrogant and unmanageable, and she declared she would show them she could become a "big shot" without an education.

Linda's arrogance and highhandedness did not originate in school. Aggressiveness, suspiciousness, and fear that people were out to control her were expressions of the defensive, persecutory nature of her personality. She had erected these defenses to cover her deep needs for maternal affection that had never been met. The caseworker undertook to help Linda redirect her aggression into channels where she could utilize her potential in the service of forceful and acceptable leadership. In mapping out a treatment plan, the agency recognized that for a girl of Linda's high intellectual caliber the school could provide both a much needed source of gratification and an opportunity for sublimation.

In arranging her reinstatement, we told the school that her behavior was a symptom that at the moment she could not manage but with which we hoped to help her. We explained that Linda's actions, admittedly irritating to those who had to endure them, were not an expression of willful malice but an armor she had put on over the years because of the hurt suffered at home. Illogically, and almost automatically, she now flew out at people in criticism and attack, fearing that unless she did so she would be attacked first. The school agreed to have Linda return on a trial basis. With its new understanding it was able to handle her in a calmer, more matter-of-fact way.

Another part of the school-agency plan was to have Linda assume some special responsibility at school to absorb her abundant energy and give her satisfaction. In addition, the responsibility was to be one in which she would not be obliged to be in constant contact with other people. Writing a column for the school newspaper proved an ideal solution. She soon began to handle this task successfully. The success brought her gratification and reduced her need to be domineering; she gradually became one of the well-regarded leaders in the school. Linda was graduated from high school with honors and went on to college to prepare for a profession.

UNDERSTANDING AND MANAGING SEXUALITY IN ADOLESCENT GIRLS

Although there is no dearth of published material about the physiological and psychological changes occurring in pubescent and adolescent girls, parents, schools, and the public at large have been slow to deal in a helpful way with the sexual overtones appearing in the behavior of this age group. A relatively large number of girls in our project were diagnosed as having hysterical character formations because of the way in which they tried to master their sexual impulses. These girls were seductive, provocative, and seemingly intensely preoccupied with sexuality. People tended to overestimate the gravity and depth of the sexuality in their behavior. They often concluded that such a girl was promiscuous—an actual or potential sex delinquent.

Because of its added worry that the girl with hysterical symptoms was a dangerous influence on other students, the school often felt an urgency to remove her. Teachers frequently admonished and warned the girl about the danger of her ways. Punishments were in the form of isolation from peers and withdrawal of privileges, for example, barring a girl from the choral group until her behavior improved.

The schools were apprehensive about adolescent girls with hysterical reactions. We believe that increasing the understanding of a school about one such girl has great carry-over value for subsequent dealings with similar girls. We explained that the flirtatious, exhibitionistic behavior is actually a defense against sexuality itself; that such a girl is fearful and guilty about her sexual impulses, and the fear and guilt ordinarily keep her from engaging in frank sexual activities. The task then is to help her accept her sexuality, find sublimations for its expression, and develop the ability to form good heterosexual relationships.

Admonitions and warnings by the school do not help because

they stimulate preoccupation with sexuality rather than help to contain it. Punishment or withdrawal of privileges usually are not effective because the girl already suffers from guilt and punishes herself for her own misbehavior. Isolating her from her peers takes away her laboratory for learning how to get along with contemporaries of both sexes. It is part of an adolescent girl's psychology to need relationships; if denied interaction with her peers, she will seek out undesirable or inappropriate companions. Barring her from an activity she enjoys takes away a healthy sublimation for her sexuality.

One important contribution an educational system can make to any adolescent's development comes from the opportunity it affords for sublimation. It offers this through the many intellectual, creative, and interpersonal activities available in school. The school's position, as far as possible, should be to encourage such sublimation rather than to cut it off.

All adolescents, not only girls with hysterical character formation, need the support of good peer relationships. This is particularly true for youngsters who have emotional difficulties. Unfortunately, the youngster who has a personality disturbance is often impaired in forming peer relationships. His friendships are few and usually of a nonconstructive kind. If he is punished for his academic malfunctioning by being denied participation in certain school activities, his chances to make healthier friendships are lessened.

PLANNED BUT SIMPLE SCHOOL MEASURES

School planning for a specific child on the basis of information given by the social agency need not involve complex therapy on the part of the school. On the contrary, the task of the school becomes easier because once it knows what will help, the things that need to be done may be quite simple. Jack's situation is an example.

Jack was an emotionally hungry boy whose ineffectual, dependent manner obscured his true intelligence and ability and interfered with his application to his school work. Casework treatment focused on giving him the warm relationship he needed to become more mature. We felt, too, that the school personnel could make a genuine contribution to Jack's development by making small, simple gestures of friendliness. We worked closely with the interested school adjustment teacher, who was of great assistance. She explained the situation to some of Jack's teachers. They were asked to say "hello" to the boy when he came into the classroom, to make some friendly personal inquiry when the opportunity presented itself. History was the one subject in which Jack had shown some interest. When he handed in a history paper of some merit, the teacher brought the paper to the attention of the class. Such recognition and signs of personal warmth meant a great deal to the boy. They were among the factors that ultimately motivated him to do better, and he began to study diligently for the first time in many years.

These school measures, for all their simplicity, were effective because they fitted Jack's special needs. They might not have been suggested for another youngster who, though suffering from similar problems of dependency, required a different approach because of different circumstances.

STEREOTYPED METHODS OF HANDLING

The forms of action taken by the school in the cases of Jack (friendly interest to increase self-esteem) and Linda (assignment of an appropriate responsibility to channel energy constructively) are time-honored school techniques for dealing with students with problems. The point to be made is that, although the techniques themselves may be excellent, they should not be administered in a stereotyped manner without reference to an individual problem. Problems, too, may be labeled with a stereotyped generalized term. For example, "learning difficulty" or "laziness" may be designated as the problem, with "improve study habits" as the prescription for cure. But our experience was that active and deliberate concentration on the school problem frequently was not beneficial but detrimental to the failing youngster. It not only ignored the real issue, but, by focusing on the final symptom, it deterred the child from solving the emotional issues behind the symptoms.

Harold, a daydreamer, was indifferent to learning and distractable. No subject appealed to him or had significance for him. He spent his time throwing spitballs, passing notes, and making remarks to amuse his classmates. His semidelinquent activities were enough to make his family and the school unhappy with him but never enough to get him into trouble with the legal authorities. Psychological testing indicated that he had an I.Q. of 140. Our agency study of Harold and his family revealed that the youngster's nonchalance about school was a final result of the long-standing nonchalance of his parents about him and his life. Both parents were intelligent but highly preoccupied people, too concerned with their social and professional activities to devote themselves sufficiently to Harold's welfare or to show an interest in him beyond their desire that he not bother them.

Not knowing the boy's history and psychodynamic make-up, the school attempted to correct his academic ineptitude by working toward the improvement of his study habits. In applying this technique to the problem it overlooked the vital question of why the boy had come to have poor study habits in the first place. More importantly, it conveyed to the youngster and his parents that the school difficulty was a simple matter that could be solved if only Harold learned how to study. The result was to increase Harold's feeling of depreciation and worthlessness. Additional homework, focus on study techniques, and the teacher's help after school did not improve the situation. Harold and his parents came to believe the problem insoluble, and everyone concerned experienced a sense of desperation that further complicated an already difficult situation.

Since the adolescent's superego is in the process of change, his controls may need reinforcement from the environment. Youngsters sometimes beg for limits by progressively greater provocation and aggression. A strict, disciplinary approach by the schools can be effective in some cases but is futile in others.

Nora's school attendance pattern was three weeks in school, then absence of a day or two. We noted a similar pattern in her part-time job and in her appointments with us. She had a schizoid personality, and out of a deep-seated fear of human beings she could not tolerate continuous social interaction. Bizarre tensions accumulated and could be relieved only by escape from the confining relationship. In a sense her truancy was self-therapeutic, enabling her to build up enough strength to again face a fearful ordeal. The truant officer handled the absences by scolding and threatening the girl. Her fear of people thus increased, she became even less able to attend school.

When misbehavior does not respond to a reasonable degree of discipline, schools, and parents, too, often lose patience and resort to threats that drastic action will follow the next repetition of the undesired act. Threats seldom work: the fearful child becomes more fearful and ineffectual; the rebellious child feels challenged and goaded. Moreover, since the threats are seldom

carried out consistently, they serve to undermine school authority
for the youngster and the classmates who witness the interplay.

Enforced "next time" warnings may be effective in dealing
with the physical exuberance of the normal child or may be the
only way of containing, for a time at least, the hyperactivity of
the impulse-ridden child. When acting-out behavior, however, is
a defense or ego adaptation to anxiety aroused by unconscious
conflicts, threats will rarely work; they may in fact precipitate
the very misbehavior the teacher is hoping to avert. Such a child
finds it hard to endure the "sword of Damocles" hanging over
him and may end the suspense by committing the forbidden act.

Extracting promises for better behavior from youngsters with
unconscious problems is likewise ineffectual and detrimental.
They may willingly make the promise and consciously wish to
keep it but, for reasons outside their conscious control, be unable
to comply. Shame and guilt then become part of their already
uncomfortable feelings; or, faced with their inability to control
themselves, they become panic stricken and the misbehavior is
exacerbated. The difficulties of these children are like the problems of the many people who want to lose weight but cannot ad-
here to a reducing diet. There are more factors involved than
simple good intent.

There were instances where a school, in the hope that kindness
might somehow provide the answer, became overly permissive
with a youngster whose actual need was for firm controls and a
facing of reality consequences. These excessively permissive
situations were most apt to occur with the adolescent who was
charming, seductive, and ingratiating. Rita was one of these de-
lightful, manipulating adolescents. Her parents covered up her
misdeeds, and a well-meaning teacher kept the full extent of her
class cutting from the knowledge of the attendance counselor.

STEREOTYPED ADVICE TO PARENTS

Even an understanding of psychological principles and a recognition that emotional forces within the child's personal life are
associated with learning difficulties can lead to stereotyped generalized handling. It is well known that constantly nagging a

youngster to achieve is not the best way to help him learn. The school may advise the parents to stop nagging their child and to let him do his own homework. But this advice may or may not be valid, depending on the specific circumstances.

The same caution applies to the categorical advice sometimes given to overprotective and overrestrictive parents. Such attitudes in parents are cause for concern and, in the long run, will need to be changed; yet if parental controls are taken off sharply and prematurely, the youngster may act out in harmful and destructive ways.

These reservations concerning the handling of students and their parents may seem to pose an insoluble dilemma in which there is no right thing to do. Our point, however, is that premature advice based on insufficient study will seldom yield the desired result. The answer lies in an individual study of the child, his parents, and his total learning situation so that recommendations that are applicable and feasible may be made. This spadework is the province of the social agency and other specialists. How the recommendations are carried out in school depends upon the understanding, imagination, and ingenuity of the educators.

Other Social Agency Responsibilities

DIAGNOSIS

We have said that the spadework to achieve an understanding of the child is the province of the social agency. School personnel do not ordinarily have the training that equips them for deep understanding of the basic psychological factors operating within an individual child. Intensive psychodynamic understanding of human behavior is a separate professional discipline. The school, of necessity, must concern itself with a large number of children, and its primary professional function is to educate. By tradition and philosophy, as well as need, teachers are geared toward understanding the broad educational requirements of the majority of their students rather than comprehending an intricate individual personality disturbance.

There are, of course, a variety of individual learning problems that teachers can solve, but these usually are problems arising from some specific aspect of the educational process itself, not from emotional conflicts. The failure of schools to fully understand the individual personality factors operating in the child can bring about some unfortunate circumstances. It may lead the school to make crucial decisions in the life of the child on the basis of what it believes are his educational needs. These measures may run counter to the youngster's basic defenses and intensify his symptomatology. For example, the school may double promote a bright child who is not doing well on the theory that he is bored with a curriculum that is too easy. This may be true for one child, and the solution may work out well. But when a school does this with a boy whose learning problem is based on a fear of competition and achievement, the double promotion simply accentuates the primary competitive fears, and the learning disability is increased. In addition, such a boy must now compete with classmates physically more mature and emotionally more advanced.

COURSE OF TREATMENT

In addition to giving the school appropriate knowledge about the personality dynamics of a child referred for counseling, the social agency should tell the school about the expected course of treatment in order to enlist its patience and continued support.

Time considerations. It is natural for the school to hope that treatment will bring rather quick results in moderating or ending troublesome behavior in school, since it bears the brunt of the day-to-day problems a child presents. It is also constantly faced with the fact that the youngster's school behavior is obstructing his education. Moreover, if the child's symptomatic behavior is impinging on the orderly learning routine of the other members of the class, an additional stress is present. In all, there are valid reasons for the school's wish that the child improve rapidly.

The school should be informed, however, when this wish may not be realized. Severe difficulties in school are usually symptomatic of deeply rooted character problems. As such, they are ingrained in the total personality structure of the child, and treatment is a slow and difficult process. Attempts to hurry changes in attitude and behavior simply defeat the desired goal.

Sometimes the counselor can make rough predictions about the prognosis and the length of treatment. If these predictions are shared with the school, their expectations will be more realistic. Suppose, for example, the youngster in treatment is a stubborn child. The counselor may say candidly, "It looks as if this child will continue to be annoying for some time. Stubbornness and opposition are his ways of handling his problems. It's going to take us a fairly long time to help him, and although the change in his personality may not be great, we do expect some improvement. Do you think you could go along with us on this?" In another situation, a girl with a hysterical character formation is acting out aggressively, and her defiance is presenting the school with a real problem in management. Knowing that girls with this character formation tend to respond rather quickly to an understanding therapist, the counselor could inform the school that chances for rapid improvement in some areas are good if the school can accept the girl's difficult behavior for just a little longer.

Preparation for relapses. It is well also to prepare the school for relapses. Not only is improvement usually slow but learning and integrating new patterns of behavior do not move forward in an unbroken line. Adolescents proverbially proceed at the rate of two steps forward and one step back. With the disturbed adolescent this process may be accentuated, and it can be anticipated that an adolescent's improvement will be interrupted by a regression to old ways of behavior. Unless the school is aware of this, it may interpret the relapse as evidence that the child is not responding to treatment and that some new, perhaps drastic, action must be taken.

Support during relapses. It is not enough to alert the school to expect regression on the part of a youngster in treatment. When it does occur, the counselor should help school personnel to see the matter in perspective. Relapses are often reactive to something that has happened to the student, for example, his disappointment that he did not get a grade that he thought he deserved. Perhaps the hospitalization of a parent, an impending court hearing, or some problem explored in treatment has increased his anxiety.

Such explanations remove the focus from the specific incidents, bolster the school's trust in casework therapy, and lead to a rational assessment of how it is best to proceed.

Keeping the school informed. The counselor, knowing the great amount of difficulty a particular student is causing at school, should recognize the plight of the teachers or school authorities. Other than just commiserating with them, he should make a point of keeping them informed of the progress of the treatment. Even a report to the teacher that a child is coming regularly for interviews has a bolstering effect. He should especially announce favorable changes that he notes in the youngster's functioning, even though there is no lessening of the school problem. If the school knows that the child is at least responding to treatment at some level, it can continue to hope that the symptoms causing malfunction in school will eventually abate. Sometimes the role of counselor and teacher switch, the teacher being the first to report some change for the better.

Changing schools. We were constantly impressed by the patience and helpfulness shown by school personnel toward the children we mutually served. On many occasions, when it was important that a difficult child remain in school until treatment had an opportunity to take effect, the teaching and guidance staffs exercised a great deal of forebearance. They were highly ingenious in devising ways to prevent the child's presence from interfering with the proper learning and teaching conditions to which the other students were entitled. If the youngster clashed with a particular teacher, the staff shifted him to another teacher whose personality appeared more compatible with his needs.

Sometimes a change of schools appeared to be the only solution to the problem. A child might persist in disrupting classroom routines to a point beyond endurance. In a very few cases, despite efforts of both agency and school to understand each other and compromise, situations arose where they disagreed about the needs of a child and the solution to his problems. For reasons it held valid, the school believed that stern measures were needed, whereas the agency believed they would deter ultimate progress. We found it extremely difficult to help the emotionally disturbed adolescent toward better school functioning unless the school environment was fairly stable and sympathetic. If to the normal treatment obstacles another environmental disability was added—either persistent unfavorable attitudes of the child toward the school or of the school toward the child—the odds against a successful outcome became very high.

Another factor sometimes pointing to the desirability of a change in schools was the negative attitudes of schoolmates toward the adolescent who had been in trouble, particularly if the offender was a girl. A number of our rebellious girls, by reason of their acting out and their association with nonconforming or semidelinquent groups, acquired a poor reputation with the rest of the student body. This problem could become troublesome for the girl who, after a period of treatment, had begun to change her attitude. She might find herself stigmatized as a bad girl whom the better groups would not accept. We found that an interim period ensued in treatment when former companions no longer sufficed and new companions were not available. This transitional period was a trying test to such girls for whom, like other adolescents, friendships in their own age group were an imperative psychological need. As one girl in our project said, "When you've been in with a bad bunch and you want to get in with good kids, that's when the trouble comes. The good kids won't take you in for a long time—if ever."

Since existing regulations did not permit changes of public high schools as long as the family remained at the same address, we sometimes arranged for a youngster's entry into a private high school. In a few cases, when the parents could not afford it, we paid the tuition. In a number of instances, a change of schools, as part of the treatment program, seemed to tip the scales favorably, and a startling improvement in school functioning took place quite soon. The adolescent's opportunity for a fresh start in a new environment plus, in some cases, the especially understanding teachers or smaller student group and more personal atmosphere in the new school made the difference.

The Emotional Component in Learning

From our study we received the impression that schools do not always appreciate the significant relationship of emotions to

learning. When our adolescents talked about school, they sometimes began by ascribing their dissatisfactions to the poor quality
of the education offered. They vaguely criticized teachers from
whom they could not learn or who they thought were not teaching properly. But it soon became evident that their real complaints
did not concern the educational aspects of school. The complaints about teachers and school environment were similar to the
complaints about parents and home environment. The issues of
genuine concern to them were those of being liked or not liked
by teachers, of being disciplined or not disciplined by school
authorities, of finding understanding of their problems in the
school. Of all youngsters, children with emotional problems are
the ones most keenly affected by the attitudes they meet in the
school staff and in the general school environment.

TEACHER-STUDENT INTERACTION

Not all students in our project were failing all subjects. Some
had a hill-and-valley pattern of learning. The youngster did fairly
well and obtained gratification in at least one or two subjects but
completely failed in other courses. Satisfactory performance in a
particular subject was frequently connected with the child's
liking for the teacher. The normal adolescent or the youngster
who has invested his energies in learning to the exclusion of other
areas of adjustment can learn from a teacher he does not like.
But the disturbed youngster can learn only when he likes the
teacher or when the subject matter interests him.

In understanding the learning process, one should not overlook
the significance of the instructor and the importance of the learning environment. Learning capacity cannot be isolated in a personality as if it were an operation in and of itself. A basic, if not
most important, psychological determinant of learning is the
child's identification with the teacher. A youngster reacts to his
teachers not simply as conveyors of skill and information but as
part of the dramatis personae of his emotional life. He looks upon
them in dichotomies: good or evil, beautiful or ugly, affectionate
or cold, permissive or authoritarian, nagging or guiding, encouraging or deterring, cooperative or competitive, selfish or al-

truistic, interested or bored, trustworthy or potentially dangerous.

We believe that teachers tend to underestimate their importance in the lives of their students. More than once we listened to a high school student recalling with nostalgic affection a teacher who had been kind to him. "I had a teacher in second grade who was real nice to me. She was so friendly and interested. But don't get me wrong. She knew the score, and she never let anybody get away with stuff."

The particular way in which the child regards a teacher depends to some extent on his relationships with his parents and represents an attitude displaced from his family life. Neither the teacher, the principal, nor the other staff members of the school with whom the child associates can extricate themselves from the way the child regards them. The child's own special emotional life determines how he learns from these individuals and how he reacts to them.

Teachers who tend to underestimate the influence they have on the lives of children also underestimate the effect of their comments upon the youngster. A chance remark to which the teacher attaches little importance may have a great deal of impact on the child. It is in this light, for instance, that one should examine the effort to control and motivate children by citing other students as good examples. Even more detrimental is using the youngster in trouble as a bad example. Thus, in reproving a class, a teacher may warn, "Sam truanted, and he had to go to Family Court. Now don't let it happen to you." Such singling out of an individual youngster as a bad example is very damaging. It tends to emphasize the child's pathology, to isolate him from the rest of the class, and to make him a ready scapegoat. If the child is in treatment and trying to improve, he may be greatly discouraged and embittered to find that he cannot separate himself from his past misdeeds.

PERSISTING SCHOOL ATTITUDES

We noted that schools sometimes lagged in altering their attitude toward youngsters who began to do better. If such a child had given considerable difficulty in the past, the school might continue to view him as the troublemaker he had been, rather than reacting to his improvement. The cumulative school records kept for each child and containing information about grades, tests, behavior, and disciplinary incidents are a valuable tool for the school in working with the student. If such material is not used in proper perspective, however, the poor impressions a youngster has made or his previous difficulties can follow him from grade to grade. Such material may color and prejudice a new teacher's attitude toward him or lead her to discipline him for some minor incident far out of proportion to the offense.

The Family Court referred Tony to us for a number of delinquencies. The school reported that he had shown an abrupt withdrawal of interest in school and frequently cut classes and truanted. After entering treatment, Tony improved rapidly and dramatically. His cutting, truancy, and stealing stopped completely. Some of the school personnel, however, continued to view this boy, unquestionably troublesome to them in the past, with irritation and a somewhat suspicious watchfulness.

One day, Tony had difficulty keeping awake and his head began to nod as the class was listening to an oral report. The teacher told him to go to the back of the room to continue his nap, admonishing him not to snore. Tony made an angry retort, and was taken to the principal's office.

Without consultation with the guidance teacher, the school administrative authorities prepared papers for his immediate transfer to a disciplinary school. When we attempted to intervene, the discipline officer quoted at great length from Tony's previous record, using this as evidence that the boy was very undesirable and had no place in the school. The offense Tony had committed was seen only in relation to his formerly unsatisfactory school history; his recent and dramatic improvement was entirely overlooked.

Need for Early Referral

Our experience in the Drop-Out Project highlighted the importance of early recognition and immediate referral for treatment of those children whose school problems are caused by emotional and personality difficulties. Because of their contact with the students, the schools are in a position to discover the youngster needing therapeutic help. We believe that referral of such youngsters at once would constitute a significant contribution toward reducing educational disabilities and preventing early school leaving.

Earlier, we noted the finding that a number of our adolescents, especially the boys, had long histories of school difficulties and observable emotional symptoms before they were referred for casework help. We similarly indicated the multiple problems occurring when school and personality difficulties become chronic. Aside from the prolonged stress and unhappiness engendered, the long continuance of basic psychological problems can so entrench them that they become increasingly resistant or perhaps impervious to treatment efforts. In addition, as school malfunction persists, academic deficiencies accumulate. The resultant educational retardation, together with the youngster's shame, discomfort, and wish to save face, become strong additional motives in the adolescent's drive to leave school.

OBSTACLES TO EARLY REFERRAL

We found many school personnel alert to the need for prompt referral and effective in persuading parents to apply for counseling for the child. As we have stated before, we were impressed with the amount of individualization given to many children within a school system as large as that of Chicago.

Certain obstacles, however, remain to be overcome if the ideal of early referral is to be achieved. Some teachers resist the use of intensive counseling services. On the other hand, there are some valid reasons why schools may be inclined to wait before utilizing the counseling services of casework agencies or clinics. They may be hoping that the trouble is temporary and will pass. Children frequently manifest difficulties that disappear without any special outside attention. Or the school personnel may wish to handle the problem by trying their own methods first. Certainly, not every child having trouble in school is emotionally disturbed or needs casework counseling, and conventional techniques of the school can clear up a large number of educational problems. When the difficulties are not responsive to the school's methods, however, continued reliance on these methods may not only complicate the problem but also create considerable delay in obtaining the treatment the child requires.

Furthermore, schools are reluctant in many instances to request the casework services of a social agency until a situation is serious and acute. They may refer only those students who are most troublesome to the school and their parents. This tendency is understandable. Teachers may be so occupied with the most troublesome youngsters or those who deviate very sharply that they have little time or opportunity to devote themselves to the milder situations. Also, schools may hesitate to ask an agency to help in situations other than the most serious if they have learned through experience there is not enough counseling service in the community to meet all the needs.

Consultant Resources

Since teachers and often school guidance personnel do not and cannot be expected to have a thorough knowledge of personality dynamics, their efforts to deal with school problems must be bolstered by specialists. These consultants, drawn from the disciplines of psychiatry, psychology, and social work, should have clinical experience in the diagnosis and treatment of emotional problems as well as thorough familiarity with the school environment. They should be an integral part of the school system and, if possible, in the school itself. Some functions of the consultant would be:

1. Educating school personnel to the importance of psychological factors in their own and students' behavior
2. Advising the classroom teacher on techniques for handling behavioral problems
3. Evaluating the effectiveness of the school's approach to problems so that ineffectual handling does not persist
4. Making case studies and complete diagnoses of those students with serious symptoms or of those who do not improve with the school's methods of handling
5. Treating on a short-term basis the children with transient or reactive disturbances to prevent their entrenchment

6. Acting as liaison between the school and the social agency to whom cases are referred for treatment

Many of the referrals to the Drop-Out Project were made by school psychologists and adjustment teachers. We believe our ability to be helpful to the school was bolstered considerably by their presence. They knew individual teachers and could approach them easily and on a personal basis. They were on the scene to interpret new bits of behavior, to make modifications in procedures, and to encourage teachers when their efforts did not bear fruit quickly.

Although we strongly favor consultant resources as an integral part of the school system, we are not ready to take the stand that long-term psychotherapy should be conducted within the school.

Danger Signals for Teachers

If the ideal of earlier treatment is to be realized, teachers need to be more familiar with the "danger signals" in children's behavior. Because human behavior is so varied and complicated, it is often difficult for parents and teachers to distinguish between behavior that is not of serious import and behavior that may be the forerunner of more serious trouble. With adolescents, particularly, these distinctions are difficult to make because the range of normal adolescent behavior is very broad.

Below are some warning signals we have noted as significant. When they appear, they call for early consultation with the school guidance specialist if one is available, or early referral to an agency qualified to work with children.

1. A sharp discrepancy between intellectual ability and academic achievement. Usually emotional difficulties are interfering with the learning process in a student of average or better intelligence if (a) standardized achievement tests show a full grade retardation in more than one area; or (b) basic skill levels are appropriate, but the student fails two or more courses or gets C's instead of A's.

2. Marked change for the worse in high school functioning as compared to performance in elementary school.

3. Youngsters who seem weak and unable to cope with situations. When these children reach adolescence, they give the impression that school and life are too difficult for them. They may adjust fairly well in the protected atmosphere of elementary school but break down quickly in the impersonal high school setting. In the eighth grade they usually view high school with considerable apprehension and may voice their concern to the teacher. Such youngsters may do well if given individual attention and support; without it they drift and are lost.

4. The overly responsive youngster who requires inordinate amounts of attention and reassurance and cannot function without it.

5. The child who has a great deal of difficulty getting started or staying interested in any project. He may never finish what he starts or he may begin with a spurt but quickly lose interest. Some of these youngsters are actually quite perfectionistic; they never finish anything because they cannot satisfy their own impossibly high standards. Others in this group seem apathetic and lethargic.

6. The child who is very much preoccupied with himself. He is moody and appears unhappy much of the time.

7. The youngster who seems somehow strange or different from other children. Fellow students may refer to him as an "odd ball." Such a child usually does not respond to or communicate with people.

8. The child who is physically present in the classroom, but emotionally absent.

9. The youngster who blames everyone but himself for his troubles—the "collector of grievances." When difficulties occur, such a child declares that everything will be all right "if," or that he "didn't do anything."

10. The youngster who is continually a behavior problem even though his misdemeanors are minor. The persistency and frequency of the behavior are the alerting signals.

11. The combative, belligerent youngsters, particularly those who seem to delight in stirring up trouble for its own sake.

12. The signs of quasi-truancy: continued tardiness, frequent absences for vague or minor illnesses, and class cutting.

In making use of the warning signals, one must consider the degree and persistence of the symptoms. Many healthy children are temporarily inefficient in school performance or occasionally behave improperly. For healthy youngsters these learning and behavior problems and their solutions contribute to the maturing process; they represent the trial and error method by which children develop their personalities.

A rough time guide to use in determining important warning signs is to consider carefully any malfunctioning that has continued for a full semester with or without intervention by the school. This is particularly true if the problem is one of both academic performance and behavior. For the very earliest school years some allowance should be made for the slow starters, but academic achievement below intellectual capacity that begins almost immediately and persists into the third or fourth grade is invariably a sign of trouble.

Some Guidelines for Social Agencies

Out of our joint work with the schools we arrived at some guidelines for collaboration that may be of use to other social agencies. These points are not new and seem self-evident; yet we found it well to remind ourselves of them, especially when zeal for an individual child made us forget occasionally the inescapable differences between schools and social agencies in dealing with children.

The school's mission is to educate all its students.

Social workers should first bear in mind that the school's chief function is the education of all its students and that it is organized to perform this task. The school cannot be expected to serve primarily as a therapeutic milieu for the emotional needs of any particular youngster, if meeting such needs interferes with the education of other students. Because of their focus on a specific youngster, social workers sometimes make requests that the school cannot reasonably fulfill. If Johnny is a dependent boy, it may be therapeutically valuable for the teacher to give him more attention. But if the attention Johnny requires is so extensive that his classmates are seriously deprived, the teacher cannot be expected to give him all the time and attention he could use.

The school's flexibility is limited.

There are limits to the flexibility of action a school can exercise toward a youngster. For instance, it may be desirable that the classroom misbehavior of a hostile, acting-out child be tolerated for a period. Within limits, this may be possible. Nevertheless, to cite an extreme example, if this youngster curses a teacher, the school may regard it necessary to suspend or expel him, whether or not this is in the best interests of therapy. The counselor who handles a child's hostile outbreaks in the privacy of an agency office is in a position quite different from a teacher who must cope with such behavior in a classroom.

Schools are responsible for educational decisions.

One of the most important facts for social workers to remember is that the school is the responsible authority over the educational life of its students. In discharging its responsibility, the school has the right to make the final decisions pertaining to the child's education. The function of the social agency is to provide the school with information to help it arrive at the soundest judgments. In making decisions, however, educators may have to consider factors not germane to therapy. The counselor should understand and be willing to accept this. His understanding and acceptance does not relegate him to a passive role in the collaboration; he can be active and vigorous in presenting his material and his point of view to the school. But if he genuinely recognizes the demarcation of function between school and social agency, he will be less prone to attitudes or actions that schools regard as an attempt to interfere with their jurisdiction and accordingly resent.

Request appropriate information from schools.

We have already mentioned that the schools have valuable information about their students and that social workers should use it. This material is generally of a descriptive nature. Counselors should not request the kinds of information schools cannot be expected to have, such as material about underlying causes of problems, subtle family relationships, or unconscious motivations. Such requests are usually unproductive and, at worst, may be irritating because of the implication that the school lacks a perceptiveness not really an integral part of its professional province.

Avoid excessive promises about treatment.

From our previous discussion about the difficulty of treating severe malfunctioning in school, it seems evident that social agencies should be wary of promising more than can be achieved in treatment. Yet the temptation toward excessive promises is subtle and many sided. It may stem from the optimistic core most therapists have as part of their therapeutic personality. It may come from the counselor's desire to obtain the fullest cooperation of the school. It may result from his efforts to give comfort and hope to school personnel who may be enduring the exasperating behavior of a particular child. And it may, of course, represent a mistake in prognosis.

It was our experience that schools are usually receptive to a realistic presentation of treatment possibilities, even when rapid or substantial improvement is not anticipated. Furthermore, a social agency that has shown correct judgment in appraising a treatment situation will gain more confidence from the school than one whose unfulfilled claims and promises result in disappointment to the school.

Make the school a genuine partner in treatment.

If we have the conviction that the help of the school is important in treatment of youngsters with school problems, we must give more than lip service to this conviction. We must act on it and make the school a true working partner in the treatment process. Schools rightfully complain that, following their referral of a student to an agency, they all too often hear little or nothing about subsequent developments.

Social agencies have an obligation to keep the school informed about the student who is in treatment. Simple professional courtesy would require this, but more is involved than the observance of amenities. Schools are interested in their students and understandably want to know how they are getting on. Moreover, the appropriate sharing of information heightens the school's sense of collaboration; the counselor who has provided reports to the school is more likely to obtain its cooperation when he makes suggestions about the child's needs.

We have mentioned that the information given to schools should be appropriate. This implies, as stated in another context, that the concepts and language used should be meaningful to people in the field of education. Yet the term "appropriate" has another important implication. The material provided should not be the kind that can be misused or misinterpreted. This exercise of judgment necessitates the counselor's knowing something about the people to whom the information is going—having some measure of their psychological understanding, their attitudes, and their respect for confidences. For example, if a teacher or administrator will be shocked rather than helped by the knowledge that a student's problems are based on severe hostility toward a parent, there is no purpose in providing this explanation.

Whenever possible, the school should be looked upon and treated as an integral part of the therapeutic team set up around the child. In many instances, schools can be drawn into the agency's basic thinking on case formulation and treatment plans. School representatives—perhaps the psychologist, adjustment teacher, or guidance counselor—can often participate beneficially in an agency case discussion or psychiatric consultation. We had many successful conferences of this kind.

In the most basic sense, however, the crux of a good working relationship between school and social agency lies not in detailed guidelines but in the fundamental respect each should have for the other: respect for the knowledge and skills of each discipline; respect for the different methods each must use in its work; respect for the mutual devotion toward children.

It is inherent in any collaborative process that disagreements may arise, but if respect exists, the impediments of rivalry or of patronizing attitudes will not consume time and energy. School and agency will be able to devote themselves to the ends to which both are dedicated—the education and the well-being of the child they are serving.

CASE ILLUSTRATIONS [1]

BETH   *Diagnosis:* Infantile-demanding character formation
        School Dynamic: Dependency

Two counselors invested a great deal of time and effort in Beth and her parents. For financial reasons the parents had delayed first their marriage and then starting a family. The mother had a severe reaction to a difficult pregnancy with the first child, a son. Two more boys were born in the next three years and then Beth was born. The mother was overwhelmed with her responsibilities, which reactivated earlier problems of hostility and rivalry with her own siblings. Unable to restrict her children's demands or properly train them, she became filled with confusion, self-blame, and helplessness.

As soon as Beth was old enough to enter school the mother began to take on housework jobs in homes where there was illness and her services soon became in demand because outside her own home she was a conscientious worker. At the time Beth came to us, the mother was working every day and was sometimes absent several days at a time; she would prepare the evening meal, leaving it on the stove to be reheated. Over the years she had withdrawn more and more from her husband, depreciated him, and

1. Identifying data have been disguised.

could not be pleased by him. She expressed utter disgust at his personal habits and would not share a bedroom with him. Arguments over money were the only verbal communication between them.

In interviews with her caseworker the mother was clinging and talkative; her conversation was rambling, vague, and confused. She was diagnosed as schizophrenic. We could not help her establish even minimal limits for the children. Although she recognized they were having difficulties, she projected the entire blame on the father. Treatment goals for her were geared to gratifying some of her dependency needs and giving her a place to ventilate the intense hostility she had for the father in an effort to lessen her depreciation of him at home.

We diagnosed the father as an infantile-demanding, oral-aggressive character. He was an infant when his own father died and his mother was unable to keep the family together. He left school to support himself and eventually secured employment in a real-estate firm. His own dependency needs were very intense, but he did have feelings of responsibility for the children. Admitting that he resented the children because they kept him tied to a bad marriage, he tried to hide these feelings from them. What other people thought was important to him, and he was shamed by the disrespect shown by his children.

The father did seem to profit from the casework relationship, but his attempts to move closer to the children and to place reasonable limits on their almost uncontrolled behavior were sabotaged not only by the mother's failure to support him but by her scornful depreciation of his efforts.

The school referred Beth for counseling because she was falling to pieces scholastically in her first semester of high school and was having trouble with her teachers.

Selected semester notations from her cumulative school record told us quite a bit about Beth, demonstrating the value of such school information:

Kindergarten: Alert, catches on quickly.
1–B: Demands attention but has winsome ways.
2–A: A beautiful child who wants to do as she pleases.

4–B: Good student, but difficult to settle down. Praise is very effective.

6–A: Underachieves because she will not apply herself. Immature.

7–B: Reads well but barely passing other subjects. Is frequently home sick.

8–A: Sassy, chatters incessantly.

The mother had not prepared Beth for counseling or even talked to her about it, so the therapist's telephone call to arrange an appointment took her by surprise. This was part of the therapist's report of the first interview:

Beth is a beautiful girl. She has large blue eyes, softly waving black hair, and a slender figure. She is aware of her loveliness but seems to draw self-certainty rather than conceit from this knowledge. She was on the surface, at least, self-possessed and well-poised throughout the interview but not in a cold, controlled fashion; she showed a lot of spark and spontaneity.

As she described them, her problems in school achievement and with the teachers seemed based on dependency needs. For example, she said she had failed Biology. On the first morning the teacher gave the students three pages of mimeographed material containing assignments for one week. Beth was discouraged by this and thought the length of the assignments was unfair, since she also had homework for other courses. After a short while the teacher told her she would never pass, so she thought if that was the way the teacher felt, she would just not try. And she did not.

She expressed an interest in completing high school so she could go to college in preparation for being a flight nurse, or a dancer. She reported very few parental controls on her behavior and said she goes out every night of the week, staying out until three A.M. on weekends. Her mother is never home and her father irritates her so that she avoids him.

We diagnosed Beth as an infantile-demanding character type with some masochistic aspects to her personality. The predominant observable complaints were demandingness and provocativeness. Provocativeness was her chief ego adaptation. With a set of "company manners" added to her physical beauty of face and figure, she made a manipulative and narcissistic approach to people. Her behavior, however, with family members, teachers, or people who put demands on her was provocative in a self-destructive way. She was strongly identified with her mother both in regard to positive attitudes toward sick people and negative attitudes toward men.

Beth was required to take on self-responsibility much too early in a setting where she had to compete for the mother's attention. Because of her physical attractiveness and through the development of charming ways, as a young child she managed to get satisfaction from adults outside the home. During the same period she secured some approval from her mother by being responsible and self-sufficient. She managed fairly well through elementary school, although her functioning was erratic both in scholarship and attendance. She was ill quite often, but her mother readily wrote excuses for the least indisposition.

At the beginning of high school, Beth's academic and social functioning deteriorated. She practically abandoned her Sunday manners, becoming easily irritated and expressing her anger by verbal and physical assault. Her illnesses became more frequent, and there were periods of depression. Sporadically, she was efficient and responsible, but then she behaved in ways that were self-harming. More and more dependent upon and clinging to an indecisive and substanceless mother, she appeared to be beating her head against the wall to get a little bit of love and attention. Disappointment was multiplied by disappointment and Beth finally left school. She sought dependency gratification in a sexual relationship, became pregnant, and then married the boy.

We saw Beth over a three-year period. There were frequent cancellations, changes of appointment, and periods of as long as six weeks that we did not hear from her. In spite of the breaks in counseling, however, either the parents or Beth would request that it be resumed. After about two years of therapy it was decided to terminate treatment. Beth's needs were considered too great to be met and the home too pathological to expect any change. When she became pregnant, however, we felt it advisable to continue service until the baby was born.

Initially, Beth related in an aggressive, provocative way. Very gradually, the caseworker became meaningful to her because of accepting, giving attitudes, and Beth began to have respect for the ideas presented for her consideration. At this stage of treatment she accepted generalizations and mild interpretations very well. Eventually, it was pointed out to her that her dependency on her mother was no longer realistic, that she could find satisfactions elsewhere, and that she could take care of herself. She made attempts to be more mature, but environmental demands and frustrations overtaxed her capacity.

There were periods when she applied herself in school. During one such period she was encouraged to study by her boy friend. When his parents moved out of the state, her mother invited him to live with the family. Beth handled her rivalry with her boy friend–sibling by regressing to infantile longings and childish behavior. She left school in a very self-damaging way, although her therapist and the school had worked out a modified program for her.

Beth was malfunctioning in all areas of her life but a general personality problem was not selected as the dynamic of her use of school. She was classified under poor management of dependency impulse because school unconsciously represented dependency for her. In elementary school, where she could get love and attention, she did relatively well academically; in high school where achievement and independence were demanded, her school functioning, admittedly complicated by other circumstances, broke down to the point where she dropped out.

Beth's school life had no specific dynamic meaning for either her mother or father; their dynamic use of school was a general personality problem. The mother lacked concern about all areas of Beth's functioning, and although the father valued school, he was too preoccupied with himself to involve himself in Beth's school life.

CHUCK   *Diagnosis:* Oral-dependent character formation,
                            passive type
               School Dynamic: General personality problem

Chuck's dependency seemed incongruous with his vigorous physical appearance. Over six feet, he was well-built and handsome. Though his I.Q. showed a potential of 120, he was at sixteen still a freshman in high school. Even this grade was far above his ability because his basic school skills were at a fifth grade level. He was failing his subjects and had started to truant.

Chuck lived with his mother and had an older sister who had just married and left home. His extreme dependence was tied up with the great emotional deprivation he had suffered. His father had been a poor provider from whom the mother separated shortly after Chuck's birth. The mother placed both children in a foster home of her own finding, and Chuck remained there until his adolescent years. Although the mother paid for their upkeep, she rarely visited the children.

In recounting his history, Chuck said his foster mother was all right, but he expressed much disappointment in his foster father who was childish and irresponsible. The foster father deserted his wife when Chuck was fifteen and the two children were returned to their mother.

The natural mother was capable in her job as a receptionist and related how she used her charm "to the hilt" to earn as much money as possible. She was extremely narcissistic and this was explained by the intense hardship she had suffered. She had been separated from her own parents and had been reared by a foster mother who mistreated her. Sadistically cruel, the latter would often express her displeasure by refusing to talk to the girl for a week at a time. Meals were skimpy. Once the foster mother deliberately held the girl's hand over an open flame when she failed to wipe off the kitchen range.

At age sixteen Chuck's mother ran away to Chicago and from then on made her own way. She was often hungry. At eighteen she married his father in order to have some financial security, only to find he would not support her. When the children came, "there were three hungry people instead of one." She decided to place the children and go to work herself.

When her "babies" were returned to her as "adolescents" she was unable to cope with the responsibility. Out of their deprivations and needs the children continuously made great emotional demands upon her. She was glad when her daughter married, and gave Chuck to the agency with a "he's your baby now" attitude. She refused to come for more than two interviews but did telephone several times during the course of Chuck's treatment. She expressed irritation that "this big boy" should always lean on her, and she demanded to know when this dependency would stop. She could not understand how a proud and independent person like herself, who had always fought her own battles, could have a son with no drive and no initiative.

Chuck was a pleasant mannered but timid youngster. Having never had his dependency needs met, he was still seeking such gratification in a manner appropriate for a much younger child. He attached himself to any adult showing an interest in him and used his good looks and personal appeal to have others do things for him, but could not actively take any steps on his own behalf.

He continued to try to obtain affection from his mother. Though she made him unhappy because she criticized and ridiculed him, he was extremely fearful of separation from her. His mother repeatedly told Chuck to get out if he didn't like the way she ran things. Once she locked him out when he came home late. He was very frightened by this and doubled his efforts to appease her. He also feared that she might marry and turn her attention to her husband.

Another facet of Chuck's passive dependency was his complete lack of interest either inside or outside school. He said vaguely there was nothing he particularly liked except television and movies. He had one friend, a tough, much older boy whom he occasionally trailed, receiving some vicarious gratification in watching the other's aggressive behavior.

Chuck was beset with painful feelings of inferiority and inadequacy. He was convinced he was stupid and could hardly believe the results when psychological tests in our agency revealed his high I.Q.

Chuck had difficulty in school from the very outset. He failed both the first and second grades, which compounded his difficulty by making him much older than his classmates. He recalled what had happened in those grades, telling his counselor unhappily, "I just didn't study any of the work the teacher gave. I just didn't do anything. I just sort of sat there, that's all." Then he brought out that while he was sitting there, he was constantly thinking of his mother and how much he wanted to be with her.

This ungratified dependency and yearning for his mother accounted for the boy's inability to master his school subjects. His energy was drained into his preoccupation with his mother and his own emotional needs, and he had little left for academic studies. The trouble came to a head when he began high school with only fifth-grade skills. He was not equipped to do high school work even if he did study. This complication, added to the emotional stress already present, resulted in the picture of discouragement and hopelessness characterizing him in high school. School could be only a place of frustration and unhappiness. An added blow came when one of his teachers told Chuck the reason he was doing so badly was that he was lazy and that no doubt his father must have been pretty lazy too. Chuck's truancy was the end result of the total situation. It was a passive kind of truanting, a drifting away when things became too much for him. As Chuck said, "I just feel like running away from the whole business."

At the beginning of treatment, because the same difficulties that kept him from mastering regular school courses would interfere with the remedial work, the boy's emotional problems had to be dealt with before he would be ready to undertake a remedial curriculum.

Chuck quickly formed an attachment to his worker and came for almost a year. He gradually made some movement toward independence, finally leaving public school to enroll in a private high school where he could take remedial classes with older students. He was employed afternoons and evenings, and this combination of school and work precluded his coming for further therapy. This was unfortunate since it was doubtful that he could maintain his gains without further treatment.

Chuck's case is an illustration of a general personality problem acting as the school dynamic; school had no special emotional meaning for him.

DAN *Diagnosis:* Masochistic character formation
      School Dynamic: Conflict in another area

Dan used school to resolve a conflict belonging to another area. The real conflict he was trying to work out was between himself and his father. In a similar manner his father used Dan's schooling in an effort to work out his own personal conflicts.

At the time of application Dan was in the second year of high school. He had an I.Q. above 140 but had failed every subject for the past two semesters. The school psychologist who referred him reported that he displayed complete lack of interest in school, did no homework, cut classes, and truanted.

Dan dropped out of school three times. His emotional struggle resulted in the wrecking of his school career and altered the pattern of his life.

The conflict between Dan and his father was primarily over the father's attempt to completely dominate the boy. A compulsive, pressuring man, he tried to live his son's life for him, acting as if Dan had no identity of his own. A combination of circumstances led to the father's using pressure for educational achievement as a chief medium for exerting control over Dan. The case is a typical example of the ways in which school can become the arena for conflicts having their roots elsewhere. It is of interest that this father's character disorder helped produce school difficulties in all of the other children in the family as well.

On the surface Dan's family was a conventional, middle-class family in comfortable financial circumstances. They owned a nice house in which they took great pride, and the father was active in politics. There were two older sisters and a younger brother.

The father worked in the payroll section of a large corporation. He suffered from deep-seated feelings of inadequacy, which he constantly attempted to overcome. One of his rationalizations for his feeling of inferiority was his lack of higher education. He believed he would have gone farther and achieved more recognition if he had had a college degree.

Dan's father was a slight man physically, meticulous and a perfectionist. He suffered from a great deal of unconscious hostility, though much of his anger was conscious. His chief method of dealing with his hostility was to use compulsive defenses. He was highly critical and faultfinding with everyone but particularly so in his own home, where he felt he had the right to control all members of the family. His relationship with each of the family members was difficult, but he was especially involved in his relationship with Dan. Over the years this relationship consisted mainly in the father pressuring and pushing the boy academically. He constantly prodded Dan about his school work, asked him about his grades, tried to tutor him, and lectured him about the values of education and the necessity of college. In addition, he was in the habit of assigning many chores, which he expected to be done with precision and accuracy. Dan, however, could never do them to his father's satisfaction. If Dan attempted to defend his manner of doing a task, his father would give him a long lecture on the right way. Even if the boy really achieved satisfactorily in some area, the father withheld praise. The youngster told his counselor despairingly that he had never been able to do anything to please his father and had no hope of ever satisfying him.

Aside from the father's perfectionistic and hypercritical attitude, his compulsiveness came out in a need to organize minute details. For example, he had typed out and posted a strict schedule for the use of the bathroom in the morning.

Dan's mother was not much help to him. Though warmer and more lenient than his father, she did not have a strong character— we diagnosed her as an oral-dependent, passive character type. Her husband's expectations made her nervous and tense. Because of his criticism that she was not strict enough with Dan, she resorted to frequent nagging and checking, so that the boy was beset by pressures from all sides.

The chief adaptation Dan had developed in his efforts to handle his anger was passivity. This passivity did not have the quality of open stubbornness; it was more like an apathetic drifting with the tide. In school he was aimless, vague, and uninterested. He showed little overt concern about his failing grades and easily admitted to his indifference. When Dan left the first public high school he attended, his parents enrolled him in a private school. He delayed registering in the new school until it was almost too late, meanwhile giving vague assurance that he would register "soon." The private school dropped him because of his excessive absences and failure to do assignments. Dan was still legally obliged to attend continuation school because of his age but did not report there until he was forced to do so by the truant officer. If he were permitted, he would sleep until noon, and he made no effort to look for a job. Dan returned to regular high school after the school authorities decided to give him another chance. After a spurt of better work, the old pattern of cutting classes and not doing assignments returned, and it was evident that the school would ask him to leave. Even in the face of this reality the boy's lassitude and drifting persisted. When it seemed essential for him to discuss plans with his counselor, he said evasively that he would handle the forced drop-out "if and when it occurred."

In his numerous drop-outs Dan clung to a significant and characteristic pattern of behavior. In response to his father's persistent driving for achievement, his prime defenses were nonachievement and passivity. In accordance with his passivity, he never actively attempted to leave school. Instead, he would oblige the school to take the initiative in asking him to leave. If he attended class, he simply sat, lending his physical presence and little else. After a time the cutting would begin, and the school finally would have no alternative but to expel him.

Dan's passivity contained a large hostile, provocative element, and the boy's behavior was very effective in frustrating his father. The father, becoming more and more upset, redoubled his lecturing about the benefits of education. He felt he had made a particularly telling point when he informed Dan that a friend of his who had dropped out of school was still a stock clerk. Dan replied indifferently this sounded like a good job to him.

Dan's use of school as a weapon in the struggle with his father was on quite a conscious level. He was well aware of the inordinate importance of education to his father and knew his failure in school hit his father in a most vulnerable spot. Dan put it this way: "If I fail, it won't hurt me; it will hurt him." Dan recognized that his father wanted him to achieve not for his own sake but to satisfy the educational goals his father wanted but had been unable to secure. He sensed that his father did not view him as a separate individual and said wearily there was no point in his going to college. Even if he did well there, it would be his father who took all the credit for the accomplishment.

Dan's use of school to resolve an outside conflict was only one element operating to ruin his school career. The factor that constantly worked against the youngster's success in school as well as his success in treatment was his severe masochistic character disorder. By the time we saw him, his character problem had become entrenched and crystallized. His masochism was evident in his over-all manner: he consistently acted in such a way as to hurt himself. His seeming unconcern about his poor grades was not genuine unconcern. Underneath he was unhappy at the way things were going in school, but defeating tendencies came out every time things became a little better for him. After casework was initiated, there would be times when Dan did better in school and pressures at home would ease up a bit. He could not tolerate such prosperity, and failure to do homework and cutting of classes would start again. This happened despite the boy's growing recognition that his behavior was self-destructive and was making him unhappy.

Projective psychological tests administered by our psychologist gave confirmation of the boy's marked passivity as his chief defense and of the severe self-defeating pattern constituting his masochistic character problem.

This case further demonstrates that school problems are virtually impossible to solve as long as the emotional conflicts creating them are not alleviated. The exacerbating factor keeping the pathology alive was the vicious circle of interaction between father and son in which the father pushed and Dan passively resisted. We were not able to break into this interaction despite intensive contact with both parents as well as with Dan. We knew at the outset that this would be a long-term, difficult treatment situation. We continued for several years with separate therapists assigned to each parent and the boy because we hoped to ultimately salvage something for this highly intelligent youngster.

We attribute the lack of success in treatment not only to the depth of the pathology in father and son but to the nature and rigidity of their defenses and their interactions. The father was not able to change. His strong need to see his son as an extension of himself persisted. His immobility in treatment seemed due to an unfortunate combination of personality elements. Not only was he rigidly compulsive but he was also infantile. In his own

family constellation he had been displaced as his mother's favorite
by the birth of twins who were sickly and required a great deal
of his mother's attention. There was little he could obtain from
his passive, uninterested father.

Thus, he came to his own marriage with great unmet dependency needs. At first he established an equilibrium by getting
dependency gratification from his wife, but the equilibrium was
upset by the birth of his children and the necessity to share his
wife. This revived his own early trauma, and he reacted by view-
ing the children as sibling rivals. The father's general defense of
compulsivity was compounded in his relationship with Dan by a
sadistic element because of his hostility at being displaced by a
boy. This accounted in part for the intensity and the intransigency
with which he pushed Dan.

The rigidity of the father's defense was dramatically ex-
emplified in treatment. Although he consciously wanted to change
and understood that pressuring Dan was making things worse,
he could not tolerate the psychological tensions or the physical
symptoms (headaches) he felt when he tried to avoid pushing
the boy. If he succeeded in halting the pushing in one area, his
neurotic need to act out in this way appeared in another area. For
example, we were able to help the father stop lecturing Dan about
college, but he then took to forcing the boy to read biographies
of famous men, and so it went. Even when Dan was functioning
relatively well and attending school regularly, his father could not
restrain from a minute questioning of the boy about every detail
of his life—what time he arose in the morning, what time he
got to school, when he returned in the evening, and so on. When
an English assignment required Dan to write ten book reports
during the course of the semester, his father worried incessantly.
At one point he complained, "The semester is almost half over.
Dan has written only six reports and he will not have time to read
four more books." The father's final rationalization in defense
of his pressuring was, "It's natural to want always to forge
ahead."

Even with the father's inability to change, we might have
helped Dan had his masochistic character structure not been fixed.
His need to harm himself, expressed in nonachievement, interfered

with his progress in counseling just as it did with his progress in school. The therapy was soundly handled from a technical point of view, but Dan frequently did not appear for appointments and finally drifted out of treatment. His failure to keep appointments often occurred just at a time when some progress was being made in counseling.

This case illustrates the need for early referral before the emotional problems become so deeply imbedded that they present an intractable treatment problem. It also points up the need for proper diagnostic understanding of the factors behind such symptomatic school behavior so that a suitable treatment plan can be instituted.

Though not referred to our agency until his second year in high school, Dan had school difficulties as far back as the fifth grade. At that time, a school report noted that Dan applied himself poorly to school work and was badly behaved. The report mentioned casually that some home problem might account for the difficulty, but no further cognizance was given to this.

An enormous amount of ground was lost between the school problem's first appearance and Dan's referral to our agency five years later. He managed to limp through grade school, always underachieving scholastically, but by the time he started high school his pathology reached the point where treatment was of no avail.

ELLEN   *Diagnosis:* **Anxiety reaction in a hysterical character formation**
             School Dynamic: **Superego revolt**

Ellen exemplifies a girl in whom adolescence touched off a wave of rebellion. Her rebellion represented the overthrow of a fundamentally strict superego, and her school difficulties were due to this revolt. We were able to help Ellen. Though her behavior was stormy, her ego was basically adequate and she had a good capacity for relationship. It was toward these factors that therapy was directed. Her diagnosis was anxiety reaction in a hysterical character formation.

Ellen was sixteen. During her four high school semesters she had cut classes, was repeatedly absent for vague illnesses, had failed many subjects despite a high I.Q., and had fallen one semester behind in grade placement. The family was Jewish. The parents were educated, cultivated people with ample income. Prestige and standing in the community were highly important to them. They had no other children.

Help was sought after Ellen wrote a letter to her mother during a six day truancy episode. At the time, her father was hospitalized with pneumonia. The letter read:

Dear Mom, I'm in an awful mess. I've been skipping school all the days you've been at the hospital with dad. I know you have been unhappy with my grades and the way I act, and I am too. There's a craziness in me that scares me and I don't know what to do. Please wake me up when you get home tonight. You've got to help me. I promise to try. I'll do anything.

Her mother became alarmed and was referred to us by friends.

A report from the school indicated that Ellen had been absent frequently, was not doing her homework, and seemed preoccupied in the classroom. In an angry outburst she had told one teacher she hated school and all its rules and regulations, "It's just like home."

The mother brought to her first interview a collection of Ellen's compositions dating from the third grade. She also stressed that Ellen had great talents in other areas as well. Her pride in her daughter's accomplishments was obvious. Her overevaluation of Ellen's ability and her pressure for achievement were attempts to fulfill her own needs through her daughter.

The mother placed the onset of Ellen's problems at the beginning of high school. Up to that time she was an "ideal child"—doing well in grade school, acting as teacher's helper, and causing the parents no trouble. Now there were difficulties not only at school but at home and with peers. Ellen was rebellious toward her parents, especially her father, whom she regarded as old-fashioned and too strict. They frequently had loud, vehement arguments. She was going with undesirable friends and at school belonged to a lower status group regarded as nonconforming.

The mother was a rigid and perfectionistic woman. Cleanliness was important to her, as were duty and high standards of accomplishment. Her guiding precept in life was that she could do anything she "put her mind to." Clinically, the mother had a compulsive character disorder. Ellen had been toilet trained early and as a youngster had been exceedingly clean. Now, under stress, she had become quite sloppy. On the positive side, the mother had real concern for Ellen; she was disturbed by her unhappiness and wanted things to be better.

Ellen's father was a distinguished looking gentleman who was precise and punctilious. His idea of proper behavior consisted of "obeying the rules, practicing self-discipline, and having other people think well of you." He was uncomfortably aware that he seemed old-fashioned but clung firmly to his belief that the proper rearing of children must be based on strict discipline and obedience. Like his wife, his was a compulsive character disorder with a rigid superego. His compulsive defenses, however, did not always work. He confessed to a violent temper and had explosive rages in which he struck Ellen and called her vulgar names.

Ellen was a tall, attractive girl with a sense of humor, though anxious and visibly tense. She seemed immature, and her rebellion had a petulant quality, very much like that of a naughty child. Her quite impulsive behavior presented one of the most acute problems because some way had to be found to modify it before irreparable damage resulted.

Ellen gave a perceptive account of the events that she thought led up to her school problems. Until the seventh grade she was a "real square." She worked for good grades, was teacher's pet, and was babied by both teachers and classmates. She had friends and, while not a leader in her group, had an important place in it. In the eighth grade she entered a different school when the family moved to a better neighborhood. Here her unhappiness began. Her new classmates were snobbish and would not accept her. She was very hurt, and school became distasteful to her. Nevertheless, she threw herself into her studies with desperate fervor. She was surprised and saddened when her classmates labeled her a "brain" and would have even less to do with her. When Ellen was graduated from grammar school, she felt she had had enough of being the good little girl. She wanted some fun and was going to have it. In high school she found acceptance with some girls who were considered fast. They taught her to "sharpen up" and showed her how to use make-up. Once Ellen's rebellious behavior had broken out, it took over. She began cutting and doing poorly at school. Her parents' reprimands served only to increase her defiance. After the truanting episode, Ellen's guilt overwhelmed her, and she wrote the letter quoted above, which was essentially a plea for help. Acting out had not resolved her conflicts and anxieties but intensified them so that she had little energy left over for productive schoolwork. The vicious circle was in full swing.

In addition to the difficulties at school and trouble at home, Ellen was seeing a non-Jewish boy whose background and milieu were very different from hers. To the consternation of her parents, who wanted her to date only Jewish boys, she proclaimed her love for this boy and her intention to marry him.

Ellen understood part of what was responsible for her school problems but not all because much of it was a result of unconscious forces. She was unaware that underneath her overt antagonism to her father she had a deep attachment to him. As a little girl she had enjoyed a close and seductive relationship with him. At adolescence the oedipal conflict was revived and intensified. Her rebellion served many purposes, but most of all it was a defense, an unconscious effort to flee from her oedipal longings for her father. If, through rebellion, she became involved in an angry relationship with her father, she was protected from facing her incestuous wishes and fantasies. Her choice of a boy friend very different from her father was another manifestation of the oedipal struggle.

The triggering factor in Ellen's truancy was her father's hospitalization. His illness stirred up unconscious guilt over her hostile and sexual feelings toward him. These tensions were more than she could tolerate, and her truancy was an effort to get relief through a kind of random, motoric activity.

Like her parents, Ellen had an overrigid superego, and in latency her chief behavior was submission to the superego. By compliance and striving for accomplishment she defended herself against the hostility to her parents aroused by their pressures for achievement. This won approval from both her parents and teachers.

With the change in grammar schools her former gratifications disappeared, and Ellen became unhappy in her mode of adjustment. Even so, she clung to her old defenses and went on achieving, though now her achievement brought no real pleasure. At adolescence, however, Ellen's instinctual needs increased and pressed more insistently for satisfaction, together with the resurgence of oedipal wishes. Thus, hunger for gratification became greater, while available satisfactions diminished. In high school Ellen had an opportunity for impulse gratification through her acceptance by the group that was acting out aggressively. At this point her submissive defenses gave way, and she rebelled against her rigid superego. A reaching out for impulse gratification, with its attendant picture of defiance, flouting of authority at school, and quarrels with parents at home became her overt behavior pattern. Dynamically, however, the most important aspect of the rebellion remained its use as a defense against oedipal longings.

Ellen eagerly entered into counseling, recognizing that she needed help. Her anxiety level, however, was very high. It soon became apparent that she could not tolerate exploration of any underlying areas touching on significant feelings and relationships or creating additional anxiety. Therefore, the treatment sessions centered mainly upon current realistic difficulties with attention to the more immediate aspects of her behavior and feelings.

The chief method of treatment used was ego support within the framework of a stable, nonanxious, nonpressuring relationship. Ellen was provided with a corrective emotional experience in which she was accepted as a worthwhile person in her own right and not on the basis of achievement or performance. When better performance came about, it was approved but only as it seemed something she wanted for herself.

Ellen's impulsiveness was the focus of considerable work by the counselor. Much of the help for this problem stemmed from the steadying influence of the counseling relationship, which helped Ellen to clarify reality, to examine her wishes, to discover her best interests, to look at her behavior more honestly, and to foresee consequences. This expanding and strengthening of the ego resulted in the gradual establishment of control of her impulses. The goal was to enable Ellen to attain better social functioning. There was no attempt at resolution of her basic conflicts, since she was not ready for more intensive treatment.

Improvement in school came about quite rapidly. Ellen attended regularly and received better grades. This improvement was fortified when circumstances permitted her to transfer to another high school. In the former school she had become known as a problem student to her teachers and had acquired an undesirable reputation among her peers because of her association with the acting-out clique. In the new school these handicaps were absent. She was able to stand out as one of the better students, in this way satisfying one of her important needs. Her grades rose to A's and B's, and she was selected to represent the school in a city-wide essay contest.

The parents were gratified with Ellen's improvement and the family turmoil diminished. Some months after the end of treatment Ellen was graduated from high school.

FERN   *Diagnosis:* Anxiety neurosis in a hysterical character formation
        School Dynamic: Reality problems

The school difficulties of most of the youngsters studied in our Drop-Out Project stemmed from emotional conflicts, but Fern was a girl whose harsh environmental situation caused both the emotional problems and the leaving of school. Basically, she had considerable emotional stamina and, in spite of the most taxing circumstances, had functioned well for a long time. When the hardships created by her environmental situation increased to an intolerable degree, however, she reacted with emotional symptoms that finally forced her to leave school. Fern had an anxiety neurosis and her general character structure was hysterical in nature.

The family consisted of Fern, her younger brother Joe, and the mother. The father, an alcoholic, had deserted the family when Joe was a baby. Since then the family had been maintained by Aid to Dependent Children. At the date of application to us,

Fern was in high school, having recently returned after dropping out for the third time.

The mother was an invalid, suffering from a disease that made her totally helpless. Incontinent and unable to feed herself, she was bedridden. Her hands shook violently, her speech was blurred, and her memory was poor.

Aid to Dependent Children provided a daytime housekeeper five days a week until 4:30 P.M. Fern had to care for her mother every evening and on weekends. This involved feeding her, lifting her to change the linen, and getting up several times during the night to give her the bedpan. This responsibility for her mother's care meant that Fern could not get away from home for any normal activities of a young girl.

At the time of referral the situation was acute. Joe had secured the mother's permission to join the Navy on his seventeenth birthday. Thus, in the near future Fern could anticipate complete responsibility for her mother. The few relatives had never been able to help; to the contrary they reminded Fern that it was her duty to care for her mother. Fern's mother would not permit friends or neighbors to sit with her because she believed that outsiders came in "only to pry." She had long made it clear that she did not want to go into a nursing home and over the years had pressed Fern to promise that she would never leave her to the care of strangers.

Although she was expected to give a great deal to her mother, Fern received no gratification in return. The severity of the mother's illness had made her totally absorbed in her own needs. Querulous, demanding, and complaining, she seemed totally unaware of the girl's difficult situation. Furthermore, she preferred Joe. Fern sadly related how her mother's face would light up when she talked to Joe, but "I do all the work and don't get any of the credit."

Fern was responsive and intelligent. She was filled with anxiety and tension, and her emotions were very close to the surface. In her first interview she poured out all her problems in a flood of feeling, bursting into bitter tears as she described her frustration over her inability to lead a normal life. Despite her efforts to control her feelings, Fern was growing increasingly irritable with her mother and became involved in frequent arguments with her. She felt extremely guilty about this.

Fern's anxiety neurosis was complicated by another symptom, spells of excessive sleeping. These came on when pressures were increased. Such stressful periods might follow disagreements with her mother or intimations from Joe or relatives that Fern must always continue to carry the burden of her mother. During these episodes she might sleep fifteen hours or more. She said she felt as if she were drugged. If awakened, she would simply fall asleep again. The sleeping was a regressive manifestation, an escape mechanism, which took over when the girl's situation and conflicts became intolerable. It was as if in sleeping she retreated from everything around her into a state of psychic exhaustion.

As is characteristic of hysterical persons, Fern also somatized. Her physical symptoms took the form of headaches, nausea, and colds. They were clearly tied in with her emotional state because when her tension was relieved, the symptoms disappeared.

The major burden of the mother's care as well as household management such as cooking, cleaning, and marketing had rested on Fern since she was ten years old. In the beginning Joe had divided the household duties with her. Though the mother was confined to a wheel chair then, she could still feed herself and direct the children at their tasks. Fern said that even with all the work she had to do during this period she was relatively happy. She thought this was because her mother was not yet so ill and was less irritable.

Unlike many drop-outs, Fern always liked school very much, and she wanted to graduate. Even with her heavy obligation at home, she did well throughout grammar school and received better than average grades in the first year of high school. She attended a parochial school, where she received considerable gratification from the nuns, who took a personal interest in her and were very kind. This meant a great deal to her.

When Fern was fifteen and beginning her sophomore year in high school, her mother, while alone, fell out of her wheel chair and hurt herself. This traumatic experience sent her into a state of shock, and from then on she grew steadily worse. Increasingly fretful and demanding, she soon became totally helpless and dependent. Joe began to refuse to do "girl's work" and was supported in this attitude by his mother.

Fern's adjustment to her life broke down. She became ill with a vague lingering infection and had to leave school. The next semester Fern enrolled at a public high school because the parochial school did not have the semester system. She remained there only a short time and dropped out again. In telling why she left the public high school, Fern touched on an issue that many of our drop-out youngsters repeated as a reason for finding school unsatisfying. Fern said she could not adjust at the public high school because it was too large and too impersonal. She thought none of the teachers seemed to care about the individual student. She felt completely lost, just "one of the mob." Obviously, this was not the entire reason for Fern's drop-out, but it was a contributory factor. The girl's great need for love made the attention of an interested teacher very important to her.

Primarily, Fern dropped out because responsibility for her mother increased her intrapsychic conflict to the point where she could no longer handle it. Although her hostility both on a conscious and unconscious level was very great, Fern also was attached to her mother. In Fern's infancy and early childhood, before her mother became ill, she had received maternal affection and care. This accounted for her adequate ego development. Now in adolescence Fern felt severely ambivalent and guilty. She expressed her ambivalence this way: "It would be so much easier if I could feel just one way about it. One part of me is sorry for mother and tells me I ought to be strong enough and courageous enough to bear this cross. The other part of me wants a chance to get out and live a normal life like other girls."

Because Fern had no means of adequately handling her emotional turmoil, she developed an anxiety state. The symptom of heavy sleeping began. Psychological struggles drained her energy, leaving little available for concentration in school. This, coupled with the diminished gratification from the new and impersonal school setting, made school unsatisfying to her, and she could not continue.

A two year period followed in which Fern was caught in the treadmill of her neurosis. She made abortive attempts at obtaining employment, but, as with so many drop-outs, the same needs and problems hampering her school adjustment also hampered her adjustment at work. For example, she had one job that she liked as long as she was in a department where the supervisor and the girls were friendly. Transferred to a department where she knew no one and where the people were cold and distant, she found it hard to do the work, began to be absent, and lost her job after two months.

Once more Fern tried attending school, but again she dropped out. Her unchanged reality continued to create emotional problems that interfered with schooling. Fern did not understand that the school problems were a product of her inner conflict as well as her environmental circumstances. Her verbalized reason for dropping out was that she now felt out of place and unhappy at school because she was a full year older than her classmates. One year later she made her fourth and final attempt to return. She now tried a private high school attended by older students in the hope that she would feel more at home. For a brief period things went well. She was regarded as a good student who was serious about her work. She was liked by both teachers and classmates. As before, the connection between Fern's unresolved personal problems and school problems was visibly demonstrated. One long holiday weekend the housekeeper was not present. Her mother was in an especially nagging mood, and Fern was upset at not being able to go out. A quarrel took place in which Fern said things that made her feel very guilty. Immediately afterward, she became exceedingly anxious and depressed, and the symptom of oversleeping recurred. She started to miss school and then had to leave when it became impossible for her to make up the work.

Our treatment of Fern utilized a variety of casework methods. The initial step was to meet the girl's dependency longings. She quickly formed a positive, dependent relationship with her counselor because she had a great capacity as well as a hunger for object relationships. The caseworker represented the loving maternal figure. This symbolic representation of the worker as the good mother was concretely reinforced by the agency's financial assistance and assurances of help when she needed it.

The counselor's acceptance and understanding of Fern's

difficult environment and of the normality of her conflictual feelings eased the girl, and her anxiety lessened. She spoke of the relief she experienced in finding someone with whom she could discuss her feelings. For the first time in her life she felt that another human being really understood all she was going through.

Because of her great guilt, Fern tended to be self-depreciating and had little self-esteem. The worker's acceptance, encouragement, and interest raised the girl's sense of worth, and Fern began to have more hope for the future. In this initial phase of treatment the emphasis was on ego supportive techniques.

The ultimate treatment goal for Fern was physical and emotional emancipation from her mother because the burden of a permanently invalided mother meant essentially the sacrifice of her life. In any case, some other plan for her mother's care had to be made eventually, since Fern could not continue functioning in the situation.

We recognized, however, that because of Fern's deep ambivalence about separating from her mother, the working out of the separation would take a long time. Treatment around this goal included an exploratory and clarification process in which Fern was helped gradually to bring out her various feelings about her mother and to think about what she wanted to do and what seemed best. She slowly gained some insight and began to move toward her wish to leave home, being bolstered by the recognition that her mother, too, would be better off in an institution with regular nursing care.

Considerable environmental work accompanied the treatment of Fern's emotional problems. Medical and dental care, as well as financial aid, were provided. We worked closely with the public agency that was assisting the mother. While helping Fern toward the ultimate goal of leaving home, we encouraged and helped arrange for her to get out more and to have greater freedom. This period of work went through many vicissitudes, both internal and external. When guilt increased or the pressures of reality became more difficult, Fern failed appointments or fell ill. Then the counselor made home visits in order to keep in touch and to reassure her of our constant interest and concern.

Fern's characteristic quality of resilience was evidence of the adequacy of her ego. As soon as external strain lessened and she received some gratification, she relaxed and felt better. The arguments with her mother also decreased. Once when Fern was ill the public agency installed a full-time housekeeper. She blossomed during the short time the housekeeper was in the home. She said she felt like a queen in being able to have a full night's sleep without getting up to attend to her mother. We were racing against time, however. We had to help her work out her conflict about her mother before her emotional symptomatology became overwhelming. As it developed, an authoritative source had to take the decision to leave her mother out of Fern's hands. It was as if Fern unconsciously arranged this.

Some time after her fourth and last school drop-out, Fern tried to ready herself to go to work. She had some ambivalence about this, equating employment with finally sealing her responsibility for her mother. In treatment we were dealing with this problem, hoping to help her separate the two issues. We could not control what went on in Fern's environment, however. The relatives and the mother were continuously pushing Fern to get a job and were highly critical of her.

The final explosion came when Joe, home on furlough, quarreled with Fern. He insisted it was her duty to find work and support her mother as long as she lived. Fern reacted with hysterical weeping, then became depressed, and again fell into deep sleep for lengthy periods. Her physical condition became critical because she was not eating and was vomiting. Altogether, she seemed to have given up.

After consultation with the agency psychiatrist, we had Fern hospitalized in a good psychiatric hospital as an emergent and protective measure. Her physical condition needed medical attention, and we felt Fern could no longer be allowed to remain at home in a desperate reality she could not endure.

The girl's hospitalization presented an auspicious time to bring about separation from the mother. We believed that recommendation by a medical authority that Fern live apart from her mother would ease her guilt by relieving her of the responsibility for the decision.

A conference with a number of agencies quickly worked out

an effective plan. The public agency made arrangements to have the mother placed and maintained in a nursing home. The attending psychiatrist at the hospital discussed with Fern his recommendation that she not return home following her discharge, but make some other living arrangements.

The speed of the girl's recovery was significant and confirmed the fact that reality issues played the predominant role in her problems. As soon as the burden of her mother's care was lifted, Fern's depression and physical symptoms markedly decreased. She readily accepted the psychiatrist's recommendation for separation and on her own found a place to live with friends. Soon afterward she obtained employment, resumed contact with girls and boys her own age, and entered into a satisfactory pattern of living. She continued to see her mother, had normal concern about her, and established a much more friendly relationship. The mother, too, adjusted to the nursing home much better than had been thought possible. She seemed able to accept the fact that her condition required the more intensive care available in a medical institution.

The solidity of Fern's adjustment was verified in her reaction to her mother's death a year later. She felt saddened but was able to continue quite adequately without undue guilt. After a time she recovered her natural buoyancy and began making plans for the future.

Casework treatment resulted in considerable improvement in Fern's functioning, but it came too late to save her school career. When treatment terminated, she had only one year of high school credits, and it was too late to make up the three lost years.

GEORGE   *Diagnosis:* Inhibited character formation
           School Dynamic: Competitive aggression

Most of the students in the Drop-Out Project were still in school, but George was one of the few who had dropped out before treatment started. He was working full time. An interested teacher who had remained in touch with him referred him because she thought it a waste that this intellectually superior boy who basically seemed interested in his education, should be handicapped by inadequate schooling.

George came in ostensibly for help with educational planning. After several interviews it became apparent that an emotional problem was uppermost in his mind. He revealed with much shame and discomfort that for some years he had been troubled by his homosexual tendencies: he felt sexually attracted to men. He had never acted upon these feelings but feared he might do so. He wanted help for this difficulty, which he regarded as "morally wrong." He wanted to be "normal like other people," to date girls, to eventually marry and have children. George was ambitious and had a great desire to be an achieving, successful man, but felt that his emotional problems prevented this.

Exploration of the case revealed that George's difficulty, from a psychodynamic point of view, was not one of homosexuality per se. More accurately, he was developing an inhibited character formation to handle competitive aggressive impulses.

George was a pleasant faced, tall, and robust boy. Superficially, he had a quick, bright manner, but we perceived his high level of anxiety. He was quite tense and perspired heavily, especially in moments of stress. It was hard for him to articulate his thoughts. When he became anxious, he would block and choke up so that he could not speak.

George was one of seven children. An older brother and two younger sisters lived at home with George and the mother. The father had deserted the family about the time George entered school and had had virtually no contact with the family since. Even before his final desertion he had been irresponsible, leaving home for periods of a month or more. Things were difficult for the family after the father left and they were often short of food and fuel. At first, they were supported by Aid to Dependent Children. Later, the mother went to work nights to maintain the family, while the oldest daughter took over the care of the children. From an early age, George worked at odd jobs after school to help out.

George could recall very little about his father. He denied having any hostility toward him for deserting the family; to the contrary, he stressed his liking for him and said he found him pleasant during his later infrequent visits to the family.

Throughout his early years George had been engaged in a struggle for his mother's love. She was preoccupied with the problem of trying to maintain her large, fatherless family and was also absorbed in the care of the two children younger than George. He felt he had not secured enough affection from his mother and as a child was irritated and angry about this. He remembered lying in bed wishing he had some woman who loved him as much as he loved her. His boyhood dream was to have enough money so his mother would not have to work. He felt close to his oldest sister, but at eleven he lost her when she married and left the household. A very bad time ensued. He felt alone and unhappy, isolated from the rest of the family. His older brother Jim, who was bigger and more adept in sports, had become the dominant person in the family, the one to whom the mother listened. He was bossy toward George and generally scornful of him. George felt most sympathetic toward his youngest sister, who, like himself, seemed to have little in common with other family members.

During this period of deep unhappiness George ran away from home several times. He often truanted from school to wander about downtown, and men tried to pick him up. During one of his runaways he was seduced into a homosexual act. Although George was extremely frightened and repelled by this experience, there was also a certain fascination in it. Since that time he had been bothered by homosexual fantasies, which occurred when he saw men to whom he was drawn.

Until this seduction George had had some relationships with girls, but now he gradually withdrew. At the time he came to us, he did not date and was ill at ease in his few experiences in mixed groups. His family thought it odd that he never went out with girls, and to forestall their questions, he would tell them he had a date and then go to the movies by himself.

To George, all sexual impulses were "bad." One of the reasons he was uncomfortable with other boys was their sexual talk regarding girls; he thought such discussions were "vulgar and indecent." Behind George's feeling that sex was "dirty and disgusting," lay his basic concern that he could not prove himself sexually adequate with a woman. The whole idea of heterosexuality frightened him because he feared that a woman would not find him desirable. Although George stressed his homosexual feelings, heterosexual feelings were very much on his mind and he frequently had fantasies about sexual relationships with girls.

What contact George was having with the opposite sex was confined to older women, who were less threatening because they did not represent eligible sexual partners. These women were friends of his oldest sister whom he visited in the sister's home and with whom he discussed intellectual matters. Earlier, George had been quite preoccupied with heterosexuality. In the elementary grades he had a crush on a girl in school and was jealous of her attention to other boys. Until he dropped out of high school he visited frequently with a girl neighbor of his own age. He did not dare make any affectionate advances to her, however, though he had many fantasies about her.

George was able to recall two experiences that had traumatic sexual implications for him. When he first entered school he wet the bed several times and had been greatly frightened when his mother threatened to cut off his penis unless he stopped wetting. A few years later he had an erection while his mother was supervising his bath. She accused him of masturbating and said it would lead to insanity.

The inhibition, whose origin was over sexual issues, had spread to many areas of George's character structure. In beginning casework treatment, he presented the picture of a quiet, unassertive, apologetic person who inhibited not only his sexual feelings but also most of his aggressive impulses. He found it very difficult to express anger or admit hostility, even though it might be realistically justified. He thought it "wrong" to show anger or dislike people.

George was self-conscious and easily embarrassed. One of his central preoccupations was his constant comparison of himself with other men, in which he always felt the other men were bigger, stronger, and better than he. George suffered from a painful sense of inferiority and carefully avoided all situations where he might be called upon to compete with men. He had never been good in sports and consequently shied away from them. When some possibility of a clash loomed on either a verbal or physical level, George would retreat. His attitude was similar in relation to competition for girls. Even on those occasions when a girl clearly showed that she preferred him to another boy, George would withdraw in favor of the other boy.

With treatment George was able to bring out more of his inner feelings and to disclose that he had a real fear of men—fear of their power and authority. Though he knew it was irrational, he had a specific dread that continued: when he rode on a bus and some big man sat beside him, he became alarmed that this man might assault him. This fear of men turned out to be George's basic psychodynamic problem, and his major defensive structure had been built up to protect him against this anxiety.

George's conflict over competitive aggression came to a head during his high school years, when he was struggling with the stresses presented by adolescence. The unsuccessful handling of this conflict was the predominant factor in George's dropping out of school. Prior to adolescence the issues of sexuality and competition are not impelling, and George, with his good intellectual capacity, had been able to make excellent marks in grammar school. High school entry roughly corresponds to the onset of adolescence, the developmental stage in which sexual competence and rivalry with other males become very important for boys. George was not emotionally equipped to deal with these problems. He tried to inhibit the impulses, isolating himself from the peer group by his oddness and unaccessibility. Moreover, his inhibition directly affected his school performance. "I would sit all tightened up in class waiting for my turn to recite. When I was called on, I choked up and just couldn't talk."

George did not enjoy high school, since he could not participate in its social life and felt like an outsider. His classmates called him a "sissy" and a "goody-goody." His marks began to slip, and by his sophomore year he was doing mediocre work. In a desperate effort to rid himself of the "goody-goody" label and thereby gain entry into social groups of boys, he gave up studying. Still he was not accepted. His discouragement and unhappiness with school deepened, and he dropped out. The reason he gave the school authorities was a need for employment in order to contribute financially at home, but George knew at the time that this was not the real reason.

The genesis of George's difficulty was an unresolved oedipal conflict, the result of his inability to work out satisfactorily the universal dilemma, of young boys around the age of five, of sexual longings for the mother, hostility toward the father as a rival, and a fear of punishment from the father for the forbidden wishes. The father's desertion occurred at a most damaging and crucial time—at the height of George's oedipal period. His unconscious wish to have his father out of the way had been gratified. Therefore, his unconscious guilt over hostility to his father and the related fear of retaliation from him became especially intense. The loss of his father deprived George of the paternal care and interest that normally help a boy to deal with oedipal guilt and fear and lead him toward masculine identification and the eventual achievement of a satisfactory heterosexual adjustment.

The twofold consequences of this unresolved conflict—fear of males because of desires for women and the lack of a suitable male with whom to identify—were the most important factors in George's developing the defense of inhibition. He attempted to handle his anxiety over rivalry with males by avoiding competition with them and acting as if he were not a man. His homosexual feelings were dynamically a secondary defense that he had erected against the emergence of the dangerous heterosexual wishes. George's ultimate need was character reconstruction, and for this, psychoanalysis would be required. It was agreed, however, in consultation with the agency's psychoanalyst, that for the present, casework was the more desirable treatment. Psychoanalysis was likely to offer more fruitful results when the boy was older and his life situation more stable. Since he was too frightened to derive the fullest benefit from analysis, the preliminary experience in casework counseling might serve as good preparation for subsequent analytic therapy. In addition, George needed help currently in achieving better social functioning and in developing plans for further education, both of which goals lent themselves to casework methods.

While the casework objectives with George were more limited

than the basic character changes that would result from psychoanalysis, an active, interpretive type of therapy was still necessary in the casework process. Throughout, the counselor alleviated the boy's anxiety about homosexual feelings and supported his conscious objections to acting upon them. The intensive work, however, was structured around an approach to his inhibitions and the various ramifications of this defense at it affected his feelings, relationships, and behavior. Through exploration and appropriate interpretive comments, he came to understand how his current behavior and attitudes had grown out of his past experiences and relationships. He was helped to recognize that his central problem was not homosexuality but fear of punishment for heterosexual desires.

The treatment medium was the relationship with a male caseworker. The counselor represented the kind father figure, providing emotional support and gratification and a model for masculine identification. Gradually, George became free enough to express some anger toward the counselor. As this was accepted and discussed, he learned from a living experience that it was not dangerous to assert himself with another man. An intensive treatment approach was possible because George had an adequate ego development and was intelligent, introspective, and motivated to work on his emotional problems.

The counselor did not initiate any direct discussion about education or suggest that George return to school. The focus was on the boy's emotional life. Nevertheless, as George's problems eased, as his inhibition diminished and anxiety lessened, he was able to make constructive plans on his own. He himself brought up the possibility of going back to high school and eventually entering college. He followed through by enrolling at public night school and made sound plans for the completion of his education. George continued his daytime employment and was able to combine work and school quite successfully. He received excellent grades and began to participate in school social groups.

George became similarly aggressive about employment. Of his own volition he decided it was time to leave his poorly paid, routine job. He obtained a more satisfying position at a larger salary and told his counselor with considerable pleasure and pride that he had won the job over many other applicants.

In social relationships George grew freer and more secure, finding it easier to talk to people. He made healthy strides in his relationship with the opposite sex and began to have occasional dates. Family relationships also became more gratifying. In pleased surprise George mentioned that his older brother must be "changing," since he was now treating George with more respect. On second thought, however, George concluded it was he who had changed and the brother's altered behavior had been mainly in response to George's aggressiveness.

Treatment came to a close at the end of eighteen months. There was a mutual understanding that at a later date George might decide upon psychoanalysis for fuller resolution of his remaining intrapsychic problems. A year later he paid a friendly visit to his counselor, requesting information about arranging for analysis. At that time he was in his last year of high school and was preparing to take college entrance examinations.

JOE   *Diagnosis:* Infantile-demanding character formation
        School Dynamic: Dependency

Joe was referred shortly before his sixteenth birthday. Although his intellectual capacity was good, he had been doing poor academic work for many years and now was failing in four major subjects; truanting and cutting had started rather recently.

Joe's family consisted of his mother and a stepfather. The mother was an attractive, likable woman. Her mother had died leaving five children ages two to twelve. Her father tried to keep the family together, but arrangements were always makeshift and there was much financial hardship. During her high school years she earned room and board by keeping house for a querulous, demanding, and moralistic aged couple. She took a commercial course in high school and after graduation was able to find and hold a well-paying clerical position in a defense plant. Almost completely dominated by her father, she acceded to his demand that she endorse her pay checks to him and also continue to work for the aged couple.

Through a girl at work she met a soldier on leave and impulsively eloped with him. In a few days he left for overseas duty and she never heard from him again. Her father was enraged by her marriage and when she told him she was pregnant he washed his hands of her. The aged couple turned her out, too, and she went to live in her girl friend's apartment. She had no medical care until the day she delivered her baby. In later years when the mother wanted to get a divorce she learned her husband had died in an automobile accident.

Joe's early years were spent in a series of foster homes, his mother paying for his care. She tried intermittently to keep him with her, but his day care presented problems. Joe's last foster home was especially poor: he was improperly clothed and generally neglected. When he reacted by becoming enuretic, his foster mother locked him in a small closet. Joe's mother immediately took him away, but since she still could not manage to have him at home with her, she sent him to a boarding school where he remained for a year.

Joe's experience at the boarding school was unhappy. He was mistreated by a group of older boys when he was unable to perform certain tasks to their satisfaction. They tied him to the top landing of a fire escape on two occasions. When Joe's mother found rope marks on his body, she withdrew him, and from then on he lived with her.

Having been deprived of his mother for so long, Joe had a great need to be close to her. He kept asking if she loved him. By the time he was nine or ten, his mother had begun to go out occasionally and neighbors sat with him. Joe hated to see his mother leave, however, and would get "sick to his stomach" after she left. Only when she married his stepfather was a normal family unit established for the first time.

Joe was a good-looking boy who made an excellent superficial impression because he was outgoing and had a great deal of ingratiating appeal. As a result of his charm and his proficiency in sports, Joe had a number of friends and was popular in the club group to which he belonged.

Within the home and in any close, significant relationship, however, Joe's outstanding characteristic was his demandingness —his expectation that people would cater to him. He made a great deal of fuss over any triviality concerning his comfort. For instance, instead of buttering his own toast, he insisted his mother be on hand to do it. Because he liked to sleep later than the rest of the family, he expected that a special breakfast be made for him. He also suggested, half seriously, that his breakfast be served in bed on holidays. As one would suspect, food had a great significance for this orally oriented boy, and he was a voracious eater.

Coupled with Joe's demanding attitude was his impatience to have his wishes satisfied. He had little tolerance for the postponement of gratification and became quite irritable if he had to wait. Although he received an ample weekly allowance on Friday, it was gone by Monday, and for the rest of the week he badgered his mother for more money.

Another trait was his ability to manipulate people so that they provided what he wanted. He used various devices from whining to threatening. He had a particular talent for making his mother feel guilty if she did not accede to his demands. He would accuse her of not loving him, and she would become extremely upset. When Joe's parents were reluctant to sign for his student driver's permit, he threatened to drive without one, pointing out that this would cause them a great deal of trouble.

Joe also used his religious precepts in an attempt to rationalize and maintain his irresponsible ways. When his mother remonstrated about his poor grades and urged him to think more about his future, he replied: "The Golden Rule means 'live and let live' to me and I'm not hurting anybody. You don't have to make good grades or be a millionaire to get into heaven—better to have people like you and I've got lots of friends."

Joe's harassing experience in the boarding school added to the emotional damage he had already suffered as a result of his unsettled life. He failed the first grade at the boarding school. After he returned to live with his mother, he entered public school. His mother begged that he be placed in second grade, and the school authorities permitted this on condition that she help him with his reading. Joe's mother told the caseworker how hard she worked with her son. She kept him up late to study in order that he might pass and every Saturday took him to story hour at a library to stimulate an interest in reading.

Joe was promoted regularly in elementary school but with grades far below his potential. His teachers, knowing his capacity, often became exasperated and kept telling him that he should do much better. While Joe never presented a serious disciplinary problem in elementary school, he was usually involved in the small annoyances created by this kind of demanding, irresponsible child. His mother was frequently called to school because of his behavior and his failure to hand in home work.

Joe's truanting began in high school. He made no attempt to hide his intense dislike of school and said he would leave just as soon as he could. His fantasy about leaving school was quite in keeping with his personality structure—it was in terms of an alluring gratification that lay in wait for him. He would get a "good-paying job" and then realize his ultimate purpose to buy a car—a Thunderbird. Joe's manipulative and threatening manner was very evident in a discussion he had with the school principal. Both he and his mother had been called in by the principal, who stated he would expel the boy unless he stopped truanting. Joe triumphantly declared that this gave him an excellent idea of how to get out of school.

Joe's mother was a person with many ego strengths and had shown great resourcefulness in dealing with numerous handicaps. Her marriage to Joe's stepfather was basically good. Genuinely devoted to her son, she was deeply concerned about his problems. She spontaneously revealed to the counselor her belief that her own attitudes had contributed to his difficulties. She felt very guilty about his early life, and in her anxiety to make up for his past deprivation she had become overprotective and indulgent. Her behavior intensified Joe's immature, demanding attitude.

Along with her overprotectiveness, Joe's mother tended to be suspicious. She constantly gave him "suggestive warnings" about things he must not do, even though there was no evidence that he would have done them. She rummaged through his room looking for sex literature, questioned him minutely about his friends and activities, and, in general, was smothering what potential the boy did have for growth.

Joe was fortunate in having a stable stepfather who not only cared about him but understood how his past experiences had contributed to the current problems. The stepfather recognized that his wife was too hovering and indulgent but hesitated to interfere, for fear of offending her. Nevertheless, Joe respected his stepfather, and the excellent relationship between them was a great asset.

On his sixteenth birthday and in the initial treatment stage Joe insisted on dropping out of school. He left school ostensibly to earn money. Following his drop-out, however, his basic demandingness could be observed in even sharper perspective than before. He made virtually no attempt to obtain a job. He slept late, obtained money from his mother on the pretext of needing carfare to look for work, and then went to the school lunch hangout to chat and eat with friends. He took a nap in the afternoon, got up for dinner, and then went out for the evening.

It became apparent that Joe would not find work on his own. It was also clear that a job was important, not only for obvious reasons but as a therapeutic necessity in the process of trying to help him toward maturity.

Despite his patent resistance to work, Joe at least verbalized a wish for employment. This fact was utilized in treatment. The counselor proceeded with a firm, reality based approach, structuring interviews around the tacit assumption that Joe wanted to work. Valuable aid came from the Illinois State Employment Service; the agency was interested and helpful about effecting a suitable placement. It was decided that Joe needed a work environment where the element of personal relationships was important and where there also were normal expectations about productivity. Although Joe was reluctant to approach the agency for an initial interview, out of his liking for his counselor, he agreed to do so when the counselor offered to accompany him, to introduce him, and to assist him with forms and procedures.

The ISES was able to place Joe in a clerical position at a large firm where the general atmosphere was benevolent and paternalistic. Obtaining this particular job turned the tide for Joe. His colleagues and superiors were friendly, and he felt proud to be connected with a well-known place of business. There was an initial period when he failed to get up on time and was late for work. Coordinated counseling efforts with the parents and with Joe, however, kept this behavior to a minimum. Gradually the gratifications inherent in the job, especially in the weekly pay checks, overcame Joe's childish wish to get something for nothing. He learned the important lesson that he could obtain satisfaction through his own efforts.

Joe progressed in treatment and profited from his experiences. On one occasion he cut continuation school, which he still had to attend one day a week. In order to make up this class Joe had to miss a day's work as well as a day's pay. He later told his stepfather that he really had learned his lesson from this experience. He said ruefully, "What fun did I have anyway on the day I skipped?" From then on the boy's attendance at work and continuation school was regular.

Counseling with Joe terminated when he was performing well on the job, was much happier at home, and was on the whole conducting himself in a more grown-up way.

Work with the parents was just as important as work with the adolescent. Joe's mother, in particular, had quite intensive counseling, and she continued in treatment for some time after Joe terminated because of her belief that she could use more help for herself.

The treatment method selected for her was one of supporting and expanding her ego. She quickly formed a relationship in which the counselor represented the benevolent and wise maternal figure. Talking readily about her problems, she was well motivated for change.

The caseworker provided her with practical advice and guidance in handling Joe. The chief focus was on aiding her to become more consistent and appropriately firm with her son and to allow him a suitable amount of responsibility. She eased up on her suspiciousness, and as she did so, her suggestive warnings and tendency to nag decreased. Other constructive changes in her attitudes toward Joe occurred fairly soon. She also achieved considerable gains in her own intrapsychic comfort, growing more relaxed and self-confident. As she hovered less over Joe, she turned more of her energies to her husband and to other satisfactions and interests.

The help Joe's mother received in dealing with him came not only from practical discussions about day-to-day functioning but from the understanding she obtained about her unconscious need to overprotect and indulge him. She came to recognize how her attempt to make up to her son for past deprivations had resulted in her infantilizing him.

The stepfather's judgment in handling his stepson was sound. As his wife changed and as he received support from the agency, the stepfather was free to assume his proper paternal role. Joe's improvement reflected not only the work with his own therapist but the healthier attitude of his parents and the total improvement in family life.

KEITH   *Diagnosis:* Overcompensated character formation
         School Dynamic: Competitive aggression

Many of the boys whose dynamic involvement in school was competitive aggression were timid and inhibited in the school setting. Keith's defenses, however, were of the opposite variety. He was tending toward an overcompensated character formation and, in keeping with this syndrome, was loud, exhibitionistic, and given to bragging. Underneath, he was quite insecure and sensitive. He was an only child, born late in his parents' marriage. The father was a simple, uneducated man who was rather quiet and passive. The mother was a self-educated, aggressive, highly emotional woman who had many intellectual interests. She depreciated her husband and often criticized him to Keith for being weak and unsuccessful.

In Keith's developmental years, his mother had been overpossessive and highly stimulating, and as a result he was stirred by more sexual feelings than he could master. His oedipal problem at adolescence was therefore more complicated than that of most other boys. Moreover, the path for the normal solution to this conflict was blocked. Because Keith did not want to identify with a depreciated father figure, he tried to deal with his unconscious oedipal anxiety through the character defense of over-compensation. By his overt behavior he attempted to remove himself from and to deny any likeness to either his weak father or his intellectual mother. Keith became part of a group of semi-delinquent boys who sneered at any idea of conformity, derided school as having no virtue, and spent much of their time riding around in cars looking for sexual conquests.

The students in Keith's school were predominantly Jewish and had conventional middle-class standards. In a further effort to escape from his own background and the conformity represented by the middle-class group, Keith denied he was Jewish. He wore clothes typical of the aggressively acting-out group: tight jeans hung low on his hips, long sideburns, and a duck tail haircut. His idea of being a man was, in his own words, "to be a sharp operator, to con, fake, and bluff your way through life." Even in his own group, Keith was not popular because of his overbearing ways. At home he was ill-tempered, shouting at and arguing with his mother.

In the classroom Keith's need to compete aggressively made him a trial to teachers. He attempted to make himself the center of attention and sulked if he did not succeed. He talked constantly, interrupted other students, and laughed loudly if they made an error. He played pranks calculated to make the teacher look foolish. Since he was out with his gang every evening, he did little studying and his schoolwork was poor. But when he received a poor grade, he argued with the teacher that the grade was unfair.

Keith had attended high school for two years when we first saw him. Barely passing, he was thinking of quitting school. A perceptive teacher referred him to the agency, sensing that something about him did not ring true, that he seemed unhappy and not as tough as his outward swagger indicated.

For a year and a half, Keith came regularly to counseling, and treatment was markedly successful. In part, this was because his character disorder was not crystallized but still in the formative stage. Keith was also well motivated for change, since his defenses were not operating successfully. Aside from his general discouragement, one of the reasons he considered leaving school was his fear that the behavior of his gang was becoming too wild. He thought it was headed for real trouble and felt vaguely that he should get away from it. He did not know how this could be accomplished, however, except by leaving school and moving into a totally new environment.

The foundation of treatment was the counselor's role as a masculine figure with whom Keith was able to identify. Through him the boy was able to obtain a firmer and more comfortable sense of masculinity. An educative process went on at the same time. Because of his lengthy association with a rowdy, lower-class group, Keith was bewildered about acceptable social behavior. He was able to discuss this with his counselor and learned about behavior suitable to the groups to which he hoped to belong.

Even more important, the interpretive approach employed in counseling resulted in insight and subsequent modification of defenses. In counseling sessions, Keith and the counselor examined his past to ascertain why the compensatory defense had arisen, what neurotic purposes it served, and how he was presently acting out certain events of his past life. The oedipal conflict was not directly interpreted but aspects of it were discussed in terms the boy could readily accept, as for example the depreciated position of his father in the household and the effect this had on Keith.

Keith participated fully and freely in treatment. He was enthusiastic and zestful. The energy that had previously gone into creating his façade of toughness was redirected. It was now used to introspect, to make discoveries about himself, and to begin social activities with a different class of peers.

As he moved along in treatment, he became able to confide his concern about his masculinity. Feeling inadequate, he feared girls would not like him for himself alone, so he had lied about his worldliness and sexual experiences in order to impress them. Keith had been ashamed that, unlike the rest of his gang, he had not had any actual sexual experience because he had not been able to bring himself to engage in sexuality on a casual basis. He was immensely relieved when he recognized that physical displays of sexual prowess were no proof of true manhood and that really mature sexuality entailed a relationship with and affection for one's sexual partner. Keith also began to understand that intellectual interests were thoroughly compatible with manliness and that being a good student meant neither becoming a "square" nor a "dopey grind," as he had feared.

As Keith gained a feeling of security about himself as a person and a male, rapid changes appeared in almost all areas of his functioning. The boy himself was surprised at the changes. He reported in a rather puzzled way that now that he was studying more his school subjects were suddenly becoming much more interesting.

Keith's relationships with girls grew easier and more gratifying. He became comfortable in dating because he no longer felt under constant pressure to "prove himself a man." The experience that reassured him the most was the discovery that girls began to like him after he gave up telling lies and exaggerations.

During treatment there was an interesting example not only of Keith's own suggestibility but of behavior often typical of adolescents. Some improvement had occurred. He had toned down his former delinquent type of dress and was becoming acquainted with the world of intellect and delving into it enthusiastically. One day he happened to attend a special exhibit of pictures at the Art Institute. Very impressed, for a few weeks thereafter Keith fancied himself a budding artist. He blossomed out in disheveled Bohemian attire and deliberately neglected his personal hygiene. He told his counselor that people stared at him on the street but he was certain they did so because his sloppy appearance convinced them he was an artist.

The boy's last stand of rebellion was to cling to his duck tail haircut. The counselor never discussed it with Keith, but one day he appeared with a becoming crew cut. He explained sheepishly that he had cut his hair only because he was looking for a summer job and thought the new haircut would be more acceptable to employers.

Neither parent participated in counseling to any extent, and we found that work with them was not essential. Keith's problems were such that he could proceed on his own, and his parents did not interfere with his treatment. His mother came in a few times, but she was not well and we did not press her to continue. She was pleased that we were working with Keith, since she felt she was too old to know how to deal with an adolescent boy. She was also gratified with his progress and found him much more reasonable at home. Keith's relationship with his father improved, too. As the boy grew more confident about his own masculinity, he began to see admirable qualities in his father, and his respect for him grew. When his mother depreciated his father, he told her easily but firmly that he cared about both his parents and he did not want to hear her say unfavorable things about his father.

At the time of termination of treatment Keith was graduating from high school and making plans to enter college. His grades had improved to the point where he was eligible for college admission. He had worked out a constructive sublimation of his exhibitionistic tendencies by becoming active in a temple drama group.

LAURA   *Diagnosis:* Adjustment reaction of adolescence in
                              a hysterical character type
                  School Dynamic: Conflict in another area

Laura's situation is particularly illustrative of adolescent problems because her behavior stemmed from a struggle with basic adolescent issues: (1) the effort to become emancipated from the parents and the attempt to overthrow the superego values they represent; (2) the striving to manage increased sexual pressures; and (3) the oedipal hostility to the parent of the same sex. Laura's difficulties were clinically transitional rather than representative of a deep pathology, but this did not mitigate the severe consequences of her behavior.

The parents were intelligent, capable people who functioned in an orderly way. The father was a quiet, conscientious man; the mother was soft-spoken and gentle. At the time of referral Laura was beginning her junior year in high school. She had two older brothers. A tall, heavy-set girl with a sharp, eager expression,

Laura was verbal and quick witted, talking explosively with an air of dramatic determination.

For some time Laura had been having school difficulties and associating with undesirable companions. But the immediate problem bringing the parents to the agency was their fear that Laura was engaging in irregular sexual conduct. Laura had in fact had no sexual experience, and actually there was no likelihood of sexual misbehavior. Her allusions to sexuality were mainly of a provocative nature aimed at arousing her mother. This provocative attitude was generally characteristic of her. She was defiant and argumentative with her parents, and they found it impossible to reason with her. Laura had attached herself to a boy of bad reputation who had had some encounters with the police. Her best girl friend was also from a delinquent group.

Laura's explosiveness was apparent in an incident involving her father. They had an argument, and her father refused to let her go out that evening. The girl raised such a shrieking clamor that her father feared the neighbors would think he was beating her. She then left a note for her mother, who was out of the home at the time, "Either you divorce that man or I am running away. And I'm not kidding about this." The parents were helpless in knowing how to deal with Laura and seemed afraid of her.

Laura's academic problems, like the rest of her difficulties, began in high school. In grammar school she did well and received excellent grades. At the time of referral she was failing three courses, was barely passing a fourth, and had a record of frequent cutting and truanting. Inattentive in class, she had given up doing any school work. Her teachers' reactions to her ranged from anger to pity, depending on their personal feelings. One teacher recommended that the girl be removed from class for the balance of the semester. Another endeavored to be helpful by keeping Laura from the notice of the attendance authority. She called the parents when the girl cut and asked them to bring her back to school. Laura's mother sought to cover up for her by writing false excuses. She was uncomfortable about doing this but was bewildered about what else to do, as she feared there would be further trouble if Laura came to the attention of the school's disciplinary personnel.

Though Laura proclaimed her hatred for school, she revealed in counseling that this dislike and her cutting and truanting had little to do with school itself. She said she was so mixed up about her troubles with her parents and friends that she "just needed time to think." Whenever her tension and confused feelings became too strong, she left school and went home. "There I would sit, listen to music and try to get things straightened out in my mind."

There was nothing seriously traumatic in Laura's previous history. For the most part she had been a happy, vivacious child, friendly with other children and affectionate with her parents. When she entered adolescence, however, she was not prepared to handle the problem of sexuality. Her mother was sexually inhibited and overreacted to normal adolescent manifestations of interest in sex; Laura unconsciously identified with her mother's inhibitions.

The family lived in a small apartment, the boys sleeping on couches in the living room. In her zeal for modesty the mother gave such constant admonitions about wearing bathrobes and closing doors that her well-meant warnings created an atmosphere of sexual stimulation and preoccupation. The result for Laura was a heightened sexual conflict when she came into adolescence. This factor, the normal oedipal rivalry, and the general adolescent push for independence combined their pressures to lead to her rebellious behavior. The rebellion was prolonged by the parents' unsure handling. With no adequate external structure for the containment of her impulses, Laura became frightened and stimulated to more rebellion.

Early in the management of the case the counselor established herself as a person not anxious about or fearful of the truculence the girl displayed. Laura therefore obtained relief from the fear of her own aggressive impulses, since she could find in the counselor a source of adult strength for control.

Treatment centered on educative methods designed to enlarge the scope of Laura's ego. Some techniques were advice giving, pointing out reality, and examining the results of her unwise behavior. As she became more firmly attached to the counselor, she was confronted with her projective defense. She had depicted herself as less favored than her siblings, and therefore justifiably angry with her parents. This was not true; Laura had not been deprived of parental affection. Following recognition of her defense of projection, she realized her own part in creating her troubles and gained more ability to control herself. Improvement was rapid and sustained, with Laura making noticeable gains in school, at home, and with her friends.

Treatment of the parents, especially the mother, was an important feature of this case. The mother's anxiety required relief. In particular, she needed to re-establish confidence in her role as a parent. Supported by the counselor, she became less fearful of Laura's anger, learned to distinguish between vital issues where the girl had to be limited and areas where yielding was advisable, and discontinued covering up for her daughter. Laura kept in occasional touch with her counselor long after formal termination of treatment. She was graduated from high school and subsequently married a suitable young man of whom her parents approved.

MAY   *Diagnosis:* Anxiety reaction in a hysterical character formation
        School Dynamic: Conflict in another area

May was in the second semester of high school when the school's attendance counselor referred her. She had a panic reaction to attending school; if forced to attend, she developed symptoms of fainting, dizziness, and vomiting. At the time of referral May was remaining away from school a week at a time, only attending intermittently.

May's father had died six months before. She had been very attached to him and reacted strongly to his death. Shortly after his death May had experienced a number of other unhappy changes in her life. Her mother took on an evening job, and May was left alone a great deal. A sister of whom she was very fond married and left home. The family moved to a new neighborhood where May had no friends. All these changes occurred as she was beginning adolescence.

May was an attractive, intelligent, highly articulate girl. When she attended school, she was liked by her classmates. She herself valued education and revealed to the counselor her hope of becoming an occupational therapist in order to help other people.

On the surface the problem seemed to be a serious and complex school phobia based on deep unconscious factors. Careful evaluation disclosed, however, that this was not the case. May was utilizing the school issue quite consciously to work out a struggle in her relationship with her mother.

In counseling, May brought out her great need for attention from her mother. Moreover, she had to have attention the instant she wanted it, and she became angry if she had to wait even a few minutes. May did not understand why she had this desperate urge for more closeness with her mother. She knew only that staying away from school to remain at home with her mother and to make constant demands on her seemed deeply satisfying.

May's mother was an ambitious woman who placed a high premium on education. Thus, May's choice of symptoms—not going to school—threatened the mother in a most vulnerable spot. Appearances were very important to her. She presented herself as a devoted, self-sacrificing mother, but she was basically cold and self-centered and had little affection to give to May. As a child the girl had experienced inconsistent warmth and mothering, though her material needs were met. Consequently, May had many unresolved oral problems.

Our case material revealed, however, that May's major current struggle was oedipal. She was having more than usual difficulty in solving the family triangle problem because of the recent death of her father. May's hostile demands on her mother were open and tenacious, but they were a defense against unconscious problems. She tried to make it appear that her relationship with her mother was that of a little girl. By emphasizing her dependency, May kept out of awareness the basic cause of her deepest anxiety—the oedipal conflict in which she was competing with mother on a sexual basis.

The most immediate goal of the casework treatment was getting May back to school. If she continued to stay away much longer, her inability to make up lost work might cause her to leave school as soon as legally possible. Because our diagnostic assessment revealed that May's school difficulties resulted from conscious factors subject to her control, we were able to help her to return to school rather early.

Since May was an intensely anxious girl, attempts to work toward insight in any areas such as the oedipal could not be undertaken for a long time. We felt that the best approach toward early help lay in establishing a strong dependent relationship between May and the counselor, who became in effect a substitute maternal figure providing the warmth and interest that May's mother had no capacity to supply. In this way her involvement with her mother and her need to act out would diminish.

This plan worked successfully. May formed a close and meaningful attachment to her counselor. She came regularly for interviews and poured out much about herself, her feelings, and her need to remain away from school. At an appropriate time the counselor mentioned that school for May had somehow become tied up with her mother and had no independent existence or value of its own. The counselor asked why this was. May responded almost inadvertently that she didn't go to school because, "it gets my mother mad. She doesn't pay enough attention to me, and I'm paying her back." This made it clear that May's absence from school was not only a conscious attempt at closeness but also a deliberate retaliation.

The counselor commented matter of factly that May was succeeding from this point of view, but drew attention to the price May was paying for this supposed "satisfaction." Was it worth the destruction of her educational prospects and her vocational goal? Also it seemed as if May's understandable wish for more attention and affection from her mother was not being fulfilled by staying away from school. As May had to realize, she was getting less, not more, from her mother.

These apparently simple comments were therapeutically potent because they were based on an understanding of May's needs and came from a counselor who had involved the girl in a close emotional relationship. May seriously considered these new thoughts, discussed them further in succeeding interviews, and

returned to school relatively soon. Resuming the life of a high
school student, she obtained gratification from doing well in her
studies, from the approbation of her teachers, and from the
friendships she made among her peers. Another area of gratification was the improved relationship with her mother, who was
pleased with the changes. These realistic satisfactions gave May
much more pleasure than her former attempts to be treated like
an infant.

As often happens in treatment, when one portion of a problem is worked out, spontaneous insight comes about in other
areas not specifically discussed. During the time May remained
away from school she became involved with a young traveling
salesman whom she promised to marry as soon as she was of age.
One day, after she had returned to school and was functioning
better, she came in to report that her boy friend was in town.
On seeing him, she suddenly realized that she didn't like him at
all. She said she finally understood why she had been going with
him: "I had been using him only as a last resort; that is, if I
wanted to quit school, I could marry him and have a good excuse for leaving." Now that she recognized her real feeling she
felt honor bound to sever her "engagement" and did so in quite
a mature way with the least possible hurt to the young man. She
began dating boys closer to her own age.

As May continued in counseling, she obtained some understanding about herself and the causes of her school problems. She
came to see that the many upsetting events occurring just as she
entered adolescence had created great stress. Understandably,
she had reacted with tension and anxiety and in an effort to obtain comfort tried to cling to her mother. When her mother
could not tend to her every moment and asked her to go to
school, May, hurt and angry, decided to "get even" by remaining
away from school even more. May and her counselor did not
delve further into the causes.

May gave no material regarding her emotional deprivation as
a child nor did she consciously recognize her mother's maternal
deficiencies. We felt it wise to leave her strong defenses intact,
since her present functioning was good and no purpose would be
served by arousing new anxieties. For similar reasons we made no

attempt to elicit material related to her unconscious oedipal conflict.

After one year's counseling, termination was planned because May had assumed a normal role in the adolescent world. She was achieving at school, getting along with her mother, finding happiness with her friends, and taking part in suitable social activities. There were clues that May needed a period of time away from treatment in order to integrate her new adaptation. We also believed that May might make additional progress on her own through the maturation of later adolescence and constructive life experiences.

Diagnostic study indicated that May's mother was suffering from a severe and rigid character disorder. An infantile-demanding type, she was fixated at the oral-aggressive phase of development. Her reaction to casework services for May, however, was favorable: she was eager that May have counseling and did not interfere with the girl's therapy. The availability of a counselor to May and the girl's increasing reliance on the treatment relationship seemed a welcome respite for her. This is understandable not only in view of the mother's particular personality traits but also because she was caught in the middle of a very trying situation: while occupied with the important task of adjusting to a job, she was faced with May's demanding and frightening behavior.

As our exploratory contact with the mother continued, it became evident that treatment aims with her must be quite limited. Despite the use of therapeutic techniques adapted to her character pattern and dynamics, she remained essentially uninvolved, although she made superficial gestures of cooperation by coming regularly for interviews. We decided that the maximum therapeutic goal would be to contain the damaging aspects of the mother's handling of May's symptoms, averting, where possible, punishment and stress. It seemed likely that May could continue to make progress under these circumstances. We also anticipated that when May was achieving adequately in school this would meet her mother's narcissistic needs. Experiencing emotional relief, she could respond in a better manner to her daughter.

The mother's contacts with the agency dwindled and ended as soon as May showed sustained improvement, and we made no attempt to keep the mother in treatment. She phoned occasionally to tell how much better things were and how pleased she was with the result of service.

CONCLUSIONS

Introduction

EDUCATION FOR ALL CHILDREN
has long been a prime goal of our American democracy. Education is a basic requisite for responsible citizenship, for maintenance of our way of life, and for successful entry into today's
complicated working world. In the United States education is
freely available and indeed is compulsory. Yet an alarmingly large
number of intellectually capable children leave school before high
school graduation. They are wasting their mental capacities, dis-
sipating their opportunities, and circumscribing their chances
for a better life.

Educational malfunctioning may well be a much more serious
problem than juvenile delinquency. Certainly in terms of numbers it is: 40 per cent of all children do not complete high school.

Schooling is the major task of the adolescent, just as earning
a livelihood is that of the adult. Acquiring an education is an important stress that the adolescent must meet, and the capacity to
adapt to this stress is a measure of the health of his personality.
What happens in school is crucial to a child and determines not
only the outcome of his vocational future and his effectiveness
as a citizen but also the integration of his personality.

Most adolescents develop the controls necessary for adapting to school life. That a large proportion of our youngsters do not or cannot deserves exploration.

What the Drop-Outs Were Like

In our project we saw 105 adolescent children referred by the Chicago public high schools as potential drop-outs. All of them had at least average mental ability but were on the verge of leaving high school before graduation.

Thus, the population consisted, by design, of children who had normal mental endowment and who, as it developed, were white, and primarily from middle-class circumstances. Because of these limitations in our sample, we cannot generalize about all drop-outs. Nevertheless, the limitations sharpen the focus and strengthen the validity of our findings for what we believe are large and important groups among all the youngsters who drop out of high school each year.

We were able to make a more thorough and detailed study of the Treatment Group of thirty-three girls and thirty-seven boys who came for four or more interviews than of the thirty-five students in the Nontreatment Group, whom we saw less often. The findings presented in this chapter are drawn from our analysis of the Treatment Group. Even though we did not have enough information to diagnose the personalities and school dynamics of the Nontreatment Group, the available information indicated that these children, too, had emotional, social, and educational problems.

The drop-out youngsters were heterogeneous in character, each with a unique personality and individual differences. Nevertheless, some striking similarities stood out.

The drop-outs had unsuccessful and unhappy school experiences.

It is theoretically possible that a student can make good use of his educational opportunities, decide that he has had all the education he needs, and then drop out at the permissible school-leaving age. We had no such students, nor do we believe there are many such youngsters in the general population.

Our drop-outs had serious and multiple school problems that interfered substantially with the educational process. Most of them were either failing in their school courses or working far below their mental capacity, a majority were also truanting or cutting classes, and about half were presenting behavior problems in school. All of the students were unsuccessful in adapting to some school requirement or regulation, and three-fourths were having trouble in more than one area of school life.

Adolescents whose emotional disturbances create school problems already have a serious, twofold difficulty. Moreover, the school problems bring in their wake a new series of stresses. Unlike some symptoms, educational problems stand out in plain view; they cannot be concealed. Children thus exposed feel resentment and shame, and loose self-esteem. Their parents are likely to voice their disappointment or anger about the school failure, adding to the youngsters' unhappiness at home. And the schools find it difficult to be sympathetic with underachieving students, especially when their behavior, as was the case in our study group, is either markedly passive or openly defiant. The outcome is that the drop-out student has many problems, and his life is onerous, with stress both at home and at school.

The drop-outs were not leaving to effect constructive plans.

The drop-outs left school because they were motivated to *run away* from a disagreeable situation; they did not feel impelled to *run toward* a definite and positive goal. Although they discussed employment, their talk was vague, aimless, or unrealistic. Most of them recognized that a high school diploma would enhance their chances for employment. The decision to drop out was the final outcome of an accumulation of school problems and the belief that it was too late to correct the difficulties. Dropping out was not only the easiest course to take but a passive, not an active, resolution of the educational problem.

In the early 1900's and through the depression years, financial stress was a major cause of premature school-leaving. Surveys in more recent years, however, have shown decisively that few children leave school because of straitened family circumstances; such was also the finding in our study. Economic deprivation can make school life more difficult and, added to other stresses, contribute to early school-leaving, but the student who drops out today is not doing so *primarily* because the family's economic situation forces him to work.

> Emotional problems were the major cause of the school difficulties and the resultant school-leaving.

The first and major hypothesis of our study was: School problems generally and early school-leaving specifically are often aspects of emotional and personality disturbances in the student. Careful diagnostic evaluation of our study group disclosed that the youngsters and their parents had serious emotional problems and that the school difficulties had resulted from emotional disturbances. Indeed, for most of the students school was only one of many areas of maladjustment.

This is not to say that realistic and environmental problems played no part in the students' lives, nor do we mean to imply that such realistic problems had no effect in deepening the school troubles as well as the emotional conflicts. The point we stress is that the basic, the predominant factor behind the school difficulty was the emotional problem.

In our group of youngsters the proof of our first hypothesis was overwhelming. It led us to the conviction that, except for those subcultural groups in which education is not an important value, the student of normal intelligence who cannot perform adequately in school and consequently drops out is almost always a student with emotional problems.

**The emotional problems of the
drop-outs were severe.**

A somewhat unexpected finding was the severity of the emotional and personality disturbances in our adolescents. We suspected that such problems would be present but did not anticipate their intensity. A very high proportion of the children (76 per cent) were suffering from character problems—maladaptations of the entire personality—in contrast to neurotic conflicts, which usually are of recent origin and more localized in effect. In a character difficulty the maladaptive behavior is widespread, rigid, and entrenched.

In addition, many adolescents with pervasive character difficulties were immature in their general personality formation and were still struggling with issues of the early developmental periods. About two-thirds of the boys and one-half of the girls were dependent children who were unwilling to assume any self-responsibility. The boys generally expressed their dependency in open helplessness and the girls by angry demands for gratification.

Neither the helpless nor the demanding youngsters were capable of the level of educational functioning required in high school. Secondary school demanded more maturity and independence than they possessed. They regarded school as an institution that not only fostered but required growing up. The helpless ones equated graduation with assuming adult responsibilities for which they were not ready and which they feared. The demanding youngsters could not adjust because they were unable to curb their frantic search for continuous and immediate dependency satisfactions.

Slightly less than a third of our youngsters had relatively mature character formations and were struggling directly with the developmental task characteristic of adolescence. This task is the integration of sexuality into the personality. In spite of their greater maturity, these students still had school problems. Most of the boys were inhibited and were in trouble because they were not achieving. Predominantly hysterical neurotics, the girls were in very serious school difficulties. Their behavior had a sexual quality that created alarm and reactions in parents and school personnel. In addition, their symptoms took the form of rebellion and acting out. Their actions not only made their school life turbulent but used up the energy that should have been going into educational endeavor.

School can take on a special psychodynamic meaning of a conflictual nature.

Emotional disturbance does not invariably result in poor school adjustment; there are maladjusted children who pour all their energies into learning to the disadvantage of other areas of life. We have observed also that some youngsters may develop severe problems in school but function quite well in their homes and communities. To learn how school became involved in the personality difficulties of our group, we formulated our fourth hypothesis: School itself has a psychodynamic meaning of a conflictual nature that is contributory to early school-leaving.

School had an unconscious and specific psychodynamic meaning for quite a large number of our students, mostly the boys. It had become involved in the dependency conflicts of some of the immature children who were afraid to grow up. Most of the more mature boys had a type of emotional disturbance that made them especially vulnerable to school problems: conflict around competitive aggression. The majority were inhibiting themselves in the face of social pressures toward aggressive masculine achievement. In high school, rivalry is intense for scholarship, sports awards, leadership, and social superiority. To the inhibited boys, seeking competence in any of these areas unconsciously represented becoming better than their fathers and carried the threat of castration. They were consciously afraid that they could not be successful and would get hurt in the process of trying to achieve. Much more security and safety lay in withdrawing from the competitive-aggressive struggle—in being nonachievers.

Some students used learning and the school environment in

an attempt to work out conflicts with their parents. They failed their courses or broke school regulations for a specific purpose: to retaliate, to arouse concern, and the like.

Although for over two-thirds of the boys school assumed a special conscious or unconscious meaning causing malfunctioning, this was true of less than one-third of the girls. The girls had equally serious school difficulties, but the majority were rebelling and acting out not in school alone but in all areas of their lives. Thus, our fourth hypothesis, that school can acquire a psychodynamic meaning of a conflictual nature, proved true for boys but not for girls. We speculate that this difference occurs because our culture considers an education more important for boys than for girls; therefore school provides a special focus for rebellion and conflict formation for boys.

Aside from the above mentioned sex difference, there were two other striking contrasts between the boys and girls.

The boys and girls differed in their approach to life and in the time of onset of the school problems.

The essence of the first, a personality difference, was that the girls created problems by their *activity*, whereas the boys caused concern by their *inactivity*. Secondly, the school problems of the boys had begun much earlier than those of the girls. The point at which school symptoms first appear is important to consider, since the earlier the recognition that a problem exists, the easier it is to resolve the problem.

The girls' symptoms did not generally appear until adolescence. Their school difficulties, as well as their emotional malfunctioning, seemed, for the most part, to be precipitated by the physiological and psychological changes of pubescence. In the elementary grades almost all of the girls had conformed and had been good students. With the beginning of adolescence, however, they displayed rebellious, acting-out behavior, often to the complete surprise of their parents and the schools. There were minor behavorial symptoms in the seventh and eighth grades but as a rule, school malfunctioning started in adolescence with entry into high school. Close examination of the histories revealed the previously hidden vulnerability of the girls to emotional problems.

Massive rebellion typically pervaded all areas of the girls' school adjustment. They became aggressive and defiant, and truancy was a frequent problem. Course failures and ultimate grade retardation were by-products of poor attendance, failure to do assignments, and misuse of class time. Because of their sudden onset, disturbances of girl students are likely to remain unrecognized until the problem is actually quite severe. From a preventive point of view, treatment should begin with the first signs of behavioral changes—especially if drop-out is to be forestalled.

In contrast, the school problems of the boys were chronic. Three-fourths of them had academic problems (usually under-functioning) in grammar school, and one-half were already in trouble by the fourth grade. Failures of certain subjects and the notation "grade repeated" were frequently found in their elementary school records. When these boys reached secondary school, they were deficient in basic reading and computational skills. Even without the concomitant emotional problems, it could have been predicted that they would have great trouble in mastering the more demanding high school curriculum.

Very early in life these boys could be characterized as passive, lacking in energy, immature in behavior. They needed much undivided attention in the classroom in order to function at even a minimal level. These personality traits were carried into adolescence, and the passive, procrastinating, ineffectual attitudes toward life were intensified. The boys now stood out more sharply than ever because their behavior and attitudes were so far removed from the masculine attributes our culture expects in adolescent boys. Truanting and class-cutting, which first became serious in high school, seemed mainly a running away from their continued poor academic performance and the increased pressure for accomplishment coming from home and school.

We have discussed certain similarities and some special sex differences among our drop-out students. A most important finding, however, was the range of variation among the children as individuals.

The drop-outs were a heterogeneous group.

Apart from the large issue of severe emotional disturbance, no other single factor could be isolated to account for school malfunctioning and premature leaving of school. Though the drop-outs had emotional problems, some kinds more frequently than others, there was no typical emotional disorder that characterized them; they ran the gamut of diagnostic classifications. In environmental aspects, the range of individual differences was also broad. The students not only came from homes of varying degrees of stability but the parents had a diversity of attitudes and character problems. In addition, some schools offered more understanding than others. Thus, the drop-outs were subject to a variety of stresses, and each youngster had his individual vulnerabilities, deficiencies, and capacities. It follows that there is no easy, over-all solution to the complex problem of school malfunctioning or early school-leaving. Help must be individualized for each student in accordance with the particular circumstances that create the emotional problems and school difficulties.

What the Parents of the Drop-Outs Were Like

Many of the parents did not involve themselves in the agency treatment plan; only a fourth came for more than five interviews.

None of the parents we were able to diagnose had a neurosis. Even the most mature were not comfortable in sexual areas. The remainder clearly had character disorders, and the majority were very immature, with characters structured around dependency needs. Most of the immature fathers were the dependent type—

weak and helpless; but half of the immature mothers were aggressive types—angry and demanding.

As one would expect, there was a high degree of similarity between character structure of the child and one or both parents.

**The parents had strong reactions
to the students' school problems.**

Some parents were shamed, others were angered by the child's school difficulties, and all reacted in negative ways. Even the well-meaning parents responded nonconstructively by withdrawing expressions of affection and instituting handicapping systems of punishments. A combination of irritation and lack of understanding led to confused and inconsistent handling, which served to aggravate an already bad situation.

**The drop-outs and their parents
had unhealthy and distorted relationships.**

Apart from the disastrous interplay occasioned by the school problems, the parents and youngsters were at odds in other areas of their relationships. The adolescent period is a time of turbulence in most families, and even calm, understanding parents occasionally run out of patience. In our drop-out group the households were often in a state of instability.

The immature mothers and fathers, minimally effective as parents during the youngster's childhood, were very inadequate in coping with the adolescent period. The physically maturing adolescents behaved in infantile ways that threatened the dependency satisfactions of the parents. The interplay in these homes was quite openly hostile.

The more mature mothers and fathers, too, had predominantly negative relationships with their children. Daughters who were trying to cope with their sexual impulses reactivated the parents' poorly resolved problems around sexuality. The parents became suspicious and restrictive, and the daughters, defiant and rebellious. The generalized passivity of the inhibited boys irritated, worried, and angered their parents. The parents nagged and pushed; the boys became more inert and ineffectual.

Regardless of the degree of maturity of parent or child, the vicious circle in process needed to be interrupted and broken.

Casework service to the parents had limited goals.

Treatment was impeded by the reluctance of many parents to involve themselves with the agency. Most of those who did come had strong defenses as could be expected in character disorders. Being very immature, they rationalized their own behavior, projected responsibility, and did not see their own role in the difficulty.

Those parents who had a strong investment in the importance of school exhibited rigid, self-righteous attitudes bolstered by society's sanction of parental concern about school malfunctioning. Quite a few parents came to the agency feeling attacked and misunderstood because of past experiences with people who had given advice.

In beginning treatment with the parents, therefore, it was necessary to focus first on lowering their defensiveness. We encouraged them to ventilate their feelings and complaints, and we created an atmosphere of sympathy and understanding. Treatment occasionally resulted in changing the parent's attitude toward the child, but in many cases our casework efforts had to be confined to containment, keeping the situation from becoming worse.

It is noteworthy that the relatively more mature mothers were much more cooperative about coming for interviews, had basically positive attitudes toward their children in spite of their deleterious reactions to the current difficulty, and often were able to accept responsibility for their part in the problem and then move ahead to change or modify their own behavior. Their children were also more mature and quicker to respond to counseling. This constellation of mature mother–mature child has a good prognosis for therapy.

Effect of Casework Service

Forty-eight per cent of the Treatment Group improved in emotional or personality functioning; 60 per cent of the forty students who remained in school improved in school adaptation; and 46 per cent of the fifty-six students of legal school-leaving age continued in school.

Our prime purpose was to determine if casework service could alleviate the personality problems that we postulated were basic to poor school functioning and the desire to leave school. We learned that treatment is a difficult and complicated task with children who are on the verge of dropping out of school. Prognosis is poor for three reasons: (1) drop-outs have serious and multiple problems (emotional, familial, educational); (2) the problems have existed for a long time and are chronic; and (3) the emotional problem is most frequently a character disturbance which by itself has a poor prognosis.

One-half of the students improved in personality functioning.

About one-half of our students improved in general personality functioning: casework treatment was able to alleviate the presenting emotional problem that interfered with the youngster's ability to manage in life. These youngsters began to live more comfortably with themselves and others. They were better equipped than before to grow into happy, productive, and responsible adults and citizens.

Based on our experience in counseling the half of our group who did not improve in personality functioning, we believe the major remedy for failure of treatment is early detection and early correction of emotional problems. For malfunctioning youngsters already in high school, one solution may lie in developing therapeutic skills for engaging and holding them in treatment. Two-thirds of the drop-outs who came for more than fifteen interviews improved in personality functioning, whereas two-thirds of those with fifteen or fewer interviews did not improve.

The drop-outs with the more mature character formations showed the greatest emotional improvement.

Two-thirds of the youngsters with more mature character structure improved in personality functioning, as compared with the improvement of only one-third of the youngsters with immature character formation. This difference is understandable, since the more mature adolescent has attained a relatively high level of personality development. A basic capacity for adequate functioning exists and can be realized if the obstacles in its path are removed or reduced by treatment.

That the mature drop-outs responded well does not imply a lack of severity in the problems they originally presented. Their malfunctioning, both in and out of school, was serious, and without help for their emotional problems, they faced a grave and uncertain future.

A number of these more mature youngsters had a neurotic form of emotional disturbance. Their improvement rate was especially high: 80 per cent achieved personality gains. Aside from having considerable ego capacity, the neurotic adolescents made progress because their problems, though severe, were of relatively recent origin. Furthermore, because they were suffering discomfort from their symptoms, they were well motivated toward treatment.

The youngsters with personality gains who continued in school improved in school adaptation.

All twelve of the boys who improved in personality functioning improved in their school life as well. Of eight improved girls, three were graduated and three improved in school adjustment. The improvement extended to all areas—academic performance, attendance, and behavior. Truancy and class-cutting were usually the first school symptoms to disappear. By contrast, and with few exceptions, the boys and girls whose emotional problems remained unchanged failed to do better in school.

The findings support our second hypothesis: Casework treatment can improve school performance by effecting a better emotional and social adjustment. We learned also that therapeutic intervention is most effective when undertaken before school problems become chronic.

More emotionally improved boys
than girls remained in school.

Casework treatment effected better personality functioning for thirteen boys of legal school-leaving age. Eight of them remained in school, and the two boys who had dropped out of school before treatment were attending night school—altogether a 77 per cent school continuation rate. Among the sixteen improved girls who were sixteen or older, three had been graduated and four remained in school—a 44 per cent continuation rate. We believe that treatment was more successful in keeping the boys in school than the girls because (1) the boys' personality problems were more school centered, and improvement of their emotional difficulties had direct and quick effects upon their school difficulties, and (2) since school is more important vocationally to boys, it coincides with their ego-ideal.

Our third hypothesis was: Casework treatment can prevent premature school-leaving. The hypothesis was substantiated for boys but proved less true for girls.

That we helped almost half of the youngsters to remain in school gains added significance in the light of our population. The students referred to us were displaying most of the classical and final symptoms associated with premature school-leaving— they comprised a group of high drop-out potential. It is likewise significant that the emotionally improved youngsters who remained in school also improved in school functioning. They not only stayed in school but were now benefiting from their educational opportunities.

Special Aspects of the Treatment Process

Treatment of the drop-out youngster, as in casework practice generally, was highly individualized, differing for each specific child according to his problems and needs. There were, however, two considerations applicable to the group as a whole: (1) the youngsters were in the adolescent phase of development; (2) their symptoms took the form of school problems. Treatment of adolescent children requires special knowledge of this age group and the therapeutic procedures appropriate to it. It is also necessary to understand how the problems with school add complications to the emotional disturbance. These cause reactions in the child and must be handled in the therapy.

School problems, however, have a further implication: they represent a symptom that the youngster is displaying in his environment. In addition to treatment of the adolescent himself, therefore, successful resolution of the difficulty in school requires work with the environment that both affects and is affected by the symptom. Of chief significance in the child's environment are the parents and school.

Treatment of parents was important for optimal help to the child. As with the children, it was an individualized process, but here, too, we learned that the existence of school problems introduced elements requiring a special approach to parents.

Collaborative work with the schools was a further essential. We found that suitable structuring of the child's school environment could make a vital contribution toward alleviating his educational symptoms and increasing his emotional growth. From our collaborative experience we gained clearer understanding of the knowledge and skills necessary for effective cooperation between social agency and school.

So far we have related our major findings and some of our ideas about premature school-leaving. Out of our special experience in working with the drop-out youngsters and our general agency experience with adolescents, we see some measures that we believe would prove helpful.

What the Schools Can Do

It is important that schools be alert for emotional problems and refer them for correction immediately.

It is necessary to give prompt attention to an individual child's problems with school and as quickly as possible to decide whether or not they are based on emotional factors outside the school's control. When school problems do not yield rather quickly to school-centered techniques, the techniques should not be continued merely out of hopefulness. This overlooks the possibility of a personality disturbance that, in turn, delays its correction. When personality problems become chronic and entrenched they are very difficult to treat. Likewise, when the student with a long history of problems related to schooling is not referred for treatment until he is on the verge of dropping out, the odds are against prevention of premature school-leaving.

It is not within the province of the schools to be able to resolve all the difficulties that students manifest. They cannot be expected to be successful in educating those whose difficulties are the result of emotional problems, and they should not look upon themselves as failures when youngsters do not adapt to school life. But schools can be alert for signs of personality malfunctioning as they manifest themselves in the school setting, and finding them, refer the children for treatment.

Some psychological orientation is highly desirable.

Educators should have an appropriate orientation to the factors that contribute to learning difficulties and poor school adjustment. Orientation to emotional factors prevents the all too easy assumption that malfunctioning in school is simply a matter of poor study habits, lack of interest, laziness, and the like, and makes possible a wider perspective that will lead to earlier detection of personality disturbances and to their earlier referral for correction.

Psychological awareness enables the school to become the educator in the larger sense of the word, to be concerned with the broader welfare of the youngster as his strengths and weakness appear in the school environment, and to make whatever efforts are possible within that environment to enhance the child's total maturation.

Tutoring is often necessary in connection with psychological treatment.

School problems of long duration cause educational gaps that must be closed in order for the youngster to perform effectively as a student. Though a school may have tried tutoring unsuccessfully before, it should be willing to give it another try when counseling has modified some of the emotional issues. Schools are in a good position to note signs of readiness for learning and then to carefully and wisely select as tutor the kind of person to whom the child can best respond.

Schools can help prevent adult character disorders.

School malfunctioning is one of the early signs of personality disturbance. Left on his own the child may adopt nonconstructive, even harmful means to master his fears and anxieties. Gradually, such maladaptations become a way of life. They do keep him from experiencing unpleasant inner feelings, but at the same time they also keep him from achieving a positive kind of happiness in healthy interpersonal relationships. At adolescence, instead of being relatively free to decide what kind of person he wants to be, the die has been cast and his character is already solidifying.

Failure in school, then, may be the first ominous sign of a budding character disorder. Prompt intervention brought about by the school's acuity in perceiving trouble and its readiness to make referral to treatment resources, provides a real service to the individual child and to society.

What the Social Agencies Can Do

Social agencies should develop specialists in the treatment of adolescents.

Because adolescents are in a complicated phase of personality development, they are a difficult group to diagnose and treat. Direct treatment experience with a large number of adolescents is necessary in order to attain the body of knowledge and the skill needed to help them. It would be advantageous, therefore, for agencies who serve a variety of age groups to assign their adolescent clients to a limited number of caseworkers. This concentrated experience would help them become specialists in the field of adolescence. They would be in a position to contribute to the general fund of information about this age group and from this larger pool of experience might come increasingly effective techniques for engaging, holding, and successfully treating adolescent youngsters.

Treatment of school problems requires special skills.

Emotionally disturbed children whose predominant symptom is a malfunctioning in school present additional considerations for treatment. Trouble at school brings into being numerous reactions and problems in the already troubled youngster and his parents.

These reactions and problems particularly affect the start of therapy.

In the beginning phase of treatment, the caseworker inherits the legacy of negative feelings and criticism the child has experienced in relation to his school difficulties. The youngster usually resists a focus on the school issue, and pressing that focus not only increases his resistance but may delay or even prevent approaching the basic personality issues behind the school symptoms. The caseworker also should be able to recognize whether or not the child uses school in a specific psychological way and if the mechanism is mainly conscious or unconscious. This knowledge helps him to decide how and at what point to deal with the school problems.

Understandably, parents and school press the caseworker for rapid improvement of the child's behavior and achievement. Their wishes must not mislead him into forcing a concentration on the school difficulty. Instead, he should endeavor, through appropriate measures, to help the parents and school tolerate the school malfunctioning at least until the caseworker has involved the youngster in a solid and meaningful relationship.

**Social workers need to become
acquainted with the schools.**

Since working with the school is a necessary part of the treatment of children with school problems, social workers should acquire an understanding of the field of education.

Therapists need a general orientation to the nature of the educational process and the philosophy and aims of educators. With such a background they will be less likely to make requests that schools cannot reasonably fulfill. They will comprehend that handling a troublesome youngster in the office of a social agency is different from the school's problem in coping with him in a mass setting. They will recognize that the authority for making educational decisions rests with the school, and that these decisions must consider many factors apart from an individual child's therapeutic needs.

Social workers should learn the organization of their local school system, know what the administrative channels are. It is very important that they understand the school personnel with whom they will work and be aware of their views and attitudes. This facilitates approaching them in an appropriate and helpful way.

Finally, the caseworker should know the particular school setting of his youngster—the school culture and socioeconomic atmosphere, the kinds of facilities available, and the school personnel with whom the child is in contact. The counselor, in short, must have some feeling of what school life is like for the youngster he is treating, what school resources can be called on, and how best to work with the educators who play an important part in the child's life.

What the Community Can Do

The community should provide resources for diagnosis and treatment of personality problems.

Resources for diagnosis and treatment should be readily available to the schools. Whether such facilities are located in the school or in the community is secondary to the necessity for providing them.

It seems advisable that within the school itself there should be social workers and psychologists whom individual teachers may consult about their students. Equally important, the school psychologists and social workers can do case studies and make diagnoses. If a student's problem can be handled in the school setting, these specialists are on the scene to help in formulating a plan, putting it into effect, watching its progress, and, when indicated, modifying the plan to meet new conditions. If the student needs psychotherapy for his problem, the specialist can make the proper referral, interpret treatment to the school, and help the social agency.

It is less certain that treatment of the personality problems should occur within the school setting. Although in some practical ways this would facilitate the student's therapy, we have questions about its over-all efficacy that require further study.

Special schools are needed.

Some students need a highly structured and controlled environment. Because of their personality difficulties they present insuperable problems in classroom management and should be removed from the regular schools both for their own sake and that of the other class members.

The special school should be therapeutically oriented—not a custodial institution. It should offer an academic curriculum—not vocational training exclusively, or busy-work courses. Its distinctive feature would be the combined educational-therapeutic milieu created by a staff of educators, psychiatrists, psychologists, and social workers.

Some provision should be made for service to drop-outs.

The recommendations made to this point have been aimed directly at early intervention in personality disturbances to facilitate better emotional and school adjustment and thus prevent premature school-leaving. But the students who actually drop out of school need help too. Some agency or service should actively keep in touch with drop-outs to assist them in locating jobs and in making good work adjustments.

The same emotional problems that create school maladjustment interfere with employment and vocational adjustment. Statistics show that drop-outs have high rates of job changes and of unemployment. With an incomplete education and few skills for bargaining in the employment world, they drift from job to job, and intermittently their support may fall upon the community resources.

At present, in our agency's current work with drop-outs, we

note that after some of the emotional issues have been resolved
and/or after the student has first-hand realization that lack of
a high school education is an employment handicap, there is an
interest in returning to school, usually on a part-time basis. With
the caseworker's encouragement and practical help in finding
and enrolling in a school, the interest often matures into an actuality. There are drop-outs in the general population who become interested in continuing their education and who would do
so with a little help.

Ideally of course, the drop-out should receive treatment for
the emotional problems that were basic to the school difficulties
and that will now interfere with other life adjustments. We believe, however, that a special service could do a great deal to help
drop-outs in making a better adjustment to employment.

**The community must become
alert to the need for therapists
trained in the problems of children and of adolescents.**

Successful casework service with elementary school children
and with adolescents, who represent separate groups with separate
needs, requires special training and skills. The professions of
social work, psychology, and psychiatry should be made attractive to young people in the process of selecting vocations. As
malfunctioning in school comes to be seen as a symptom of
personality disturbance that requires correction before school
adaptation can improve and school-leaving be averted, there will
be a growing need for the services of these professions.

Finally, the community should have no illusions about the
enormity of the drop-out problem nor about the quality, quantity and cost of the service necessary to prevent young people from dropping out of school. But in the long run the
cost is less than that created by the loss of potentially skilled persons and the continuation of emotional disorders resulting in expensive community expenditures for many years after school-
leaving and perhaps intermittently during the rest of life.

Some Alarming Educational Trends

Learn more, and learn it faster.

In response to a variety of pressures, high schools all over the country are substantially increasing the demands on students. The trends toward upgraded curricula, increased pressures for educational achievement, heavier work loads, and earlier graduation are well established. "Education for survival" and "education as a tool in preparedness," phrases heard increasingly often, add to the sense of urgency surrounding the educational process.

We do not question the necessity or the soundness of this movement. We do want to raise some danger signs based on our drop-out study and our agency practice, which is now heavily concentrated on school problems. We are sure that the majority of bright children feel challenged and respond well to the increased demands. We are equally sure that other children are harmed by them.

An educational program designed for acceleration and higher achievement that does not take into account emotional readiness as well as intellectual capacity will inevitably accomplish the reverse of its objective with some youngsters. We have noted a substantial increase in referrals of adolescents whose educational problems were precipitated by just such intensification of the schools' demands. Many simply could not stand the increase in the expectations and the greater competitive effort this entailed. It is interesting that they not only felt they had failed themselves and their parents, but that they had also failed their country. The intent of the schools is to motivate, but some youngsters can be overly motivated.

Get rid of the misfits.

We note another disturbing trend: the schools and the community are displaying a growing impatience with students who have problems with school. In part, this impatience stems from the concern that such students interfere with the progress of the other students—and they do. In part, it stems from discouragement and disappointment that these students have not responded to the many attempts to help them with their problems. The impatience is particularly strong when the youngster's behavior is of an aggressive, attacking, or clowning nature. Such acting out places maximum stress on the tolerance of adults, and does not evoke a sympathetic response.

For academically underachieving childen of legal school-leaving age, school behavior is among the more important factors in determining whether the school encourages a student to remain in school or to leave. For younger, underachieving children, the nature of the school behavior influences the school's willingness to work with the youngster within the regular school system rather than transferring him to a disciplinary school where possibilities for academic reclamation are far fewer.

School personnel are in the most difficult position of constantly balancing the welfare of the majority of students against the individual needs and demands of youngsters with problems. This conflict cannot be eliminated. Our study does demonstrate, however, that a combination of skillful, objective handling by school personnel and therapeutic attention to emotional difficulties by social caseworkers is effective in reducing the number of youngsters with school problems. Unless we can provide these services to more young people, the drop-out toll will remain high, and the pressure "to get the kids out" will mount. The children with school and personality problems will be shifted from the schools to the community where we are less effective in dealing with them. Until we give these youngsters every opportunity to resolve their problems, it is we and not they who fail.

Our country believes in universal education. But for our intellectually capable children there is education only for those who are problem free. We are deeply concerned with the large number of youngsters whose potential energies go entirely to waste, children for whom there has not been an adequate appreciation of the real difficulties with which they are involved—

the emotional and social problems that interfere with both personality and school functioning.

Any program to take maximum advantage of the potentialities of our future citizens must include facilities for helping the youngsters whose adaptation to school is hampered by personality conflicts.

STATISTICAL PROCEDURES [1]

The original data on the 105 cases were in the form of detailed case records. We reported all interviews with the student and his parents and, except for a few cases where no parent was seen, had a complete social history for each child. Usually included were one or more reports from the school.

The two social workers and staff psychologist who had conducted most of the counseling drew up a list of factual variables they thought would be shared by all the students. Shortly afterward, the male social worker left the staff. The director of the study (who also supervised the casework), the consulting psychiatrist, the research consultant, and the two remaining counselors worked together to define terms and to devise systems for diagnosing the adolescents and determining the dynamic use of school made by each student and his parents (see Chapters 2–4).

With the aid of the research consultant, a coding plan was evolved in which each category of each variable could be represented on an IBM punch card. The social worker and the psychologist did all the coding. Factual variables such as age,

1. Dr. Benjamin D. Wright, who prepared this section, was our research consultant and is Associate Professor of Education, Department of Education, University of Chicago.

family composition, and the like, were coded independently; but the items having to do with evaluative judgments, such as diagnosis, were coded by the two raters' decision after reading the case material together. In cases of doubt or disagreement they consulted the director of the study or the psychiatrist, or both.

After thoroughly discussing the coding system of the factual variables, both coders independently rated the same sample of ten cases to see how much they agreed on code use. They found that the code was effectively explicit and that there were few disagreements. Nevertheless, whenever there was any uncertainty during the coding, the two coders discussed the facts together and made a combined judgment. In some cases they sought further information from other agency personnel in order to make the representation of the case in the coding system as correct as possible.

The final set of 105 code sheets was punched into a deck of 105 IBM cards to obtain a frequency distribution for each variable. Analysis of these tabulations showed those variables that were irrelevant or coded into too many categories, and reasonable reductions in coding complexity were suggested.

The first deck of 105 cards was then changed to a second deck of 105 cards coded more efficiently and more appropriately for the actual data. Successfully abstracted from the case material at this point were thirty-one variables that were reasonably common to the group of 105 students. Thirty-one variables admit to 465 bivariate analyses—an impossible number, in general. Five variables, however, had special prior status. Marked *sex* differences had been noted during the counseling process. Since the project was treatment oriented, *length of treatment* became an important consideration. The frequency table of number of interviews attended showed a marked tapering in the number of students who dropped out of counseling after three interviews. The Treatment Group was then defined as cases having four or more interviews. Seventy students fell into this group: thirty-three girls and thirty-seven boys. The Nontreatment Group, those having three or fewer interviews, consisted of thirty-five students: twelve girls and twenty-three boys. As *personality improvement in treatment, character formation,* and *final school status* were also of fundamental interest in this study, they, too, were designated as independent variables. The analysis of the remaining twenty-six variables was confined to exploring their dependency on these basic five. Actually, among the group of seventy students who comprised the Treatment Group only twenty-four of these dependent variables were effectively relevant. Following is a list of all the variables.

Independent Variables

1. Sex
2. Number of interviews
3. Personality improvement
4. Final school status
5. Character formation

Evaluative Variables

6. Predominant observable complaint
7. Psychodynamic issue
8. Defenses
9. Mother's diagnosis
10. Father's diagnosis
11. Mother's attitude
12. Father's attitude
13. Student's school dynamics
14. Mother's school dynamics
15. Father's school dynamics
16. Improved school functioning

Factual Variables

17. Age
18. IQ
19. Home composition
20. Number of siblings
21. Social class status
22. Prior service
23. Elementary school problems
24. High school problems
25. School action
26. Actionable antisocial offenses
27. Employment status at case closing
28. Number of interviews, mother
29. Number of interviews, father
30. Months case open
31. Termination terms

Variables three and five under Independent Variables also were Evaluative Variables and coded along with the latter.

Thus, the task of analysis was reduced to an examination of the ten relationships among the five independent variables; the fifty-eight relationships between sex and length of treatment and the twenty-nine variables over all 105 children; the forty-eight relationships between personality improvement and character formation; the twenty-four dependent variables over the seventy children who had tangible treatment; and the twenty-four relationships between school status and the twenty-four dependent variables over the fifty-six children for whom school status data were relevant.

The relationships analyzed were examined by bivariate frequency tables. In most cases a natural dichotomy in each variable was apparent, and the productive tables were condensed into fourfold contingency tables. These tables show the statistical evidence supporting relationships between the independent and dependent variables.

Two descriptive statistics were computed for each table. The first is a measure of the degree of association existing in the table. The h index of order association counts the excess proportion of ordered pairs oriented in the direction of the association. This index can vary from zero to one and, where a suitable convention about direction is followed, can have a plus or minus sign. We have not used signs in our tables, since the actual direction of association is easily apparent from the table itself. The nearer this index is to a value of one, the stronger the association observed in the table. An index of one indicates that all pairs are oriented in one direction. A description of this index appears on pages 282-284 of W. Allen Wallis and Harry V. Roberts, *Statistics: A New Approach* (New York: The Free Press of Glencoe, 1956).

The second descriptive statistic is a measure of the degree of improbability of frequencies observed in the table if it is hypothesized that there is no relationship at all between the two variables compared. The p value listed is based on the chi-square distribution with one degree of freedom and is sometimes called the descriptive significance level of the association observed in the table under a null hypothesis of no true association. The formula used and a discussion of this kind of analysis can be found on pages 429-431 of Wallis and Roberts' book.

Even after reducing the comparisons to be made to those exploring the impact of the five independent variables on the twenty-three to twenty-six dependent ones, there remained 130 tables to examine. Only about a fifth of these revealed evidence to suggest conclusions concerning association between independent and dependent variables. Because of the large number of tables examined, the statistical significance of any one table should be taken with a grain of salt. On the other hand, the expected rate of independent statistically significant tables at the 5 per cent level, when there is no real association, is one in twenty or six to seven in 130.

In research embracing so many variables it is not possible to establish that any small set of the large number of possibilities are "the causes" of any school difficulty. Nevertheless, these tables do represent a summary of the evidence available from this study. From them plans can be drawn for more definitive studies of specific clues in understanding school drop-out.

To summarize: each two-by-two table was annotated, first with a measure of association counting the balance of the data in favor of a relationship between the dependent and independent variable summarized in the table, and second with a descriptive significance level appraising the table in terms of the hypothesis of no relation underlying the distribution of numbers. These two statistical commentaries help the reader to weigh the evidence in each table in two ways: the amount of evidence in favor of the relationship, and the improbability of the evidence under the hypothesis of no real relation.

Statistical Tables

Table 1—Source of the Sample: by Schools

	Girls	Boys	Total
Amundsen	4	6	10
Austin	5	3	8
Central Y	1		1
Fenger	3	6	9
Harrison	3	2	5
Hawthorne		1	1
Hyde Park		2	2
Kelvyn Park	1	1	2
Lake View	4		4
Lane		2	2
Logan Continuation		2	2
Montefiore	2		2
Morgan Park	3	2	5
Roosevelt	2	1	3
Schurz	2	6	8
Senn	5	2	7
Spalding		1	1
Steinmetz		4	4
Sullivan		1	1
Taft	6	7	13
Tuley	1	2	3
Von Steuben		3	3
Waller	1	2	3
Washburne Trade	1	3	4
Westcott Vocational	1	1	2
Totals	45	60	105

Table 2—Elementary School Problems: Differences between the Treatment and Nontreatment Girls and Boys in Occurrence of Elementary School Problems

	TREATMENT GROUP			NONTREATMENT GROUP			BOTH GROUPS		
	Girls (33)	Boys (37)	Total (70)	Girls (12)	Boys (23)	Total (35)	Girls (45)	Boys (60)	Total (105)
Problem	33%	76%	56%	17%	48%	37%	29%	65%	49%
No Problem	64	19	40	83	39	54	69	27	45
Insufficient Evidence	3	5	4		13	9	2	8	6

Table 3—Analysis of Elementary School Problems by Problem Area: Differences between the Treatment and Nontreatment Girls and Boys in Frequency of Occurrence of Various Elementary School Problems

	TREATMENT GROUP			NONTREATMENT GROUP			BOTH GROUPS		
	Girls (33)	Boys (37)	Total (70)	Girls (12)	Boys (23)	Total (35)	Girls (45)	Boys (60)	Total (105)
Attendance Only	2	1	3		1	1	2	2	4
Performance Only	2	7	9		1	1	2	8	10
Behavior Only	3	5	8	1		1	4	5	9
Attendance and Performance	1	2	3	1	2	3	2	4	6
Attendance and Behavior	1		1		1	1	1	1	2
Performance and Behavior	2	12	14		6	6	2	18	20
Attendance, Performance and Behavior		1	1					1	1
No Problem	21	7	28	7	9	16	28	16	44
Insufficient Evidence	1	2	3	3	3	6	4	5	9

Table 4—High School Problems: Difference between the Treatment and Nontreatment Girls and Boys in Occurrence of High School Problems

	TREATMENT GROUP			NONTREATMENT GROUP			BOTH GROUPS		
	Girls (33)	Boys (37)	Total (70)	Girls (12)	Boys (23)	Total (35)	Girls (45)	Boys (60)	Total (105)
Problem	97%	100%	98%	67%	91%	83%	89%	97%	93%
No Problem	3		2	17		6	7		3
Insufficient Evidence				16	9	11	4	3	4

Table 5—Analysis of High School Problems by Area: Differences between the Treatment and Nontreatment Girls and Boys in Frequency of Occurrence of Various High School Problems

	TREATMENT GROUP			NONTREATMENT GROUP			BOTH GROUPS		
	Girls (33)	Boys (37)	Total (70)	Girls (12)	Boys (23)	Total (35)	Girls (45)	Boys (60)	Total (105)
Attendance Only	3	4	7	1	2	3	4	6	10
Performance Only	2	4	6		6	6	2	10	12
Behavior Only									
Attendance and Performance	12	12	24	5	6	11	17	18	35
Attendance and Behavior	2		2				2		2
Performance and Behavior	1	8	9	1	3	4	2	11	13
Attendance, Performance and Behavior	12	9	21	1	4	5	13	13	26
No Problem	1		1	2		2	3		3
Insufficient Evidence				2	2	4	2	2	4

Table 6—General Background Information: Differences between the Treatment and Nontreatment Girls and Boys in Occurrence of Each Variable among the Subgroup

	TREATMENT GROUP			NONTREATMENT GROUP			BOTH GROUPS		
	Girls (33)	Boys (37)	Total (70)	Girls (12)	Boys (23)	Total (35)	Girls (45)	Boys (60)	Total (105)
Middle-class Home	52%	86%	70%	58%	78%	71%	53%	83%	70%
Lower-class Home	48	14	30	42	9	20	47	12	27
Insufficient Evidence					13	9		5	3
Both Natural Parents in Home	42	62	53	58	57	57	47	60	54
Both Natural Parents Not in Home	58	38	47	42	43	43	53	40	46
No Sibling or One Sibling	27	54	41	50	39	43	33	48	42
More Than One Sibling	73	46	59	42	57	51	65	50	56
Insufficient Evidence				8	4	6	2	2	2
IQ 110 or Over	39	54	47	8	39	28	31	48	41
IQ Under 110	55	27	40	59	39	46	56	32	42
Insufficient Evidence	6	19	13	33	22	26	13	20	17
Actionable Offenses	52	35	43	25	9	14	45	25	33
No Actionable Offenses	45	62	54	67	82	77	51	70	62
Insufficient Evidence	3	3	3	8	9	9	4	5	5

Table 7—Predominant Observable Complaints— Treatment Group*

	GIRLS (33) POC I	GIRLS (33) POC II	BOYS (37) POC I	BOYS (37) POC II	TOTAL (70)
Ego-Dystonic					
Negative Self-Image	4	4	2	9	19
Anxiety	4	4	6	1	15
Total	16		18		34
Per cent	48%		49%		48%
Poor Coping Ability					
Passivity	0	1	9	4	14
Dependency	1	1	7	1	10
Total	3		21		24
Per cent	9%		57%		34%
Alloplastic Complaints					
Minor Social Misbehavior	3	2	3	0	8
Hostile Social Approach	2	2	2	2	8
Immature Activity	5	2	0	0	7
Actionable Offenses	2	2	1	1	6
Total	20		9		29
Per cent	61%		24%		41%
Twelve Other Categories	12	10	7	13	42
Total	22		20		42
Per cent	67%		54%		60%
No POC II Listed					
Total	5		6		11
Per cent	15%		16%		16%

* All but eleven of the seventy students had two POC's.

Table 8—Character Formation—Treatment Group (33 Girls, 37 Boys): by Developmental Issue

	GIRLS Number	GIRLS Per Cent	BOYS Number	BOYS Per Cent
Early Ego Phase				
Preoral	4	12%	5	13%
Oral-Dependent	2	6	8	21
Oral-Aggressive	12	36	11	30
Subtotal	18	54%	24	64%
Later Ego Phase				
Anal	3	9%	3	5%
Phallic	11	33	10	27
Subtotal	14	42%	12	32%
Insufficient Evidence	1	3%	1	3%

Table 9—Specific Defenses—Treatment Group: Frequency of Defenses Occurring at least Six Times among Girls and Boys*

	Girls	Boys
Overt Defenses		
Provocation	10	7
Passivity	0	11
Acting out	9	1
Withdrawal	3	7
Overcompensation	1	7
Random activity	5	1
Direct gratification	4	2
Stubbornness	2	4
Covert Defenses		
Repression	7	5
Identification	2	8
Reaction formation	4	3
Depression	3	4
Inhibition	2	4
Fantasy	1	5
Somatization	5	1

* Thirty-nine of the possible sixty-three different defenses occurred in the Treatment Group, and the schedule made provision for listing up to three defenses per student. The total number of defenses was 188. Table 8 lists the defenses occurring six or more times. Not all of the seventy Treatment Group students are represented in this table, and some individuals have more than one defense listed. Thus, the focus is on kinds of defenses rather than number of students.

Table 10—Defenses—Treatment Group: Frequency of Occurrence of Subcategories of Covert and Overt Defenses among Girls and Boys*

	GIRLS' DEFENSES				BOYS' DEFENSES			
	Covert	Overt	Total	Per Cent	Covert	Overt	Total	Per Cent
Impulse-Source	1		1	1%	3		3	3%
Impulse-Mode	23	27	50	72	24	24	48	53
Impulse-Object	3	5	8	12	13	9	22	24
Affect State	3	2	5	7	2	10	12	13
Conscious Adaptations	5		5	7	5		5	6
Total	35	34	69		47	43	90	
Per cent	51%	49%			52%	48%		

* At least one and up to three defenses per student have been recorded in this tabulation. Care was taken, however, to record an incidence of only one defense when a student had more than one defense in the same subcategory. This occurred among sixteen girls and ten boys and, in all but four of these twenty-six cases, in the subcategory Impulse-Mode.

Table 11—Mothers' Diagnoses by Developmental Issue— Treatment Group: Forty-nine Mothers Diagnosed

	Girls' Mothers (23)	Boys' Mothers (26)	Total (49)	Per Cent
Early Ego Phase				
Preoral	5	5	10	20%
Oral	9	14	23	47
	14	19	33	67%
Later Ego Phase				
Anal	4	5	9	19%
Phallic	5	2	7	14
	9	7	16	33%

Table 12—Fathers' Diagnoses by Developmental Issue— Treatment Group: Twenty-seven Fathers Diagnosed

	Girls' Fathers (12)	Boys' Fathers (15)	Total (27)	Per Cent
Early Ego Phase				
Preoral	1		1	4%
Oral	7	7	14	52
	8	7	15	56%
Later Ego Phase				
Anal	2	7	9	33%
Phallic	2	1	3	11
	4	8	12	44%

Table 13—Relationship of Father-Mother-Student in Character Formation (Twenty-three Students, Nine Girls and Fourteen Boys)

		FATHERS			
		Preoral	Oral	Anal	Phallic
M O T H E R S	Preoral	1 Preoral Girl	2 Preoral Boys 1 Oral Girl		
	Oral		2 Oral Girls 2 Oral Boys 1 Phallic Girl 1 Phallic Boy	4 Oral Boys 1 Anal Boy 1 Phallic Boy	
	Anal		2 Oral Boys	1 Oral Boy 1 Anal Girl 1 Phallic Girl	
	Phallic				2 Phallic Girls

Table 14—Coincidence of Character Formation

	Character formation same for student and both parents	Student character formation same as one parent	Student character formation different from either parent	Total
Observed Frequency	8	10	5	23
Expected Frequency*	1	9	13	23

$x^2 = 54.03$

* Expected on the hypothesis there is no tendency for character formation to coincide.

Table 15—Relationships around Maternal Attitude

STUDENTS' PERSONALITY IMPROVEMENT

	MATERNAL ATTITUDE		
	Positive	Other	TOTAL
Students Improved	13	16	29
Students Not Improved	6	22	28
Total	19	38	57

$h = 0.497$; $x^2 = 2.535$; $p = 0.11$

MOTHERS' EGO PHASE (FORTY-SEVEN MOTHERS DIAGNOSED)

	MATERNAL ATTITUDE		
	Positive	Other	TOTAL
Early Ego Phase	6	25	31
Later Ego Phase	11	5	16
Total	17	30	47

$h = 0.803$; $x^2 = 9.12$; $p = 0.004$

NUMBER OF MATERNAL INTERVIEWS

	MATERNAL ATTITUDE		
	Positive	Other	TOTAL
Five or Fewer Interviews	6	25	31
Six or More Interviews	13	13	26
Total	19	38	57

$h = 0.612$; $x^2 = 4.68$; $p = 0.04$

Table 16—Outcome of Treatment: Neurotics versus Character Disturbances (Sixty-eight Students Diagnosed)

| | PERSONALITY FUNCTIONING | | |
	Improved	Not Improved	TOTAL
Neurotics	13	3	16
Character disturbances	20	32	52
Total	33	35	68

$h = 0.748$; $\chi^2 = 7.33$; $p = 0.007$

Table 17—Character Formation in Relation to Outcome of Treatment (Sixty-eight Students, Thirty-two Girls and Thirty-six Boys, Diagnosed)

| | GIRLS | | BOYS | | TOTAL | |
	Improved	Not Improved	Improved	Not Improved	Improved	Not Improved
Early Ego Phase						
Preoral	1	3	2	3	3	6
Oral-Dependent	0	1	3	5	3	6
Oral-Aggressive	5	8	5	6	10	14
	18		24		42	
Later Ego Phase						
Anal	2	1	1	1	3	2
Phallic	8	3	6	4	14	7
	14		12		26	
	$h = 0.666$		$h = 0.324$		$h = 0.407$	

Table 18—Length of Treatment in Relation to Outcome of Treatment*

| | PERSONALITY FUNCTIONING | | |
	Improved	Not Improved	TOTAL
Fifteen or Fewer Interviews	12	25	37
Sixteen or More Interviews	22	11	33
Total	34	36	70

$h = 0.612$; $\chi^2 = 6.89$; $p = 0.01$

* Fifteen was the median number of interviews.

Table 19—Terms of Termination in Relation to Outcome of Treatment

| | PERSONALITY FUNCTIONING | | |
	Improved	Not Improved	TOTAL
Mutual Agreement	11	2	13
Unilateral Decision	17	33	50
Total	28	35	63*

$h = 0.83$; $\chi^2 = 8.78$; $p = 0.003$

* Seven cases still current.

Table 20—Relationship between Elementary School Problems and Improvement

| | PERSONALITY FUNCTIONING | | |
	Improved	Not Improved	TOTAL
Problems in Elementary School	13	31	44
No Elementary School Problems	26	10	36
Total	39	31	70

$h = 0.615$; $\chi^2 = 6.86$; $p = 0.01$

Table 21—Relationship between Mothers' Character Structure and Students' Improvement (Forty-nine Mothers Diagnosed)

| | PERSONALITY FUNCTIONING | | |
	Improved	Not Improved	TOTAL
Early Ego Phase	12	21	33
Later Ego Phase	10	6	16
Total	22	27	49

$h = 0.49$; $\chi^2 = 2.01$; $p = 0.15$

Table 22—Improved School Functioning (Seventeen Girls, Twenty-three Boys)

| | GIRLS | | | BOYS | | |
School Problem	Number with Problem	Number Improved	Per Cent Improved	Number with Problem	Number Improved	Per Cent Improved
Academic Performance	17	5	29%	23	15	65%
School Attendance	11	5	45	12	8	67
Classroom Misbehavior	9	3	33	11	6	54
Students Showing Improvement in One or More Areas		6	35		16	69

Table 23—School Functioning versus Personality Functioning
(Seventeen Girls, Twenty-three Boys)

	PERSONALITY FUNCTIONING		
School Functioning	Improved	Not Improved	TOTAL
Improved	18	6	24
No Change	2	14	16
Total	20	20	40

$h = 0.909$; $\chi^2 = 12.60$; $p = 0.0005$

Table 24—School Status versus Personality Functioning
(Twenty-eight Boys Sixteen Years of Age or Over)

	PERSONALITY FUNCTIONING		
	Improved	Not Improved	TOTAL
Left School during Treatment	3	9	12
In School, Over Sixteen Years of Age	8	8	16
Total	11	17	28

$h = 0.50$; $\chi^2 = 0.90$; $p = 0.34$

Table 25—Actionable Antisocial Offenses versus School Status

	In School	Left School	Total
Problem	5	18	23
Not a Problem	21	12	33
Total	26	30	56

$h = 0.72$; $\chi^2 = 7.95$; $p = 0.008$

Table 26—Students' Character Level versus School Status

	In School	Left School	Total
Early Ego Phase	9	19	28
Later Ego Phase	17	11	28
Total	26	30	56

$h = 0.53$; $\chi^2 = 3.51$; $p = 0.07$

Table 27—Relationship between Attendance Problems and
School Status for Students over Sixteen Years of Age

	In School	Left School	Total
Attendance Problem	17	27	44
No Attendance Problem	9	3	12
Total	26	30	56

$h = 0.653$; $\chi^2 = 3.65$; $p = 0.06$

Table 28—Relationship between Attendance Problems and Actionable Antisocial Offenses for the Drop-Out Population of Thirty Students

	Antisocial Offenses	No Antisocial Offenses	Total
Attendance Problem	17	8	25
No Attendance Problem	1	4	5
Total	18	12	30

$h = 0.789$; $\chi^2 = 2.25$; $p = 0.03$

REFERENCE OUTLINES

I. *Predominant Observable Complaints*

A. *Physical complaints—
    functional*
  1. Hypochondriasis
  2. Psychosomatic condition
      (somatization)
  3. Conversion reactions

B. *Psychic complaints*
  1. Distortion of reality
    a. autistic behavior
    b. social withdrawal
    c. autistic fantasy
    d. bizarre ideation
  2. Anxiety constellation
    a. anxieties
    b. fear
    c. phobias
  3. Obsessive-compulsive
      constellation
    a. guilt
    b. compulsions
    c. perfectionism
    d. preoccupations—
        obsessions

  4. Depressive constellation
    a. sadness
    b. depression
    c. easy crying
  5. Negative self-image
    a. self-depreciation
    b. lack of self-confidence
    c. inferiority feelings
  6. Inadequate identity
      formation
    a. lack of life goals
    b. unsettled values
    c. variable attitudes
    d. unsettled relationships
    e. poor body- and
        self-image
  7. Dependency constellation
    a. dependency
    b. helplessness
    c. clinging
    d. demandingness
  8. Passivity constellation
    a. insufficient motivation

b. lack of effortful
    activities
c. resistance to pressure
d. procrastination
9. Inhibition constellation
    a. shyness
    b. timidity
    c. social constriction
    d. limited aggressiveness
10. Attention inadequacy
    a. distractibility
    b. poor concentration
    c. daydreaming
    d. learning interference
11. Self-overestimation
    a. boasting
    b. exaggeration
    c. exhibitionism
12. Immature activity
    a. hyperactivity
    b. impulsive behavior
    c. clowning
    d. giggling
    e. restlessness
13. Sexual complaints
    a. autoerotic: fantasy,
        masturbation
    b. perversions
    c. sexually provocative
        behavior in talk,
        dress, and actions
    d. heterosexual
        experiences
14. Addictions
15. Hostile social approach
    a. hostile competitiveness
    b. provocativeness
    c. stubbornness
    d. suspicion and distrust

C. *Social complaints*
    1. Minor social misbehavior
        a. mischief-making
        b. disobedience
        c. bullying
        d. lying
        e. provocative acting out,
            including fighting
    2. Actionable antisocial
        offenses
        a. running away
        b. delinquent gang
            association
        c. vandalism
        d. stealing
        e. assaultive behavior
        f. drinking
        g. breaking curfew

D. *School complaints*
    1. Learning difficulty
        a. learning disability
        b. learning block
        c. nonachievement
        d. speech disturbance
    2. Decathexis of school
        a. loss of interest
        b. nonparticipation in
            educational process
    3. Attendance problems
        a. tardiness
        b. unexplained absences
        c. cutting
        d. truancy

E. *Environmental problems*
    1. Economic need
    2. Personal or family member
        illness
    3. Subculture problem
    4. Negative parental
        management

II. *Characterological Diagnostic Classifications*

- A. *Preoral phase*
  1. Impulse-ridden character
  2. Emotionally unstable character
  3. Schizoid character: simple, paranoid, mixed
  4. Inadequate ego development
- B. *Oral phase*
  1. Oral-dependent character formation
     - a. Infantile dependent
     - b. Oral-dependent, passive
     - c. Oral-dependent, aggressive
  2. Oral-aggressive character formation
     - a. Passive type
     - b. Aggressive type
       - i. infantile-demanding
       - ii. hypomanic
       - iii. depressive
       - iv. cyclothymic
       - v. masochistic
- C. *Anal phase:* Compulsive character formation
- D. *Phallic phase*
  1. Hysterical or anxiety-ridden character formation
  2. Inhibited character formation
  3. Over-compensated character formation
- E. *Genital phase:* Genital character formation

III. *Defenses*

Covert Impulse-Source
  Displacement
  Symbolization

  Repression
  Somatization
  Symbolization

Covert Impulse-Mode, Simple
  Conversion
  Denial
  Erotization
  Fantasy
  Inhibition
  Intellectualization
  Introversion
  Rationalization
  Reaction formation

Covert Impulse-Mode, Complex
  Asceticism
  Compulsiveness
  Conscientiousness
  Depression
  Fixation
  Masochism
  Perfectionism
  Regression
  Restitution

Sublimation
Undoing

Covert Impulse-Object
Decathexis
Depersonalization
Identification
Incorporation
Introjection
Projection

Covert Affect State
Blocking
Denial—affect
Isolation

Covert Conscious Adaptations
Conscious denial
Conscious displacement
Conscious fantasy
Renunciation
Suppression

Overt Impulse-Mode, Simple
Direct gratification
Identification with the aggressor
Random activity

Overt Impulse-Mode, Complex
Acting out
Corrupting
Manipulation
Passivity
Provocation

Overt Impulse-Object
Altruism
Avoidance
Blaséness
Clowning
Mania
Megalomania
Narcissism
Omnipotence
Withdrawal

Overt Affect State
Affect swings
Apathy
Counterphobic maneuvers
Direct discharge
Dramatization
Exhibitionism
Overcompensation

IV. *Dynamic Use of School—Student*

A. School difficulty is the result of unsuccessful handling of impulse or need.
   1. Sexuality
   2. Competitive aggression
   3. Hostile aggression
   4. Dependency
   5. Other
B. School difficulty is the result of maladaptive superego reactions.
   1. Revolt
   2. Superego lacunae
C. School difficulty is the result of the student's attempt to use the school to resolve a conflict belonging to another area of life.
D. School difficulty is only one manifestation of a general personality problem.

E. School difficulty is the result of reality problems.
   1. Economic need
   2. Physical illness
   3. Education not a value in subculture
   4. Other

V. *Dynamic Use of School—Parents*

A. Student's school life exacerbates parent's problem of impulse or need.
   1. Sexuality
   2. Competitive aggression
   3. Hostile aggression
   4. Dependency
   5. Other
B. Parent's involvement in the student's school life is the result of maladaptive reactions to the superego.
   1. Rigid
      a. submission
      b. revolt
   2. Inadequate
      a. lacunate superego
      b. inconsistent superego
C. Parental involvement in the student's school life is the result of an overvalued school ego-ideal.
D. Student's school life receives no special focus; it is just another element in the parent's generalized personality disturbance.
E. Student's school life is used by the parent in an attempt to resolve a personality conflict belonging to another area of life.
F. Parent's reality problem affects his involvement in the student's school life.
   1. Economic need
   2. Physical illness
   3. Education not a value in the subculture
   4. Other
G. No psychopathology nor reality-based problems influence parent's involvement in the student's school life.

A GUIDE FOR TEACHERS

Quite early in our study we began to put to good use what we learned in the course of counseling children with serious school problems. The following informal talk, which was given to a group of principals and teachers, is an example.

There will always be problems in the classroom, just as there are in all areas of living. Since problems are ever-present, they must be handled. Large classrooms, insufficient resources in the schools and community, and other pressures make this task more difficult. In addition, not many of us really like problems, and we tend to avoid them as long as possible.

Unless adequate time is allowed and resources are mobilized, however, problems have a way of becoming more serious. Then they require more time and create a great deal more irritation. All of us know teachers have a most difficult job and are probably the recipient of more advice than any other group these days, unless it be parents. It seems somewhat presumptuous for a nonteacher to offer advice. I do so because we at the Scholarship and Guidance Association are wrestling with the same problems and with the same feelings.

In our day-to-day counseling we have come upon some ideas that have been of value and comfort to us during the long, emotionally draining hours. It is our hope that they may also be of value to teachers, parents, and other adults who spend a great deal of time with children.

1. Behind almost every classroom problem is an emotional problem. All children are different and behave in accordance with their own personality and life experience. Always remember, therefore, that children act the way they do for a reason.

Understanding the reason why a child manifests mean and malicious behavior is vital and can be a great source of comfort. Frequently a child's anger has nothing to do with the teacher but is related to other factors in his life. Very often we see and react only to the end results of problems, just as we can see only the tip of an iceberg. When a child creates trouble, our first reaction should be, "What is wrong with this youngster to make him behave this way?" not "Look what he is doing to me." Remember, when the goal is to control the child's expression of angry emotions, the adult must first contain his own feelings, hard as this may be.

2. It is not possible for teachers to get along with all students or to handle all classroom problems with equal success. Personal clashes occur in the classroom as they do in other areas of living. What can be a severe problem and a cause of anxiety for one teacher may be handled quite easily by another. At one time or another, all of us have said, "I just can't stand this kid."

It makes sense to have some flexibility in assignment, transferring a pupil within the school or even to another school to take advantage of a teacher's highly individual strengths. Teachers should not be required to "fight out problems" to their solution or failure. The classroom is not a battleground on which to win victories.

3. Many teachers expect and look forward to the kinds of gratification that come from teaching the intelligent, alert, eager youngster. There are also gratifications in aiding a maladjusted child to benefit from what the teacher and educational system have to offer. "There is more rejoicing in heaven over the salvation of one sinner than over ten righteous men."

4. Don't be the kind of teacher who is impossible to please. Youngsters seldom improve dramatically; behavioral changes evolve slowly and with many setbacks en route. Progress should be related to where the youngster was when he started to improve rather than to where you would like him to be. There is no way that a youngster who has been troubled for a long time can suddenly become "all good." Patience and fortitude are highly essential qualities. More than one child has been lost because we gave up too soon.

5. We may have higher expectations of good behavior for the youngster who has been in difficulty for a long time than for the child who seldom misbehaves. A good student explodes once in a while, and the school tolerates his misbehavior. The same behavior in the problem child may put into motion all the disciplinary machinery. But youngsters who are in the process of working out their difficulties will also have "off days." We sometimes forget that when a habitual truant becomes an occasional truant, this is really marked progress. Lapses do not necessarily mean that he is reverting to his previous behavior.

6. In handling disciplinary problems, make sure that the punishment fits the crime. Relate it to the offense and to the youngster who has committed the offense and not to the way you feel as an individual about the youngster's behavior. It is fairly easy to make big troubles out of little ones. Discipline is necessary but should not be automatic. The way it is administered can either alleviate or aggravate the problem.

We are all familiar with the technique of trying to control or change behavior by using others as examples. "Why can't you be more like Tommy?" "Don't associate with Jack. He will get you in trouble." Probably Tommy will not be hurt by being held up as a good example. But Jack could become the classroom or neighborhood scapegoat and, guilty or not, be automatically associated with all the misdeeds that occur. It is seldom, if ever, that anything constructive results from recalling to the child and his classmates the wrong things he has done.

7. It is important to study carefully the informtaion we have about troubled youngsters and to use it to its fullest—not to pre-

judge but to understand and to search out clues for handling the problem. It is all too easy to use previous information about a child as a basis for expecting the worst; for convincing yourself that the troublesome behavior will continue, that sins will be repeated.

8. Don't underestimate yourself. The observations of teachers are of great importance in understanding the troubled child, and a therapeutic attitude is of substantial benefit. All learning occurs in the relationship between pupil and teacher. There are factors within this relationship itself that contribute to successful teaching over and above the subject matter and specific teaching techniques.

9. Know your strengths and your limitations. Refrain from making recommendations that seriously affect a child's living or family situation. For example, a recommendation that a youngster be placed away from his family can begin a serious and complicated action and should have the most careful study.

10. Use to the fullest the resources available to you within the school system and the community. Seeking help does not mean that you have failed as a teacher; rather it is an indication of good and sound judgment. Think of yourself as a general practitioner who calls on the specialist. No one can expect that a teacher can or should resolve all problems. There is enough trouble for everyone.

11. Remember that being called to school can be a frightening experience for parents. Often what they learn about their children comes as a surprise. In addition, they may be ashamed, embarrassed, or angry. However parents react, attacking them seldom accomplishes anything. There are really few parents who deliberately set out to be bad parents, though it is true that some are inadequate—even destructive. It is easy to become angry with parents because we see what is happening to their children. But inadequate parents will not suddenly become adequate nor will destructive parents suddenly become constructive as a result of a conference with a teacher, an interview with the school psychologist, or a session with a counseling agency.

12. The philosophy of the school about problem youngsters

makes an important difference in how helpful the school and the teacher can be. Consciously or unconsciously, the school's attitude will affect and often characterize the manner in which problems are handled.

SELECTED BIBLIOGRAPHY

After Teen-Agers Quit School: Seven Community Programs Help Would-Be Workers. (Bulletin No. 150). Washington, D.C.: U.S. Department of Labor, Bureau of Labor Standards, 1951.

Alexander, Franz. *Fundamentals of Psychoanalysis.* New York: W. W. Norton & Company, Inc., 1948.

Allen, Charles M. *Combating the Dropout Problem.* Chicago: Science Research Associates, Inc., 1956.

Berman, Sidney. "Psychotherapeutic Techniques with Adolescents," *American Journal of Orthopsychiatry,* 24:2 (April, 1954), 238–245.

Bowman, Paul H., and Charles V. Matthews. *Motivations of Youth in Leaving School.* (Cooperative Research Project No. 200.) Washington, D.C.: U.S. Office of Education, 1960.

Diagnostic and Statistical Manual, Mental Disorders. Washington, D.C.: American Psychiatric Association, 1952.

Dillon, Harold J. *Early School Leavers—A Major Educational Problem.* New York: National Child Labor Committee, 1949.

Erikson, Erik H. "The Problem of Ego Identity," *Journal of the American Psychoanalytic Association,* 4:1 (1956), 56–121.

Experiment in Guidance of Potential Early School Leavers. New York: Board of Education of the City of New York, 1956.

Freud, Anna. *The Ego and the Mechanisms of Defense.* New York: International Universities Press, Inc., 1946.

Freud, Sigmund. "Instincts and Their Vicissitudes," *Collected Papers*, vol. IV. London: The Hogarth Press, 1925.

High School Dropouts. Washington, D.C.: Research Division, National Education Association of the United States, 1959.

Johnson, Adelaide M., M.D., and S. A. Szurek, M.D. "Genesis of Antisocial Acting Out in Children and Adults," *Psychoanalytic Quarterly*, 21:3 (1952), 323–343.

Josselyn, Irene. *The Adolescent and His World*. New York: Family Service Association of America, 1952.

——. "The Ego in Adolescence," *American Journal of Orthopsychiatry*, 24:2 (April, 1954), 223–237.

Lorand, Sandor, and Henry I. Schneer. *Adolescents: Psychoanalytic Approach to Problems and Therapy*. New York: Paul B. Hoeber, Inc., 1961.

McCreary, William H., and Donald E. Kitch. *Now Hear Youth: A Report on the California Co-operative Study of School Drop-Outs and Graduates*. (Bulletin of the California State Department of Education, Sacramento, XXII, No. 9.) October, 1953.

Pearson, Gerald J. H., M.D. *Adolescence and the Conflict of Generations*. New York: W. W. Norton and Company, Inc., 1958.

——. *Psychoanalysis and the Education of the Child*. New York: W. W. Norton and Company, Inc., 1954.

Report on Holding Power in the Grand Rapids, Michigan, Public Schools, May, 1953. Holding Power Committee of the Grand Rapids Board of Education.

Sklansky, Morris A., M.D. "Character Disorder in Adolescence." Paper presented at Fiftieth Anniversary Professional Meetings of Scholarship and Guidance Association, Chicago, 1961. (To be published.)

——, and Solomon O. Lichter. "Some Observations on the Character of the Adolescent Ego," *The Social Service Review*, 31:3 (September, 1957), 271–276.

School Drop-Outs. Washington, D.C.: Research Division of the National Education Association of the United States, 1952.

School and Early Employment Experience of Youth: A Report on Seven Communities, 1952–57. Washington, D.C.: U.S. Department of Labor, Bureau of Labor Statistics, August, 1960.

Social Work in the Schools: Selected Papers. New York: National Association of Social Workers, 1960.

Syracuse Youth Who Did Not Graduate: A Study of Youth Who Withdrew From School before Graduation, 1946–1949. Syracuse, N.Y.: Board of Education, Research Division, 1950.

Tesseneer, R. A., and L. M. Tesseneer. "Review of the Literature on School Dropouts," *Bulletin of the National Association of Secondary School Principals*, 42 (May, 1958), 141–53.

Trend Tables on Youth Employment and School Enrollment. Washington, D.C.: U.S. Department of Labor, Bureau of Labor Standards, March, 1957.

Why Do Boys and Girls Drop Out of School, and What Can We Do About It? Work Conference on Life Adjustment Education, Chicago, Illinois, January 24–27, 1950. (Circular No. 269.) Washington, D.C.: U.S. Government Printing Office, 1950.

Youth Employment and Juvenile Delinquency. (Report No. 1463.) Washington, D.C.: U.S. Government Printing Office, 1956.

INDEX